SIMON BRYANT

SIMON BRYANT BEGAN HIS COOKING CAREER WORKING IN THAI AND INDIAN RESTAURANTS IN MELBOURNE. IN 1995, HE JOINED THE RANKS OF THE HILTON ADELAIDE'S KITCHEN BRIGADE, WHERE HE WORKED FOR A TIME AT CHEONG LIEW'S CELEBRATED GRANGE RESTAURANT BEFORE BECOMING EXECUTIVE CHEF OF HILTON ADELAIDE IN 2001.

FROM 2006 TO 2009, SIMON CO-HOSTED FOUR SERIES AND 152 EPISODES OF THE ABC'S IMMENSELY POPULAR TV SERIES *THE COOK AND THE CHEF*, ALONGSIDE FOOD ICON MAGGIE BEER.

MOVING ON FROM HILTON ADELAIDE IN 2009, SIMON IS CURRENTLY AN AMBASSADOR FOR ANIMALS ASIA, PENS MAGAZINE ARTICLES ON ETHICAL FOOD PRODUCTION AND MAINTAINS AN ACTIVE INTEREST IN ISSUES SURROUNDING ANIMAL WELFARE PRACTICES. HE IS ALSO A SEMI-COMPETENT GARDENER AND COMMITTED VEGIE EATER.

SIMON BRYANT'S
VEGIES

LANTERN
an imprint of
PENGUIN BOOKS

INTRODUCTION

This book has been growing for more than two decades. These are the recipes I've cooked for myself, my friends and my customers over the years. This is the food I eat at home, and the food I am passionate about. Yes, the recipes are minus meat and fish, and yes, I care deeply about the ethical and environmental impact of eating animals, but I believe in vegies for a whole heap of reasons – most importantly, I love the taste of them. Even after all this time working as a chef, I still get great satisfaction from cooking when I'm 'off-duty'. I have a small vegie patch at home and it never fails to amaze me that a seed, a pile of dirt, some water and a little care combine to create something good to eat – it's important never to forget this is a bit of magic!

There is a world of flavour in properly grown vegies. If you think your vegetables are boring, they probably are. Are they just a little too perfect, as though they were manufactured by a machine? Are they available every day of the year, even when they are out of season? You may just be buying the wrong vegies from the wrong places... Real vegies should vary from season to season and harvest to harvest. I like vegies that are gnarly, misshapen, a bit dirty and authentic – vegies that look like they've come from the soil, not the factory production line. (Consistency in size and colour is for the production of shoelaces, not food.) This is why I love farmers' markets. The vegies are most likely seasonal, local and fresh. You can have a chat with the grower and a taste of the produce, and perhaps even learn a cooking tip or two. (I always like looking at the growers' hands: the more weathered they look, the more I trust their produce!) My job is to turn the vegies into a meal with the minimum of fuss and then just let the produce shine.

This book is divided into seasons, but I have taken a few liberties here and there with apologies to seasonal purists. It's also important to note that each Australian state and territory has its own seasonal cycle and micro-climates, so pockets of produce may be a bit out of sync with your part of the country. My aim, however, is to inspire and guide you, not dictate to you. By all means hit the market with a recipe in mind, but be flexible too: if something stunning catches your eye, just buy what looks good, and get creative. At the end of the day, good produce cooked with love will always taste better than the best recipe in the world made with bad produce and cooked without care.

As a final note, while all the recipes in this book are meat- and fish-free, I am reluctant to call it a vegetarian cookbook. Sometimes I think we are obsessed with classifying and labelling what we eat. To my mind, there are just two types of food: good and bad. Good food is thoughtfully produced, carefully sourced and respectfully cooked; it's flavoursome, nourishing and sustaining. When you sit down to eat a dish from this book, I hope your first thought is not, *This is vegetarian*, but rather, *This is good food*. If it is, then I have done my job.

INGREDIENTS

DAIRY

I try my best only to use dairy products from cows that have walked and grazed on pasture. The overheads for farmers who respect the welfare of their herds are higher so you are going to pay more for their products, but the taste is a million times better (and if that doesn't swing you, just think of the extra cost as an ethics tax). The flavour of milk should fluctuate as the pasture changes with the seasons, so if you notice subtle variations in taste throughout the year, you should congratulate the farmer for responding to the environment: it also means the cows are well cared for. As far as cream goes, I'm not a fan of the reduced-fat stuff, as thickening agents, such as vegetable gums or gelatine, are often added to create the illusion of richness. I tend to choose double (rich) cream or clotted cream, and just use less.

I use a lot of ghee in my cooking, as it brings a rich nutty flavour and lush full palate to Indian dishes. Making ghee is similar to making clarified butter, only the solids are caramelised during the separation process. All you do is heat top-quality butter in a heavy-based saucepan over medium heat and simmer for 30–50 minutes until the water evaporates. When the fizzing and bubbling subsides, you'll notice that the white solids at the bottom of the pan start to turn nut-brown and caramelise. When these solids are a deep brown and the butter is golden with a nutty aroma, strain the butter through a piece of muslin. Store the ghee in a sterilised jar (see page 223) in the fridge.

EGGS

We all know that if we want to make life a little better for chooks, we should buy only free-range eggs. However, Australia does not have a national independent certification system that applies to the whole industry, and the term 'free-range' is often bandied about more as a marketing term than a reality. I recommend you look for eggs certified by FREPA (Free-Range Egg and Poultry Association) or ACO (Australian Certified Organic), or those with the RSPCA 'Choose Wisely' accreditation.

FLOURS

I use an array of flours in my recipes, often because a certain type is particularly suited to a specific cuisine or dish, but also to incorporate a variety of different grains into my diet. I use atta flour for making Banana pooris (see page 87) and Chapattis (see Basic recipes). All good Indian grocers will stock atta flour, but you can make your own mix by blending 4 parts plain flour with 1 part wholemeal flour. I use besan (chickpea) flour for making Spinach pakoras (see page 119) and Onion bhajis (see page 178). For pasta and pastry, I use strong plain flour. Try Four Leaf Milling (fourleafmilling.com.au) or Laucke (laucke.com.au) for excellent Australian flour.

LEGUMES

Lentils can be tricky to get to grips with, as the same ones are often known by several names, derived from different Indian dialects. Unhulled (whole) red lentils are actually brown-skinned lentils; when hulled (skinned), they're orangey-red on the inside. Toovar (or toor) dal are tiny hulled and split lentils that are pale yellow. Urad dal (sometimes called black gram) is black when whole, and creamy white when hulled. It has wonderful thickening properties, so I often add it to dishes to give a hint of body. Chana dal is made from hulled and split desi chickpeas, which are the darker and denser of the two main varieties of chickpeas. Most chickpea recipes in this book call for the kabuli (or garbanzo) variety, which is bigger, lighter in colour and less starchy than the desi.

Australian farmers are now growing a fantastic variety of legumes. Chickpeas have nitrogen compounds in their root systems (essentially a store of fertiliser) and when the plant dies, the remaining nitrogen is released into the soil – a little bequest to the land and the crops that follow. So if you are eating local chickpeas, you might just be buying from a farmer who has learnt the benefits of crop rotation (and has left the phosphates on the shelf). A homegrown lentil, chickpea or bean also saves on energy costs. Best of all, once you have tasted a new-crop Australian legume, you'll never buy a dusty old imported one again! Try Nolans Road (nolansroad.com) or my own brand, Dirt(y) Inc (dirtyinc.com.au) – shameless self-promotion, I know . . .

HERBS AND SPICES

I can't live without fresh herbs and use tons of them in my cooking. As a rule, robust, woody herbs, such as rosemary and thyme, are better added at the start of cooking, while soft, delicate herbs, such as coriander and parsley, are best added at the end. There are exceptions: really young shoots of rosemary or thyme can be finely chopped and chucked in just before serving, while coriander stems and parsley stalks impart brilliant flavour to stocks or soups.

Whenever possible, I avoid hydroponically grown herbs. These little guys look pretty enough, but flavour is often lacking, if not non-existent, and they tend to wilt pretty quickly too. I find this with coriander especially: hydro just doesn't work as well in Asian-style dishes that require the pungent flavour of the root. I always look for the telltale signs when choosing this herb: thick stems and slightly woody roots mean it was grown in dirt. I always have herbs growing in my garden and I use the bolting tips, as well as the flowers, in my cooking – you might notice some dishes are garnished with spidery end-of-season coriander fronds. If you don't grow your own herbs, make friends with your Asian grocer and farmers' market growers – they're more likely to have the good stuff.

Like herbs, spices are one of the foundations of good cooking. Unfortunately, most are stored in less-than-ideal conditions for extended periods of time before being ground and packaged. Their volatile oils are lost in the process and they become dusty and dehydrated long before they reach your kitchen, let alone your plate. I will go to ridiculous lengths to get good spices, because they make such a difference to a dish. My advice is to buy whole spices from reputable merchants; try Herbies (herbies.com.au). Unless otherwise specified, the black pepper in this book is always roasted and cracked (simply roast whole peppercorns in a cast-iron pan over low heat until aromatic, then cool and grind in teeny batches). White pepper is freshly pounded using a mortar and pestle. Salt is sea or river salt flakes, unless you're salting cooking water, in which case table salt is fine.

NATIVE INGREDIENTS

If I had my way, we'd be growing native foods on every median strip! We should absolutely be eating more of these guys. The desert species (desert limes, quandongs, bush tomato and saltbush) are hardy and water-wise and, because they haven't been selectively grown for appearance, shape and colour, they're packed full of nutrients. I try to incorporate their bold flavours into everyday dishes, using warrigal greens and desert lime to make pesto (see page 100), and adding native spices to salad dressings. I urge you to start researching these great Australian ingredients and either grow your own seedlings (go to aussiefoodplants.com.au) or find a reputable distributor. I recommend Outback Pride (outbackpride.com.au). The ingredients are top-notch, and the project provides jobs and horticultural training for indigenous Australians – the true custodians of this land and its food.

OILS

To get the best from your oils, buy them in small quantities and get through them briskly. In Australia, we are spoilt for choice for sensational olive oils. Don't be fooled by fancy labels – some little guys produce wonderful oils at a smidge of the price (I buy mine from a local olive grower at the market). Taste the new season's oils around late winter and buy what you like.

Oils for Asian cooking are usually chosen for their higher smoke point, which makes them suitable for rapid cooking over high heat. I use a lot of 'flavour-neutral' oils, such as canola, grapeseed, rice bran and soybean. The term is a bit loose – not all the oils are flavourless – but these oils will not dominate the other ingredients in a dish. You'll notice that I often just list flavour-neutral oil in a recipe, and leave you to make the call, but occasionally I'll specify a particular type of oil if a certain viscosity is needed. Canola oil, for example, is best for Pumpkin tempura (see page 159) as it makes the batter crisp and light. I always buy non-genetically modified, cold-pressed canola oil.

Virgin coconut oil gives dishes a powerful flavour that is second to none. It may be high in saturated fat, but you really don't need to use much to gain the benefits in taste, texture and aroma. There are just two points to note. Firstly, always use virgin, rather than processed, coconut oil. (Processed or hydrolysed coconut oil contains trans fats, which we all know are bad news.) Secondly, be careful not to confuse coconut oil with palm oil: different plant, different oil, different story. The stuff that is destroying orang-utan habitats is generally palm oil. However, there are still ethical matters to consider when buying virgin coconut oil. Look for a fairtrade product that ensures fair wages for the farmers and comes from a longstanding coconut plantation that has not required mass clearing of land. For virgin coconut oil and other fairtrade organic foods, go to Beach Organics (beachorganics.com.au); for local peanut oil and an array of niche oils, including pumpkin seed oil, try Hardings Fine Foods (hardingsfinefoods.com.au).

To avoid spillover when deep-frying, never fill your wok or pan above one-third capacity. Oil spillovers happen when using moist ingredients and an over-full or over-hot wok or pan. I keep a small fire blanket in my home kitchen, just in case. Blanketing oil spillovers is a safe and effective way of preventing a bad situation from getting worse.

VINEGARS

You just can't skimp on vinegar. Some of the country's best winemakers make spectacular vinegars and it's an art. It takes time, love and excellent grapes. A dish can be spoiled by poorly made vinegar, so don't baulk at splashing out a bit. You'll notice I use aged sweet red vinegar in a number of recipes, which is a full-bodied, wood-barrel-aged, slightly sweet red vinegar. I prefer to use it instead of imported balsamic vinegar, but balsamic will do if you can't get hold of it.

Verjuice also pops up a bit. Made from pressed unripe grapes, it works in dishes where a delicate acidity is required. Vincotto is a sweet, robust condiment made from reduced grape must. Great Australian vinegars are available from Coriole Vineyard (coriole.com) and Maggie Beer (maggiebeer.com.au). Shaohsing is a staple Chinese cooking wine. It's available from Asian supermarkets, as is rice vinegar.

SAUCES AND PASTES

I use a few different soy sauces in this book. Light soy is thin, paler brown soy sauce; it brings a distinctive saltiness to dishes. Dark soy is aged longer than light soy and has caramel added; it's thick and sweet, and deeper in colour. Cuisine-specific soys also have slightly different flavour characteristics. It's more important that you get the *style* of the soy correct, i.e. light, dark or thick, than the country of origin. Having said that, Thai light soy is specified because it has a slightly sweet, slightly salty flavour, and I use it in place of fish sauce in vegie recipes. Kecap manis is a thick, syrupy soy sauce. Vegetarian (or mushroom) oyster sauce adds saltiness and sweetness but, most importantly, works as a thickener and emulsifier to bring sauces together.

Vegetarian belacan is a fermented soy product that I use to mimic the savoury umami flavour of fermented shrimp paste. It's a little hard to find and you may receive blank stares when you ask for it in Asian grocers – it happens to me all the time! Your best bet is to find a shop owned by a Malaysian or Singaporean. Otherwise, just contact me via my website and I'll point you in the right direction.

TOFU

People generally start looking at their shoes when I talk about tofu, but it's really important to pick the right sort for each dish. Tofu is made by coagulating soy milk, then pressing the curds. Types vary according to the drainage process and the pressure applied when setting the tofu, as well as the setting agent used (either salt or acid). The real wobbler is silken tofu, which is just set in tubs; you will often find it broken through soups or used in desserts. The medium-firm varieties (often referred to as silken firm) are drained in muslin and maybe lightly pressed. The really firm, bouncy varieties are well-drained and pressed; they're often used in curries and stir-fries. (Are you looking at your shoes yet?) When deep-frying tofu, it's important never to use second-hand oil: you want a completely pure flavour.

SPRING

With the arrival of spring,
my vegie patch doubles in size.

Salad leaves shoot upwards and beanstalks reach to the sky. The first zucchini and capsicums arrive, all young and tender, and a few decent tomatoes pop. At the market, asparagus is plentiful and broad beans are at their best. Tropical fruit makes its way into greengrocers as the wet season up north kicks in. By late spring, the stallholders have something new to offer daily. All kinds of berries begin to trickle in and the clove-y scent of basil fills the air.

At this time of year, warm salads and lots (and I mean lots) of herbs become mainstays on my menus. Light, aromatic soups are also an easy option when I want to smash something up for an early dinner, then go out and enjoy the evening sunshine. It seems a shame to cook the new season's young, sweet beans, greens and peas – a quick steam or stir-fry will retain their freshness and do them justice.

BIRCHER MUESLI WITH ORANGE AND TROPICAL FRUIT

SERVES 6

2 CUPS (180 G) UNSTABILISED OATS

1 CUP (250 ML) FRESHLY SQUEEZED
    ORANGE JUICE

1 RIPE MANGO, CUT INTO FAT
    MATCHSTICKS

½ SMALL PINEAPPLE, CUT INTO
    2 CM CHUNKS

½ VANILLA BEAN, SEEDS SCRAPED

½ CUP (125 ML) POURING CREAM

1 TABLESPOON HONEY

½ CUP (80 G) ALMONDS,
    ROUGHLY CHOPPED

6 SPRIGS MINT

It seems bircher muesli is almost compulsory on cafe breakfast menus these days but, in my experience, all too often it's badly made. The secret to good bircher is using unstabilised oats. Most rolled oats are steamed, a process that prevents them from becoming rancid and thus prolongs their shelf-life. This is all well and good, but unstabilised oats (ones that haven't been steamed) are just so much creamier. They're not hard to find; health-food shops and good supermarkets stock them. Just buy them in smaller quantities and make sure you eat them up quickly.

You can tweak this recipe to your taste, using any seasonal fruit and nut combo that you like. You can also soak the oats in apple juice, if you prefer, but my favourite is freshly squeezed orange juice.

1 Soak the oats in the orange juice for at least an hour (2 hours is ideal).

2 Place the mango matchsticks and pineapple chunks in a bowl, add the vanilla seeds and mix to combine.

3 Stir the cream and honey through the soaked oats.

4 To serve, layer the oats and fruit in glasses or bowls. Finish with a scattering of chopped almonds and a sprig of mint.

ASPARAGUS AND BLACK GARLIC WITH QUINOA

SERVES 4 AS A STARTER OR A SIDE

⅔ CUP (110 G) RED QUINOA SEEDS

SALT FLAKES AND CRACKED
BLACK PEPPER

100 ML EXTRA VIRGIN OLIVE OIL,
PLUS A SPLASH TO SERVE

2 TABLESPOONS VERJUICE
(SEE INGREDIENTS)

¼ TEASPOON GROUND FENNEL

3 CLOVES BLACK GARLIC, PEELED
AND THINLY SLICED

2 BUNCHES ASPARAGUS, TRIMMED
AND CUT INTO THIRDS

DOZEN OR SO NASTURTIUM FLOWERS

1 HANDFUL DILL SPRIGS

This dish is bursting with big flavours. The smoky black garlic and nutty red quinoa work brilliantly with the liquorice undertones of the fennel, and the peppery nasturtium flowers inject a bit of spring to an otherwise earthy dish. If you look around your neighbourhood at this time of year, you'll find them popping up all over the place, so get door-knocking. Otherwise, you'll find the flowers in selected greengrocers. Watercress is a good alternative.

Black garlic is worth seeking out if you are a vego and miss the meaty flavour that brings out the inner caveman in all of us. This is because when you ferment garlic, the same substance that forms when you sear meat (melanoidin) is created. Good specialty greengrocers stock black garlic. It lasts for ages, so why not grab some and have a little culinary play?

1 Rinse the quinoa for a minute or so in a colander under cold running water, then drain. Place the quinoa, 1 teaspoon of salt and 2 cups (500 ml) of water in a heavy-based saucepan over high heat and bring to a simmer. Stir, then cover with a tight-fitting lid and turn down the heat to low. Cook for 12–15 minutes or until most of the water has been absorbed, the quinoa is tender to the bite and some of the quinoa have popped open and split.

2 Combine 4 tablespoons of olive oil with the verjuice, fennel and garlic to make a dressing. Use a fork to fold the dressing through the quinoa.

3 Preheat a grill-plate or char-grill pan over medium heat. Rub the asparagus with the remaining oil and ¼ teaspoon of salt. Grill for about 2 minutes on each side or until the asparagus is a little blistered.

4 Divide the quinoa among plates and arrange the seared asparagus on top. Scatter with nasturtium flowers and dill. Add a splash of olive oil and some cracked black pepper to serve.

SPINACH SAMBAL TEMPEH
with BABY SHISO

SERVES 4

200 ML FLAVOUR-NEUTRAL OIL
(SEE INGREDIENTS)

400 G TEMPEH, RIPPED INTO
BITE-SIZED PIECES

1 ONION, SLICED LENGTHWAYS

4 TOMATOES, DICED

3 TABLESPOONS BURNT CHILLI SAMBAL
(SEE BASIC RECIPES)

1 BUNCH SPINACH, LEAVES PICKED
AND CUT IN HALF IF LARGE, STEMS
CHOPPED INTO 1 CM LENGTHS

1 TABLESPOON THAI LIGHT
SOY SAUCE (SEE INGREDIENTS)

2 TABLESPOONS VEGETARIAN OYSTER
SAUCE (SEE INGREDIENTS)

1 TEASPOON CASTER SUGAR

¼ TEASPOON SALT FLAKES

1 PUNNET BABY SHISO OR 1 BUNCH
THAI BASIL, LEAVES PICKED

STEAMED JASMINE RICE, TO SERVE

I'm not a huge fan of tempeh straight from the packet, but when it's deep-fried, it's a whole new ballgame. The key is to over-fry it slightly; the tempeh may look a little unappetising, but the texture and taste benefit greatly from the technique. It allows the fried meaty tempeh to suck up the stir-fry sauce and take on a lot of flavour.

Shiso or perilla (whatever you want to call it) has become more widely available in Asian grocers over the last few years. The purple variety is used in Japanese pickled plum (umeboshi), and it has a unique flavour that works perfectly in this dish. This recipe is best with baby shiso, but if you can't get hold of any, simply substitute mature shiso leaves or Thai basil.

1 Heat the oil in a medium-sized saucepan over medium heat until just shimmering (about 180°C). Add the tempeh and deep-fry for 3–5 minutes or until it is a deep golden brown. Remove the tempeh with a slotted spoon or spider and drain on paper towel. Reserve 3 tablespoons of the cooking oil.

2 Preheat a wok over high heat until just shimmering. Add the reserved oil and swirl it around the wok, then add the onion and stir-fry until softened. Add the tomato and continue to fry for 3–5 minutes or until the tomato is mushy and broken down; add a splash of water if it starts to stick. Add the Burnt chilli sambal and the spinach stems and stir-fry for a minute or two, then add the spinach leaves and allow them to wilt thoroughly, coating them with the sambal as you go. Add the soy sauce, oyster sauce, sugar and salt and stir to combine, then add 4 tablespoons of water to help steam the spinach. Stir until a thick sauce forms, then fold in the tempeh and allow it to warm through.

3 Turn out the spinach sambal tempeh into bowls and top with shiso or Thai basil. Serve with steamed jasmine rice.

DUKKAH SOFT-BOILED EGGS with ROCKET AND HARISSA

SERVES 4

1 CUP (250 ML) EXTRA VIRGIN
OLIVE OIL

BIG PIECE PITA BREAD, RIPPED INTO
BITE-SIZED PIECES

8 FREE-RANGE EGGS

1 LARGE HANDFUL ROCKET

2 TABLESPOONS HARISSA
(SEE BASIC RECIPES)

BIG PINCH OF SUMAC

DUKKAH

1 CUP (160 G) ALMONDS

1 CUP (150 G) HAZELNUTS

1 TABLESPOON CORIANDER SEEDS

1 TABLESPOON CUMIN SEEDS

½ CUP (75 G) SESAME SEEDS

½ TEASPOON SALT FLAKES

¼ TEASPOON BLACK PEPPERCORNS,
COARSELY POUNDED OR GROUND

½ WHOLE NUTMEG, FINELY GRATED

I like eggs, but I like chickens better. They're amazing birds: social, intelligent and a joy to watch when they're happy and well looked after. Definitions of what 'free-range' means under various industry schemes can differ greatly (see Ingredients for more info) and some eggs are more free-range than others. I urge you to ask suppliers a few simple questions. Farmers' markets are particularly good for this, but any reputable egg producer should be able to answer any queries you may have. If you don't ask, nothing will change and, believe me, in the majority of cases, change is needed for the welfare of these splendid creatures.

The dukkah recipe makes way too much for this dish, but it's handy to have in the pantry to serve with extra virgin olive oil and good bread, and it will easily keep for up to 6 months.

1 For the dukkah, preheat the oven to 180°C fan-forced (200°C conventional). Place the nuts, coriander seeds, cumin seeds and sesame seeds on a baking tray and roast for 10 minutes. Leave to cool, then grind coarsely in a food processor. Add the salt, pepper and nutmeg and combine. Store the dukkah in an airtight container in the pantry.

2 Place a small saucepan over medium heat and add the oil. Fry the pita until golden. Remove with tongs or a slotted spoon and leave to drain on paper towel. Reserve 2 tablespoons of the cooking oil.

3 Fill a large saucepan with cold water and add the eggs. Heat over medium heat and when the water reaches a simmer, turn the heat down to low. Simmer the eggs for 3 minutes, then remove with a slotted spoon. Run them under cold water to cool, then peel away the shells.

4 Place 1 tablespoon of the reserved cooking oil in a bowl, add the eggs and roll them around to coat. Add 4 tablespoons of the dukkah and roll the eggs to coat. Carefully slice the dukkah-coated eggs in half lengthways.

5 Arrange the rocket on plates with the fried pita and dukkah-coated eggs. Drizzle with harissa and the remaining tablespoon of oil and sprinkle with sumac to serve.

BOK CHOY AND RICE NOODLES WITH BLACK SESAME AND SPRING ONION OIL

SERVES 4

½ BUNCH SPRING ONIONS

150 ML FLAVOUR-NEUTRAL OIL
(SEE INGREDIENTS)

1 TEASPOON DARK SOY SAUCE
(SEE INGREDIENTS)

1 TEASPOON LIGHT SOY SAUCE
(SEE INGREDIENTS)

2 TEASPOONS VEGETARIAN OYSTER
SAUCE (SEE INGREDIENTS)

500 G FRESH RICE NOODLES

3 BUNCHES BOK CHOY, LEAVES HALVED
LENGTHWAYS IF LARGE

BIG PINCH OF SALT FLAKES

1 TEASPOON BLACK SESAME SEEDS

Spring onion oil is a staple in my pantry. It's so easy to make and can turn a simple meal into something a bit special. In this dish, the light soy, dark soy and oyster sauce combine to give a salty–sweet balance, perfect for both the noodles and greens. Go easy on the black sesame seeds as they can be quite overpowering. (And if you're not a fan of the bitter black variety, just substitute white sesame seeds and ramp up the quantity.) This dish is great with any Asian greens, not just bok choy. If you want to turn it into a more substantial meal, add some tofu, or serve it with the Pickled cabbage and soybean stir-fry on page 28.

1 Thinly slice a little of the green parts of the spring onion on an angle to make about 2 tablespoons of garnish, and set aside. Roughly cut the remaining green and white parts into 5–6 cm lengths and place them in a small saucepan with the oil. Place the saucepan over low heat and leave to infuse for 30 minutes.

2 Strain the oil, discarding the spring onion. You should have 80–100 ml of spring onion oil. Allow to cool for 10 minutes or so, then add the soy sauces and oyster sauce. Pour the sauce into a large mixing bowl and set aside.

3 Set a lightly oiled bamboo steamer over a saucepan of simmering water. Steam the noodles and bok choy for 2–3 minutes or until tender. Add the noodles and bok choy to the sauce, then add the salt and sesame seeds and toss through.

4 To serve, divide the noodles and bok choy among bowls and garnish with sliced spring onion greens.

SEAWEED AND LETTUCE SALAD

SERVES 4 A STARTER OR A SIDE

200 ML FLAVOUR-NEUTRAL OIL (SEE INGREDIENTS)

2 GOLDEN SHALLOTS, HALVED LENGTHWAYS AND VERY FINELY SLICED

SALT FLAKES

5 G DRIED WAKAME

120 ML EXTRA VIRGIN OLIVE OIL

1 TABLESPOON LEMON JUICE

PINCH OF CASTER SUGAR

2 TABLESPOONS AGED SWEET RED VINEGAR (SEE INGREDIENTS) OR BALSAMIC VINEGAR

1 HANDFUL ANY NICE LETTUCE (FRISEE, WHATEVER)

1 HANDFUL BABY SPINACH LEAVES

1 HANDFUL ROCKET LEAVES

1 SMALL GREEN OAK LETTUCE, LEAVES SEPARATED

1 HANDFUL BASIL LEAVES

1 SMALL BUNCH DILL, LEAVES PICKED

PICKLED CABBAGE AND SOYBEAN STIR-FRY (SEE PAGE 28) OR PLANTAIN CURRY (SEE PAGE 31), TO SERVE (OPTIONAL)

We are 'lucky' enough in Australia to have thriving patches of wakame seaweed that appear to have arrived in ballast water from Asian vessels. I say 'lucky' because wakame is considered to be invasive – it grows a little too well in some areas, to the detriment of native species. Still, it's an amazing sight, with its fronds dancing in the current. The Australian wakame industry is very much in its infancy, but if you can get your hands on some local stuff (often sold blanched and frozen), you will be pleasantly surprised. If not, just grab some dried wakame from an Asian grocer. If you are opting for the latter, try and get the longer strands rather than the tea-leaf style, as big chunks of seaweed work really well in this dish. There are all sorts of health benefits associated with wakame, but I really just like its slippery texture and subtle ocean flavour. It works brilliantly with the crisp lettuce in this salad and the pinch of sweetness in the dressing.

1 Place the flavour-neutral oil in a small saucepan over low heat and add the shallot. Cook for 2 minutes or until the shallot is pale brown and slightly crispy. Remove with a spider or slotted spoon and drain on paper towel, then lightly sprinkle with salt. Reserve 2 tablespoons of the cooking oil and set aside to cool.

2 Simmer the wakame in boiling water for a minute or two to rehydrate, then drain. Chop it into bite-sized pieces, then set it aside.

3 Combine the olive oil with 2 teaspoons of salt and the lemon juice, sugar, vinegar and cooled cooking oil to make a dressing.

4 Combine the salad leaves, herbs, wakame and dressing in a bowl. Tip out onto a serving plate and shower with fried shallots.

5 Serve the salad as a starter, or as a side dish with the Pickled cabbage and soybean stir-fry or Plantain curry.

CANDIED LEMON AND BARBECUED HALOUMI WITH BABY CHARD AND PUMPKIN SEEDS

SERVES 4 AS A STARTER OR 2 AS A MAIN

- 4 CLOVES GARLIC, VERY FINELY SLICED LENGTHWAYS
- 150 ML PUMPKIN SEED OIL (SEE INGREDIENTS; USE EXTRA VIRGIN OLIVE OIL, IF UNAVAILABLE)
- SALT FLAKES AND CRACKED BLACK PEPPER
- 4 TABLESPOONS PUMPKIN SEEDS
- 1 LEMON, SLICED INTO 4 MM-THICK ROUNDS
- 1 TABLESPOON DARK BROWN SUGAR
- JUICE OF 2 LEMONS
- 2 BIG HANDFULS BABY RAINBOW CHARD, LEAVES TORN AND STEMS CUT INTO 3 CM LENGTHS
- EXTRA VIRGIN OLIVE OIL, FOR FRYING
- 300 G HALOUMI, CUT INTO 1 CM SLICES
- 1 HANDFUL WILD ROCKET LEAVES
- 40 G LAVOSH

With chewy slices of lemon, crunchy garlic, crispy pumpkin seeds and smashed-up lavosh, this spring salad is full of robust flavours and textures. Some pumpkin seed oils can be overpowering (this depends on the degree of roasting the seeds have undergone before pressing). I prefer to use an oil that is at the lighter and more viscous end of the spectrum. I suggest you have a taste of whatever oil you are using and, if necessary, blend it with some extra virgin olive oil to tone it down. Be careful not to overcook the garlic or you will end up with bitterness permeating the whole dish. Remove the garlic from the oil when it's golden brown; the colour will deepen as it cools.

1 Place the garlic in a very small saucepan with the pumpkin seed oil. Simmer over low heat for about 10 minutes or until the garlic is just golden brown, then lift it out with a slotted spoon or spider, keeping the pan on the heat. Drain the garlic on paper towel and sprinkle with a pinch of salt. Add the pumpkin seeds to the hot oil and fry for a minute or two until they deepen in colour and smell nutty. Lift out the seeds with a slotted spoon or spider, drain on paper towel and season with salt. Leave the oil to cool in the pan; this will be used for the dressing.

2 Preheat a barbecue grill-plate or char-grill pan over medium heat. Bring a litre of water to the boil in a small saucepan over medium heat. Pop in the lemon slices for 30 seconds or so, then remove them with a slotted spoon and drain on paper towel. Sprinkle with a little brown sugar on each side. Grill the lemon slices for 30 seconds or so on each side until they have dark brown grill-marks and are well caramelised in places. Leave to cool, then cut each lemon slice into eight little triangles.

3 Place the remaining sugar and the juice of 1 lemon in a tiny saucepan over low heat and heat until the sugar dissolves and forms a light caramel; be attentive to prevent it from burning. Set aside.

4 Saute the chard stems briefly in a little olive oil until softened, then add the leaves and heat until just wilted. Deglaze with the remaining lemon juice, then transfer the chard to a large bowl.

5 Place greaseproof paper on the grill-plate or char-grill pan and add the haloumi (this is a mess-proof option – you get the smokiness without the melted cheese everywhere!). When grill-marks appear on the haloumi, use a thin spatula to flip it over, and grill the other side. Remove the haloumi from the heat and when it has cooled a little, rip it up into small pieces.

6 Add the rocket to the chard and toss the haloumi through. Add 3 tablespoons of the reserved pumpkin seed oil, ½ teaspoon of salt and a grinding of black pepper and toss to coat the leaves. Smash up the lavosh into bite-sized pieces and arrange on a serving plate. Top with the dressed leaves and haloumi. Sprinkle the garlic chips, pumpkin seeds and candied lemon triangles over the top and drizzle with the lemon caramel.

GREEN BEANS, GREEN CHILLI AND THAI BASIL WITH HOMEMADE COCONUT MILK

SERVES 4 AS PART OF A SHARED MEAL

1 COCONUT

1 TABLESPOON VIRGIN COCONUT OIL (SEE INGREDIENTS)

200 G GREEN BEANS, TAILED

1 TEASPOON SALT FLAKES

1 TABLESPOON THAI LIGHT SOY SAUCE (SEE INGREDIENTS)

1 BUNCH THAI BASIL, LEAVES PICKED

2 KAFFIR LIME LEAVES, THINLY SLICED

1 LONG GREEN CHILLI, SLICED, SEEDS AND ALL

JUICE OF ½ LEMON OR LIME

STEAMED JASMINE RICE, TO SERVE

PASTE

1 TABLESPOON CORIANDER SEEDS

2 TEASPOONS CUMIN SEEDS

¼ TEASPOON MACE BLADES

4 GREEN CARDAMOM PODS

4 GREEN BIRD'S EYE CHILLIES, SEEDS AND ALL

1 ONION, ROUGHLY CHOPPED

4 CLOVES GARLIC, PEELED

2 STALKS LEMONGRASS, WHITE PARTS ONLY, CHOPPED

2.5 CM PIECE GALANGAL, PEELED AND THINLY SLICED

ZEST OF 1 KAFFIR LIME

1 BUNCH CORIANDER, ROOTS AND STEMS SCRAPED AND CHOPPED

2.5 CM PIECE FRESH TURMERIC, PEELED OR ½ TEASPOON GROUND TURMERIC

2.5 CM PIECE GINGER, PEELED

1 TABLESPOON VEGETARIAN BELACAN (SEE INGREDIENTS)

½ TEASPOON WHITE PEPPERCORNS

This recipe calls for you to make your own coconut milk. Sure, you can buy a tin, but it's really not that hard to extract milk from a fresh coconut – and nothing tastes quite like it. Mature coconuts have less water than young ones, so choose one that makes a sloshing sound when you shake it. When you crack it open, have a bowl ready to catch the coconut water; you can drink this or use it to add a wonderful perfume to other dishes (see the Vietnamese cabbage rolls on page 39). To extract the flesh for the milk, break the coconut shell into pieces with a smash or two, then hold the husk side against your palm and run the coconut flesh over a really coarse cylindrical grater. Whiz the grated flesh in a food processor with water, then strain the mixture through a sieve. (You can also get a second wash of thinner milk from the grated coconut flesh.) The milk is best used within a few hours. Of course, if you're in a hurry, you can buy a top-quality tin instead, but if you do, just remember coconut milk and cream are different, and a recipe will state either depending on the degree of richness required.

1 To make the coconut milk, place one hand firmly underneath the coconut. Hold the coconut over a small bowl, ready to catch the coconut water. Smack the coconut bang in the middle with the back of a cleaver and it will crack. Rotate it a quarter of a turn and smack it again. Repeat in this way until the coconut splits in half, catching the water in the bowl. Grate the coconut flesh and whiz it up in a food processor with 1 cup (250 ml) of water. Strain it through a fine chinoise or sieve, pushing with the back of a ladle to extract all the milk. Set aside.

2 For the paste, dry-fry the coriander seeds, cumin seeds, mace and cardamom in a small, heavy-based frying pan over medium heat for a couple of minutes, shaking the pan occasionally. Meanwhile, blend the chilli, onion, garlic, lemongrass, galangal, kaffir lime zest, coriander roots and stems, turmeric, ginger and belacan to a paste in a food processor, adding a smidge of water to facilitate blending. When the roasted spices have cooled slightly, grind them with the white peppercorns in a spice grinder or pound using a mortar and pestle. Add the ground spices to the paste.

3 Heat the coconut oil in a saucepan over medium heat and add the paste. Fry for a few minutes, stirring constantly, until the aroma of raw spices disappears. After 5 minutes or so, fold in the beans and fry for a couple of minutes, then add the coconut milk, salt and soy sauce and simmer for a couple of minutes or until the beans are just tender to the bite. Add up to a cup (250 ml) of water if the coconut sauce is too thick; you are aiming for an ample amount of sauce, rather than a pile of beans with a little sauce sticking to them! Divide the beans among bowls. Rip up the basil and scatter it over the top, along with the kaffir lime leaves and green chilli. Add the lemon or lime juice. Serve with plenty of steamed jasmine rice.

BROAD BEAN DIP
WITH SMOKED PAPRIKA

SERVES 12 AS A DIP OR 6 AS A STARTER

500 G BROAD BEANS IN PODS
  (TO YIELD 200 G PODDED)

2 SMALL WAXY POTATOES
  (SEE PAGE 117), PEELED AND
  ROUGHLY CHOPPED

2 TABLESPOONS EXTRA VIRGIN OLIVE
  OIL, PLUS A DRIBBLE FOR SERVING

SALT FLAKES AND CRACKED
  BLACK PEPPER

BIG PINCH OF SMOKED PAPRIKA

JUICE OF ½ LEMON

A FEW MINT LEAVES, FINELY CHOPPED

A FEW BASIL LEAVES, FINELY CHOPPED

FLAT BREAD, LAVOSH OR CIABATTA,
  TO SERVE

I'm generally not a broad-bean peeler. It seems a bit fiddly and wasteful to me. In this recipe, however, a double-peel is necessary to create a dip with a smooth texture and vibrant colour. For this reason, I use older broad beans for this as it seems such a shame to double-peel a sweet young bean. Waxy spuds are a must, as the beans really benefit from their creaminess. The dip will keep in the fridge for a couple of weeks: just pop it in a sterilised jar (see page 223) and cover it with a little olive oil to form a seal. This versatile dip is also delicious folded through fresh pasta or used as a base for risotto with some fresh basil chucked in.

1 Fill a saucepan with a litre or so of water and bring to a simmer over medium heat. Pod the broad beans, and blanch them for 3–4 minutes, then drain and leave to cool. Slip the bright green beans out of their skins and set them aside.

2 Place the potatoes in a saucepan of lightly salted cold water. Bring to a simmer over medium heat and cook until tender. Drain well.

3 Heat the olive oil in a medium-sized saucepan over medium heat. Add the potatoes and broad beans and fry for 1–2 minutes, then add 100 ml of water and cook for another 3 minutes. Season with 1 teaspoon of salt and a good grinding of black pepper. Use a stick blender or food processor to blend the mixture to a chunky paste.

4 Transfer the paste to a bowl and garnish with paprika, a squeeze of lemon, mint, basil, some more pepper and a dribble of olive oil.

5 Serve as a dip with flat bread or lavosh alongside or spread over toasted ciabatta for a more substantial starter.

PICKLED CABBAGE AND SOYBEAN STIR-FRY

SERVES 4

3 TABLESPOONS PEANUT OIL

2 SMALL RED CHILLIES, VERY FINELY DICED, SEEDS AND ALL

4 CLOVES GARLIC, CRUSHED

2 TABLESPOONS PICKLED CHINESE CABBAGE, DRAINED AND CHOPPED

500 G FROZEN SHELLED SOYBEANS

½ TEASPOON SALT FLAKES

½ TEASPOON SUGAR

200 G MARINATED SPICY TOFU, SLICED INTO THIN STRIPS

2 TABLESPOONS VEGETARIAN OYSTER SAUCE (SEE INGREDIENTS)

STEAMED JASMINE RICE, TO SERVE

This simple stir-fry must be the most requested recipe in my repertoire. Whenever I cook it for friends, I'm always asked to write down the details. Even tofu-haters seem to enjoy the mealy little soybeans.

Don't get too bogged down by the pickled Chinese cabbage. It's basically there to add salt and vinegar and some crunchy texture. You'll find an array of pickled Chinese greens sold in little tins at Asian grocers; pickled mustard greens would work just fine. The frozen soybeans and marinated spicy tofu are also widely available in Asian grocers, but plain firm tofu will do if you can't find the spicy version.

1 Make sure you have all your ingredients ready to go as this is a fast dish to cook! Preheat the wok over the highest heat for a minute or two, then add the peanut oil and swirl it around. Add the chilli and garlic and cook until lightly browned, then add the pickled cabbage and cook for a further minute. Add the soybeans, salt and sugar and fry for a couple of minutes. Add the tofu and oyster sauce and adjust the seasoning to taste, adding more sugar and salt if you think the dish needs it.

2 Serve with steamed jasmine rice.

PLANTAIN CURRY

SERVES 4

5 PLANTAINS, PEELED AND CUT INTO
  2 CM CHUNKS

SALT FLAKES

1 TEASPOON GROUND TURMERIC

½ TEASPOON CHILLI POWDER

100 ML PEANUT OIL

1 TEASPOON FENNEL SEEDS

4 CINNAMON STICKS

5 OR 6 CURRY LEAVES

1 ONION, FINELY DICED

2 LONG GREEN CHILLIES, SLICED IN
  HALF LENGTHWAYS, SEEDS AND ALL

2 CUPS (500 ML) COCONUT MILK
  (BUY TOP-QUALITY TINNED OR
  MAKE YOUR OWN, SEE PAGE 26)

JUICE OF 1 LEMON OR LIME

STEAMED JASMINE RICE AND
  CHAPATTIS (SEE BASIC RECIPES),
  TO SERVE

I first ate a plantain curry in the Rapid Creek markets in Darwin. I asked a few questions and scribbled down a few notes and I eventually ended up with this recipe, which has become a bit of a quick and easy fave. Although they belong to the banana family, plantains should not be eaten raw; instead you should cook them as you would potatoes. For the uninitiated, the appearance of the fruit versus the flavour of the final dish never seems to add up. It seems our Western brains just *want* to taste banana and this causes all sorts of little 'food malfunctions' in our senses! For this curry, you are ideally after green plantains with a yellowish tinge; this means there will still be a fibrous texture and bite to the finished dish.

1 Place the plantain in a large bowl and toss with 1 teaspoon of salt and the turmeric and chilli powder. Heat the oil in a frying pan over medium heat and, working in batches, fry the plantain chunks a few at a time for 5 minutes or so or until golden brown. Set the fried plantain aside, reserving the cooking oil and spice residue in the pan.

2 Preheat a medium-sized saucepan over medium heat and add the reserved oil and residual spices. Add the fennel seeds, cinnamon and curry leaves and cook for 1 minute until aromatic, then add the onion and chilli and saute until the onion is soft and translucent. Add the coconut milk, 1 cup (250 ml) of water and 1 teaspoon of salt. Add the plantain and cook for 5–6 minutes or until it's tender (like a cooked spud). Remove the pan from the heat and add the lemon or lime juice.

3 Serve the curry immediately with steamed jasmine rice and Chapattis.

SILVERBEET AND BAKED PANEER

PINCH OF SAFFRON THREADS, SOAKED IN A SMIDGE OF WARM WATER FOR 30 MINUTES

100 ML NATURAL YOGHURT, LIGHTLY WHIPPED

SQUEEZE OF LEMON JUICE

GOOD PINCH OF AMCHOOR (DRIED MANGO POWDER)

3 TABLESPOONS GHEE (SEE INGREDIENTS)

2 ONIONS, DICED

4 CLOVES GARLIC, CRUSHED

1 TEASPOON FRESHLY GRATED TURMERIC OR ½ TEASPOON GROUND TURMERIC

2 TEASPOONS CUMIN SEEDS

SALT FLAKES

1 TABLESPOON GROUND CORIANDER

6 SMALL TOMATOES, DICED

1 BIG BUNCH SILVERBEET, LEAVES ONLY, SLICED INTO 4 CM WIDTHS

½ BUNCH CORIANDER, LEAVES PICKED

1 LONG GREEN CHILLI, SLICED, SEEDS AND ALL

PAPPADAMS, TO SERVE

PANEER

1.8 LITRES MILK

160 ML DOUBLE (RICH) CREAM

70 ML WHITE-WINE VINEGAR

This is loosely based on the classic Indian dish saag paneer. Making the paneer may seem challenging but, believe me, it's easy and well worth the effort. This is the simplest form of cheese-making, whereby you add vinegar to hot milk and stand back with amazement as the curds form. A gentle touch is required to scoop the curds, but once you master the technique for this and the pressing of the curds, you will feel an incredible sense of accomplishment. Baking the paneer is not essential, but it does push the dish into a whole other dimension. (If you like, you can just make the cheese and rip it up into chunks *sans* baking – it's still a winner.) I also prefer the texture and iron-rich flavour of wilted silverbeet over the cressy flavour of the more traditional spinach, but by all means use spinach if you prefer. Amchoor is a tangy powder made from dried green mango. It's available from Indian grocers.

1 To make the paneer, line a 15 cm conical strainer with a 50 cm square of muslin, letting the excess hang over the edges. Place the milk in a heavy-based saucepan over low heat and bring it up to just below a simmer. Fold in the cream, and heat gently, stirring with a spatula to prevent sticking. When the mixture begins to foam up – just before it simmers over – stir it with a spatula to create a little whirlpool, then turn off the heat and pour in the vinegar in a steady stream. Leave it for 4 minutes – don't touch! Carefully scoop out all the curds with a flat fine strainer and gently place them in the muslin. Gather together the cloth to form a big ball. Tie string around the top and squeeze out the excess liquid very gently, then place in a wide shallow tray or bowl. Put a plate on top and press with something weighing about 1 kg for 30 minutes: the pan full of leftover whey usually does the trick. A little liquid will be squeezed through the cloth during pressing. Transfer the pressed paneer to the fridge and leave for 40 minutes to firm up.

2 Preheat the oven to 200°C fan-forced (180°C conventional). Mix the saffron and its soaking liquid into the yoghurt. Unwrap the paneer, place it on a lightly oiled baking tray and dollop the saffron yoghurt over the top. Bake until the yoghurt is dark brown with a few black crispy bits. Hit the paneer with the lemon and amchoor.

3 Heat the ghee in a large saucepan over medium heat and saute the onions and garlic until softened. Turn up the heat, add the turmeric, cumin seeds, 1 teaspoon of salt and ground coriander and fry for a minute or so until aromatic; some of the cumin seeds should pop a bit. Turn down the heat to low and fold in the tomato, along with any juices. Simmer for 10 minutes or until the tomato is soft. Turn up the heat, fold in the silverbeet and stir. Add 3–4 tablespoons of water and place a lid on the pan. Cook for 3–5 minutes or until the silverbeet has wilted, then check the seasoning, adding salt to taste.

4 Divide the silverbeet among plates and top with a few spoonfuls of baked paneer. Sprinkle with coriander and chilli, and serve with pappadams.

TOMATO RASAM

SERVES 6

**100 G TOOVAR DAL (SEE INGREDIENTS),
WASHED AND DRAINED**

2–3 CM PIECE GINGER, GRATED

½ TEASPOON GROUND TURMERIC

2 TEASPOONS GHEE (SEE INGREDIENTS)

¾ TEASPOON BROWN MUSTARD SEEDS

¾ TEASPOON CUMIN SEEDS

**½ TEASPOON HULLED AND SPLIT URAD
DAL (SEE INGREDIENTS), GROUND**

6 OR 7 CURRY LEAVES

CORIANDER LEAVES, TO SERVE

**CHAPATTIS (SEE BASIC RECIPES),
TO SERVE**

STOCK

450 G RIPE TOMATOES, CHOPPED

800 ML WATER

**1 TABLESPOON TAMARIND
CONCENTRATE**

¼ TEASPOON GROUND TURMERIC

2½ TEASPOONS SALT FLAKES

5 CLOVES GARLIC, BRUISED

**4 DRIED RED CHILLIES, ROUGHLY
CHOPPED, SEEDS AND ALL**

1 STICK CASSIA BARK (SEE PAGE 177)

6 OR 7 CURRY LEAVES

**1 BUNCH CORIANDER,
STEMS AND ROOTS SCRAPED,
LEAVES RESERVED**

PINCH OF ASAFOETIDA (SEE PAGE 141)

¾ TEASPOON GROUND CUMIN

¾ TEASPOON GROUND CORIANDER

This thin, aromatic soup is perfect for warmer spring weather. I find the hotter the weather gets, the hotter I want my soup – and by heat, I mean chillies! If you're not convinced, you might want to halve the amount of dried chillies in the recipe. The first tomatoes of the year, in late spring, lack the sweetness of fat summer tomatoes, but as this dish is predominantly about sourness, it's not an issue. You'll find toovar dal at Indian grocers, but if you can't get hold of it, you can substitute yellow split peas, and the rasam will still be delicious.

1 Place the toovar dal, ginger and turmeric in a medium-sized saucepan with 800 ml of water. Bring to the boil over medium heat, then reduce the heat and simmer for 1 hour, stirring occasionally, until the dal is really soft. In the last 10 minutes, stir more frequently and slightly mash the dal. Take the pan off the heat, cover with a lid and leave to rest for 10 minutes.

2 Meanwhile, combine all of the ingredients for the stock in a saucepan and simmer over low heat for 1 hour. Strain the stock through a colander, pushing it through with the back of a ladle to extract all the juice, then add the stock to the dal and mix through.

3 Heat the ghee in a small frying pan over high heat, then add the mustard and cumin seeds, urad dal and curry leaves; they will pop and crackle. Immediately transfer this mixture to the dal, working quickly to avoid burning the spices. Stir through to allow the urad dal to thicken the soup slightly.

4 Return the pan to low heat to warm through. Serve the rasam topped with coriander leaves and accompanied by Chapattis.

SPINACH, CHICKPEA AND CHAAT MASALA POTATO SALAD

SERVES 4

1 CUP (200 G) KABULI CHICKPEAS (SEE INGREDIENTS), SOAKED OVERNIGHT IN COLD WATER

500 G SLIGHTLY WAXY POTATOES (SEE PAGE 117)

1 TEASPOON GROUND TURMERIC

4 TABLESPOONS EXTRA VIRGIN OLIVE OIL

2 SMALL ONIONS, DICED

3 CLOVES GARLIC, CHOPPED

1½ TABLESPOONS CHAAT MASALA

5 LARGE HANDFULS BABY SPINACH

1 GOOD-SIZED BUNCH CORIANDER, STEMS AND LEAVES ROUGHLY CHOPPED

1 LONG GREEN CHILLI, SLICED, SEEDS AND ALL

1 BUNCH SPRING ONIONS, GREEN PARTS CUT INTO 2.5 CM LENGTHS

SALT FLAKES

JUICE OF 1 LEMON

Seek out the kabuli variety of chickpeas for this spring salad: they're bigger and paler than the darker, smaller desi variety (see Ingredients). Either will do here, but kabuli give a lighter end result. Frying the cooked chickpeas ensures they brown up nicely and their flavour becomes pleasantly nutty. I always choose waxy potatoes for a dish where structure is important. They hold their shape and texture as they cool, and won't crumble through the salad.

The chaat masala is the real hero of this dish, however. This spice mix just makes everything soar. Ground coriander and ginger play an important role in this blend, but it is the sourness of the amchoor (see page 32) that makes the chaat masala work so well with the spinach and chickpeas.

1 Drain the chickpeas, discarding the soaking water. Place them in a saucepan and cover with cold water. (The less water you use, the quicker the chickpeas will cook, so cover them by just a few centimetres and top up the water during cooking if necessary.) Bring up to a simmer over medium heat and cook for about 1 hour until tender to the bite, then drain and set aside.

2 Place the potatoes in a saucepan of lightly salted cold water and add the turmeric. Bring to a simmer over medium heat and cook the potatoes until tender. Drain well and cut into 2.5 cm chunks, then transfer to a large bowl and cover to keep warm.

3 Meanwhile, preheat a medium-sized saucepan over medium heat and add half the olive oil. Gently saute the onion and garlic until the onion is translucent and soft. Add the chickpeas and chaat masala, then turn up the heat and cook for 5–6 minutes or until the chickpeas are slightly coloured, stirring as you go to prevent burning. If they start to stick, add a little water.

4 Add the chickpea mix (including any chaat masala left in the pan) to the potato. Add the spinach, coriander, chilli, spring onion, salt, lemon juice and remaining olive oil and toss together. Check the seasoning, then serve.

BROAD BEAN RISOTTO with MINT and PECORINO

SERVES 4

- 1 KG BROAD BEANS IN PODS
  (TO YIELD 400–450 G PODDED)
- 2 HANDFULS FLAT-LEAF
  PARSLEY LEAVES
- 2 HANDFULS MINT LEAVES
- 6 SPRIGS MARJORAM, LEAVES PICKED
- 1 HANDFUL WATERCRESS,
  LEAVES PICKED
- 2 TABLESPOONS EXTRA VIRGIN
  OLIVE OIL
- 1 ONION, FINELY DICED
- 3 CLOVES GARLIC, CRUSHED
- 200 G ARBORIO RICE
- 4 TABLESPOONS DRY WHITE WINE
- SALT FLAKES AND CRACKED
  BLACK PEPPER
- 60 G UNSALTED BUTTER, CHOPPED
- GRATED ZEST AND JUICE OF 1 LEMON
- 60 G PECORINO, GRATED, PLUS EXTRA
  SHAVED PECORINO TO GARNISH

When it comes to making the perfect risotto, it's useful to know a bit about the starches found in different sorts of rice. For fried rice (see page 153), you need to inhibit the starches as this keeps the grains separate and fluffy; for risotto, however, you need to bust out the starches in order to produce the desired creaminess. The first way to do this is to maintain heat: adding cold water to the risotto rice will inhibit the release of the starches, so it's essential that your stock or water is simmering. The second way is to deglaze with wine: adding acid will help extract the starches from the plump little grains. Finally, it's important to constantly stir the risotto: this will not only prevent sticking, but will also help to disperse the starches into the stock. These three techniques will give you a really creamy risotto.

Adding lots of cheese, salt and butter to your risotto may deliver a sensational first spoonful, but it's my opinion that the last mouthful should make you want more and a light touch is the best way to achieve this. That said, you can never have enough herbs! They're often dealt with as though they're silver leaf, with a sprig placed here and there (almost inviting you to pick them up and discard them). This risotto is jam-packed full of pureed herbs and most of the flavour comes from them. Don't double-peel the broad beans for this one; not only will a lot of the earthy flavour be lost, but the rice needs a contrasting robust texture to avoid a baby-food consistency.

1 Bring 1 litre of water to a simmer in a saucepan over low heat. Pod the broad beans but don't peel them, then place them in a steamer basket set over the pan. Steam for 5 minutes or until tender, then set aside, leaving the water simmering.

2 Put half of the parsley, mint, marjoram and watercress in a food processor, add a splash of water and blend to a green paste.

3 Preheat a medium-sized saucepan or sauteuse over medium heat. Add the olive oil and saute the onion for a minute or two, then add the garlic and cook until softened. Add the rice and stir to coat with the oil; if it seems dry, add a little more oil. Toast the rice for a couple of minutes, then turn the heat up to high. Wait a few seconds, then deglaze with the wine and add a teaspoon or so of salt. When the wine has evaporated, add ½ cup (125 ml) of the hot water and reduce the heat to medium–low. Stir, and when the liquid has been absorbed, add another ½ cup of water. Continue in this way, adding ½ cup at a time, for about 15 minutes or until the rice is al dente and all the water has been absorbed. Add the pureed herbs, butter, lemon zest and juice, broad beans and grated pecorino and stir through. If the risotto is too dry, add a touch more water.

4 Finely chop the remaining herbs, reserving a few sprigs of each for frou-frou. Divide the risotto among bowls, top with the herbs and shaved pecorino and season with lots of black pepper. Serve immediately.

SPRING

VIETNAMESE CABBAGE ROLLS

SERVES 4–6 AS A STARTER

100 G RICE VERMICELLI NOODLES

12 SAVOY CABBAGE OUTER LEAVES

½ BUNCH VIETNAMESE MINT, LEAVES PICKED

½ BUNCH MINT, LEAVES PICKED

½ BUNCH CORIANDER, LEAVES PICKED AND STEMS RESERVED (SEE BELOW)

½ LONG CUCUMBER, FINELY SLICED

1 CARROT, PEELED AND CUT INTO MATCHSTICKS

¼ ICEBERG LETTUCE, FINELY SLICED

1 LONG RED CHILLI, FINELY SLICED, SEEDS AND ALL

DRESSING

½ TEASPOON WHITE SUGAR

JUICE OF 1 LIME

4 TABLESPOONS THAI LIGHT SOY SAUCE (SEE INGREDIENTS)

2 TABLESPOONS COCONUT WATER (SEE PAGE 26)

2 CLOVES GARLIC, PEELED

1 LONG RED CHILLI, FINELY SLICED, SEEDS AND ALL

2 RED SHALLOTS, PEELED AND SLICED

½ BUNCH CORIANDER, STEMS FINELY CHOPPED (SEE ABOVE)

PINCH OF SALT FLAKES

Some people would argue that Vietnamese rolls are nothing without the traditional dipping sauce, nuoc mam cham, but I reckon they're pretty good with this variation made with Thai soy sauce and coconut water. Besides, the herbs deliver heaps of flavour – the key is using the freshest herbs you can lay your hands on. I use savoy cabbage when making these little numbers, because it has such a vibrant colour and a robust texture and flavour. That's just my personal preference, however, and you may want to use Chinese cabbage instead, which is more pliable and so a little easier to work with.

1 Soak the noodles in a bowl of lukewarm water for 10–15 minutes until soft. Drain, then cover with a tea towel and set aside.

2 Blanch the cabbage leaves in boiling salted water for a minute or until they are just soft and pliable enough to roll. Drain on a tea towel.

3 Meanwhile, combine the herbs in a large bowl. Add the cucumber, carrot and lettuce and mix well.

4 To make the dressing, combine the sugar, lime juice, soy sauce and coconut water in a bowl. Using a mortar and pestle, pound the garlic, chilli, shallot and coriander stems to a paste, then add to the bowl with the salt. The dressing should be a little chunky, and hot, sweet, sour and spicy.

5 Place a cabbage leaf on your work surface. Combine a small amount of the noodles and a handful of the herbs and vegetables in a separate bowl, mix together and dress lightly. Place in the centre of the cabbage leaf. Fold over the edge that is closest to you, then fold both sides in and roll into a cigar shape. Place the filled cabbage roll on a serving plate, seam-side down, or secure it with a toothpick. Continue with the rest of the cabbage leaves, noodles and herb and vegetable mix to make 12 rolls. Mix the leftover dressing with the chopped chilli to make a dipping sauce, and serve.

LAVENDER AND ORANGE BROCCOLI WITH COUS COUS

SERVES 4

1 CUP (200 G) COUS COUS

¾ CUP (180 ML) BOILING WATER

½ CUP (125 ML) EXTRA VIRGIN OLIVE OIL, PLUS EXTRA FOR DRIZZLING

SALT FLAKES AND CRACKED BLACK PEPPER

1 HEAD OF BOLTING BROCCOLI OR ½ HEAD OF REGULAR BROCCOLI, TIPS SHAVED

JUICE OF 2 ORANGES

FINELY GRATED ZEST OF 1 ORANGE

1 TEASPOON DRIED LAVENDER FLOWERS

2 TABLESPOONS CHOPPED THYME

¼ BUNCH FLAT-LEAF PARSLEY, LEAVES PICKED AND FINELY CHOPPED

4 SPRIGS TARRAGON, LEAVES PICKED AND CHOPPED

1 TABLESPOON AGED SWEET RED VINEGAR (SEE INGREDIENTS) OR BALSAMIC VINEGAR

This recipe came about when I needed to use up some broccoli that was on the bolt. Towards the end of spring, the warmer temperatures cause the broccoli to flower, rendering the vegetable inedible. Before this happens, you can salvage the tiny little heads (they look like mini individual broccoli plants) for this salad. The stems become a little tough so I suggest you soup them up – they are absolutely full of flavour. If you don't grow broccoli, just shave little 5 mm bunches off any tight well-formed head of broccoli or – and this is one of my favourite variations – use a caulibroc, a pale green cauliflower and broccoli hybrid.

The lavender flowers are not just a wacky addition for the sake of it. I once made this salad with herbes de Provence (lavender, thyme, savory, basil and fennel) and concluded that the lavender and thyme were the real stars. The addition of tarragon and parsley works for me, but I suggest you have a mess around and see what you like.

1 Place the cous cous in a glass or ceramic bowl. Mix the boiling water with 1 tablespoon of olive oil and 1 teaspoon of salt and pour over the cous cous. Fork through, then cover with plastic film. Leave to stand for 5 minutes, then remove the film and run a fork through the cous cous again to separate the grains.

2 Place the broccoli, orange juice and zest, lavender, thyme, parsley, tarragon, vinegar, remaining olive oil and salt and pepper to taste in a large bowl and mix well.

3 Place the cous cous on a serving plate and top with the broccoli salad. Drizzle with a little extra olive oil, if you think it needs it.

CARROT AND FRIED TOFU SALAD WITH CHILLI PEANUT SAUCE

SERVES 6

2 CUPS (500 ML) FLAVOUR-NEUTRAL OIL
(SEE INGREDIENTS)

400 G FIRM TOFU, BROKEN INTO
BITE-SIZED CHUNKS

⅓ CUP (50 G) RAW PEANUTS

SALT FLAKES

200 G GREEN BEANS, TAILED

200 ML CHILLI PEANUT SAUCE
(SEE BASIC RECIPES)

1 SMALL CUCUMBER, QUARTERED
LENGTHWAYS AND SEEDED,
THEN SLICED

1 LARGE CARROT, PEELED AND
CUT INTO MATCHSTICKS

1 LARGE HANDFUL SHREDDED
CHINESE CABBAGE

1 LARGE HANDFUL SHREDDED
ICEBERG LETTUCE

4 SPRING ONIONS, DARK GREEN PARTS
ONLY, CUT INTO 3 CM LENGTHS

1 CUP (80 G) BEAN SPROUTS

4 HARD-BOILED FREE-RANGE EGGS,
QUARTERED

JUICE OF 1 LEMON

This is basically a gado gado of sorts, but I dare not call it that because purists will point out there's carrot in there, which is a no-no for authentic gado gado. With a bucketload of raw vegies and squeaky beans, this dish screams freshness, whatever you want to name it. I always think it's funny to watch what chefs eat at the end of a shift, having been surrounded by an array of exotic, gourmet ingredients all evening. More often than not, it's something really simple. By the end of a long day prepping and a long night cooking, my appetite is often completely obliterated and I am well past hunger. This simple salad, however, is one of the dishes that I will always gladly tuck into.

1 Preheat the oil in a wok over medium heat until just shimmering (about 180°C). Add the tofu and deep-fry for 5–6 minutes or until it's a deep golden colour, then remove with a slotted spoon and leave to drain on paper towel. Add the peanuts to the oil and deep-fry for 1–2 minutes until golden, then remove with a slotted spoon or spider and drain on paper towel. Lightly season with salt.

2 Bring a saucepan of salted water to the boil and blanch the green beans for 5 minutes. Drain, then refresh in iced water. Drain again and set aside.

3 Gently warm the Chilli peanut sauce over low heat. Divide the cucumber, carrot, cabbage, lettuce, spring onion, bean sprouts and green beans among serving bowls and top with the eggs and tofu.

4 Pour the warm sauce over the vegies and sprinkle with the fried peanuts. Squeeze lemon juice over the top and serve.

CHINESE GREENS with GARLIC and SICHUAN PEPPERCORNS

SERVES 4

3 TABLESPOONS FLAVOUR-NEUTRAL OIL
(SEE INGREDIENTS)

4 CLOVES GARLIC, PEELED AND BRUISED

2 TEASPOONS SICHUAN PEPPERCORNS
(OR MORE TO TASTE, DEPENDING ON
HOW SPICY YOU LIKE IT)

1 BUNCH BOK CHOY, LEAVES HALVED
LENGTHWAYS IF LARGE

1 BUNCH WATER SPINACH, LEAVES
SLICED IN HALF, STEMS RESERVED

1 TEASPOON SALT FLAKES

3 TEASPOONS SHAOHSING
(SEE INGREDIENTS)

STEAMED JASMINE RICE OR FRIED
JASMINE RICE WITH SOYBEAN
SPROUTS (SEE PAGE 153), TO SERVE

I'm always amazed at how many people say, 'How did you cook the vegies?' when I serve these greens alongside a really complicated dish that took days of preparation! It just goes to show that the simple stuff is often the best. The secret is that Sichuan pepper and garlic are infused into the wok oil before the greens are added.

Spring is the last time to get the best-quality Asian greens before the heat knocks them on the head. When I'm feeling lazy, I often just grab an assortment of Chinese greens from the market and cook them up with a little steamed rice for dinner – it's so quick and easy. Choose whatever greens look good at the time, but try to aim for a variety of different flavours and textures, from Chinese broccoli (gai lan) with its sturdy stems and slightly bitter taste, to delicate water spinach and tender, juicy bok choy.

1 Preheat a wok over high heat. Add the oil and swirl around the wok, then add the garlic and Sichuan peppercorns and, when aromatic (about 10 seconds or so), scoop them out. Be careful not to burn the Sichuan peppercorns or they will taint the oil. Discard the peppercorns but reserve the garlic.

2 Add the bok choy and water spinach stems to the wok and stir-fry for a minute. Add the water spinach leaves and salt, and stir-fry to coat with the oil. Add the shaohsing and 1 tablespoon of water and chuck a lid on top. Rattle the wok once or twice, then turn the heat off; the greens will take a minute to steam through. Return the garlic to the wok.

3 Serve immediately with steamed jasmine rice or Fried jasmine rice with soybean sprouts.

CRISPY NOODLES WITH SPRING ONION, CORIANDER AND YELLOW BEAN SAUCE

SERVES 4

2 CUPS (500 ML) FLAVOUR-NEUTRAL OIL
(SEE INGREDIENTS)

90 G VERY FINE RICE VERMICELLI NOODLES

PINCH OF SALT FLAKES

1 TABLESPOON SCRAPED AND CHOPPED
CORIANDER ROOTS

2 CLOVES GARLIC, PEELED

2 TABLESPOONS PEANUT OIL

150 G PRESERVED YELLOW SOYBEANS,
PUREED (OR YELLOW BEAN SAUCE)

50 G GRATED COCONUT PALM SUGAR
(SEE PAGE 52)

4 FREE-RANGE EGGS, WHISKED

2 TABLESPOONS TAMARIND CONCENTRATE

JUICE OF 4 LIMES

100 G DEEP-FRIED TOFU PUFFS, SLICED

1 OR 2 LONG GREEN CHILLIES,
SEEDED AND VERY FINELY SLICED
INTO LONG STRIPS

200 G BEAN SPROUTS

CORIANDER LEAVES, TO GARNISH

CRISPY SHALLOT CHIPS (SEE BASIC
RECIPES), TO GARNISH

1 BUNCH SPRING ONIONS,
DARK GREEN PARTS ONLY,
CUT INTO FINE MATCHSTICKS

¼ TEASPOON FRESHLY GROUND
WHITE PEPPER

Yellow beans, which give this dish its characteristic savoury flavour, are fermented preserved soybeans. The jars are often labelled 'yellow bean sauce' in Asian grocers, even if they contain whole beans. I actually prefer to buy the beans whole and puree them myself, as the pureed versions often have flour in them, which can result in a sauce that is a little thick and heavy. The final sauce should have the consistency of a pancake batter and coat the noodles well.

You need very thin rice vermicelli noodles for this, as they are dumped straight into the hot wok dry and allowed to puff up. I always enjoy this part, because the noodles expand so exponentially – it reminds me of the thrill of popping corn when I was a kid. But be warned: there's a very narrow time margin before the noodles burn, so work quickly and in small batches.

1 Heat the flavour-neutral oil in a wok over medium heat until just shimmering (about 180°C). Break the noodles into fist-sized bunches and, working in small batches, add them to the wok and fry for about 30 seconds–1 minute or so or until they puff up and go crispy. Remove them with a slotted spoon or spider and drain on paper towel.

2 Pound the salt, coriander root and garlic to a paste using a mortar and pestle. Preheat the peanut oil in a medium-sized saucepan over medium heat and fry the paste, then add the pureed yellow beans and fry for 3–5 minutes or until slightly caramelised and starting to stick a little. Add the palm sugar, then remove the pan from the heat and fold in the eggs gradually, whisking as you do; the eggs should thicken instantly, but you need to whisk them briskly to avoid scrambling them. If the sauce doesn't thicken to a pancake batter consistency, return the pan to low heat and continue whisking. Add the tamarind and lime juice.

3 Place the crispy noodles on plates, add the tofu, chilli and bean sprouts and pour the yellow bean sauce over the top. Garnish with coriander leaves, crispy shallot chips, spring onion and white pepper.

CELERY, FENNEL AND LEEK RISOTTO WITH KIDNEY BEANS

SERVES 4

½ CUP (100 G) DRIED RED KIDNEY
    BEANS, SOAKED OVERNIGHT
    IN COLD WATER

2 TABLESPOONS EXTRA VIRGIN
    OLIVE OIL

1 ONION, FINELY DICED

3 CLOVES GARLIC, CRUSHED

1 TEASPOON FENNEL SEEDS

200 G SHORT-GRAIN BROWN RICE

4 TABLESPOONS DRY WHITE WINE

SALT FLAKES AND CRACKED
    BLACK PEPPER

1 CUP (250 ML) FLAVOUR-NEUTRAL OIL
    (SEE INGREDIENTS)

3 STICKS CELERY, DICED, ANY YOUNG
    YELLOW LEAVES RESERVED

70 G UNSALTED BUTTER

2 LEEKS, WHITE PARTS ONLY,
    RINSED AND DICED

1 BULB FENNEL, DICED,
    FRONDS RESERVED

Using short-grain brown rice for risotto may not give you the characteristic smoothness of arborio rice, but the kidney beans bring a lovely creaminess to this dish. You could always add a few knobs more butter and some grated parmesan, if you wish, but I really like the body of this risotto without all the richness.

The second round of vegies – the celery, leek and fennel – popped in at the last minute should be *just* tender. I admit it's tempting to be lazy and throw them into the pan with the onion and garlic at the start of cooking and do a 'one-pot wonder', but the texture of the freshly sauteed vegies contrasts brilliantly with the soft earthiness of the rice and kidney beans.

To garnish, deep-fry the young celery leaves that are tightly wound on the inside of the bunch. They lack the bitterness of the more robust outer leaves, which are really only good for your chooks.

1 Drain the kidney beans, discarding the soaking water. Place them in a saucepan and cover with cold water. Bring up to a simmer over low heat and cook the beans for about 1½ hours until really tender to the bite. Drain and set aside.

2 Heat 1.3 litres of water in a saucepan over medium heat. Meanwhile, preheat a medium-sized saucepan or sauteuse over medium heat, add the olive oil and saute the onion and garlic until softened. Add the fennel seeds and rice and stir to coat with the oil, then turn up the heat and deglaze with the wine. Add the drained kidney beans and 2 teaspoons of salt. Add the hot water a ladle at a time, waiting for the liquid to be absorbed by the rice before adding another. Cook for 40 minutes, stirring as you go, until the rice is tender and the beans are creamy.

3 Meanwhile, heat the flavour-neutral oil in a small frying pan or saucepan over medium heat. When the oil is shimmering (about 180°C), pop in the celery leaves; give them a few seconds and a turn to crisp up, then remove with a slotted spoon or spider and drain on paper towel. Season with a pinch of salt and set aside.

4 Preheat a medium-sized saucepan over medium heat, then add the butter and leave to sizzle until it is nut-brown. Add the diced celery, leek and fennel and ½ teaspoon of salt and saute for about 5 minutes or until tender. Tip the vegies into the rice and stir gently to combine.

5 To serve, spoon the risotto into bowls and top with the fennel fronds and fried celery leaves. Season with black pepper.

PEA RICE PANCAKES

**SERVES 4 AS A SNACK
(MAKES 8 SMALL PANCAKES)**

½ CUP (100 G) PAR-COOKED DRY
BASMATI RICE (PATU PONI)

½ CUP (100 G) BASMATI RICE

3 TABLESPOONS HULLED AND SPLIT
URAD DAL (SEE INGREDIENTS)

1 TEASPOON SALT FLAKES

1 TABLESPOON GHEE (SEE INGREDIENTS)

1 ONION, DICED

½ CUP (160 G) SHELLED FRESH PEAS

1 LONG GREEN CHILLI, CHOPPED,
SEEDS AND ALL

1 SMALL HANDFUL CORIANDER
LEAVES, CHOPPED

1 CM PIECE GINGER, CHOPPED

COCONUT CHUTNEY (SEE BASIC
RECIPES), TO SERVE

Making these crispy little numbers may seem like a lot of effort, but most of the work is done by the rice and dal gently fermenting away by itself with no input required from the cook. It can be a little hard to achieve fermentation on a winter's day, but I find spring weather to be just right.

I love having a little peek the morning after making the batter and seeing how it has grown and become thick and fluffy. The resulting sour flavour of the pancakes is absolutely unique, and it lends itself to a variety of vegies beyond the suggested pea and onion combination.

You'll find par-cooked basmati rice labelled as 'patu poni' in Indian grocers. I have absolutely no idea why you use equal quantities of raw and par-cooked basmati rice in this batter, but this is the way the dish was shown to me and I just follow the recipe because it works!

1 Combine the patu poni and basmati rice in a large saucepan and cover with plenty of water. Leave at room temperature to soak for 3–4 hours. Soak the urad dal in a separate saucepan for the same amount of time.

2 Tip off the water from both pans so that they contain roughly an equal ratio of water to soaked grains (but don't get too fussy; you can add water later, if need be). Blend the rice to a thick paste in a food processor, and then the urad dal. Combine the rice and dal in a large bowl and add the salt. The mixture should look like a pancake batter. Cover the bowl with plastic film and leave in a warm spot overnight.

3 By the morning, the batter should have increased in size by about a third and look like a thick, fluffy pancake batter. Add a little water if it has become too gluey.

4 Preheat a small saucepan over medium heat. Swirl a teaspoon of ghee over the bottom of the pan and pour in the batter to form a layer that is 5–8 mm thick; you may need to tilt and swirl the pan to allow it to spread. Cook for 3–5 minutes or until slightly coloured, then dump an eighth of the onion, peas, chilli, coriander and ginger on the uncooked side. Flip over the pancake and cook for a further 2–3 minutes or until set. The first one might be a little sticky, but persevere and you will find they get easier! Transfer the pancake to a plate and cover with a tea towel. Repeat to make 8 pancakes, adding another teaspoon of ghee every second pancake if necessary.

5 Serve the pancakes warm with Coconut chutney.

GRAPEFRUIT, COCONUT AND MANDARIN SALAD

SERVES 4 AS A STARTER

2.5 CM PIECE GALANGAL, PEELED AND CUT INTO 3 MM SLICES

1 TABLESPOON RAW PEANUTS

3 BIRD'S EYE CHILLIES

4 TABLESPOONS SHREDDED COCONUT

3 TABLESPOONS GRATED COCONUT PALM SUGAR

1 TABLESPOON TAMARIND CONCENTRATE

½ TEASPOON SALT FLAKES

3 TABLESPOONS PEANUT OIL

2 CLOVES GARLIC, CRUSHED

2 RED SHALLOTS, FINELY SLICED

200 G FIRM TOFU, CRUMBLED

2 YELLOW GRAPEFRUIT, PEELED AND CUT INTO 1 CM DICE

3 MANDARINS, PEELED AND CUT INTO 1 CM DICE

1 TEASPOON FINELY DICED GINGER

1 TEASPOON THAI LIGHT SOY SAUCE (SEE INGREDIENTS)

CORIANDER LEAVES OR BOLTING CORIANDER SPRIGS, TO GARNISH

I never tire of citrus and coconut together. This recipe is a vegetarian approximation of Thai betel-leaf parcels, which are usually made with prawns. I've recreated the texture of the pounded dried prawns using fried crumbled tofu; it brings a nice chewiness to the salad. If you have the time and inclination, try freezing a block of firm tofu for a day or two, then defrost it, squeeze out the excess water in a tea towel and proceed with the recipe. I don't know what happens to the structure of the tofu behind the closed door of the freezer but it becomes really pleasantly chewy for some reason, which is just perfect for this!

Coconut palm sugar is derived from the nectar of the coconut palm. Unlike palmyra palm sugar, this renewable crop has been harvested for centuries without destructive deforestation. That said, not all coconut palm sugars are created equal. In my opinion, the king is the fairtrade coconut palm sugar available from Beach Organics (beachorganics.com.au).

You can, of course, take your inspiration from the traditional Thai dish and serve the salad on individual betel leaves instead.

1 Preheat a small saucepan over medium heat. Add the galangal slices and dry-fry them for a minute or so on each side. Add the peanuts and dry-fry for about 5 minutes, shaking the pan to avoid burnt spots. Transfer the galangal and peanuts to a food processor with the chilli and 3 tablespoons of shredded coconut and whiz to form a paste.

2 Preheat the oven to 180°C fan-forced (200°C conventional). Roast the remaining tablespoon of shredded coconut for 8 minutes or until crisp but not coloured. Set aside.

3 To make a dressing, place the palm sugar and 100 ml of water in a small saucepan over low heat and warm very gently until the sugar has dissolved. Add the galangal and peanut paste and simmer for a few minutes until slightly thickened, then remove from the heat and add the tamarind and salt.

4 Preheat a frying pan over medium heat. Add the peanut oil and fry the garlic, shallot and tofu for 3–5 minutes or until just starting to colour. Transfer the tofu to a bowl and add the grapefruit, mandarin, roasted coconut, ginger and soy sauce and combine.

5 Arrange the salad in bowls and pour the dressing over the top. Garnish with coriander.

SNOWPEA TENDRILS AND LENTIL SPROUTS WITH SOY, TAHINI AND LEMON DRESSING

SERVES 4 AS A STARTER OR A SIDE

1 TABLESPOON FLAVOUR-NEUTRAL OIL
(SEE INGREDIENTS)

4 HANDFULS SNOWPEA TENDRILS

¼ TEASPOON SALT FLAKES

1 CUP (80 G) LENTIL SPROUTS

1 TEASPOON SESAME SEEDS, TOASTED

DRESSING

1 TABLESPOON LIGHT SOY SAUCE
(SEE INGREDIENTS)

3 TABLESPOONS TAHINI

1 TABLESPOON LEMON JUICE

2 CLOVES GARLIC, CRUSHED

1 TABLESPOON WATER

PINCH OF CASTER SUGAR

I am an avid sprouter. There's always something in a hemp bag hanging in my kitchen; if it sprouts, I'll eat it! (Believe me, I have tried to sprout the maddest things.) Sprouting is like vegie gardening for those with low attention spans and a demand for instant results. It never ceases to amaze me that you can grow food from seed in 4 days without soil. My all-time favourites are lentil sprouts – they have a really delicious earthy flavour.

To sprout your own, get yourself a hemp bag (in my opinion, the best sprouting medium) and some seeds or legumes; I go for top-quality, preferably organic, stuff. Place the seeds or legumes in a large bowl with plenty of cold water and leave for 1 day at room temperature. Discard the soaking water, then rinse them under cold running water until it runs clear. Moisten the hemp bag and pop in the seeds or legumes, then hang the bag up in an airy place in your kitchen, preferably out of direct sunlight. Every day, put the bag in a bowl of fresh room-temperature water for about 30 minutes. Swirl the bag around and run a little fresh water over the top until the water runs clear. Give the corners a light massage to avoid clumping, then drain and re-hang. Bingo – 3–5 days later, you'll have sprouts! Bung the bag in the fridge and the sprouts will last a week. You can use them in salads or the Fried jasmine rice with soybean sprouts on page 153, or just snack on them. What are you waiting for? Get sprouting!

Snowpea leaves are those young guys with a few little wispy tendrils coming off the stems, ready to latch onto anything for climbing traction. They have a great texture and delicate flavour – nothing like the sad shoots that were on every pub meal in the 1980s, along with an orange slice. The combination of soy and tahini was introduced to me by Cheong Liew. I have a dog-eared, water-damaged, food-splattered notebook that has a note in my writing saying, 'Many tahini, a little soy, water and acid.' I have no idea what recipe this was used in at the time, but it remains a staple dressing for me.

1 Mix together the dressing ingredients with a whisk, adding a little more water if needed to achieve the consistency of mayonnaise.

2 Preheat a wok over high heat. Add the oil and swirl it around, then throw in the snowpea tendrils and salt. Coat with the oil for a few seconds, using tongs to twist the tendrils around the wok. Add a splash of water and toss once, then remove from the heat. The whole process should take about 10 seconds.

3 Place the snowpea tendrils on a plate and top with the lentil sprouts. Spoon over the dressing, sprinkle with sesame seeds and serve.

GOJI, APPLE, PINE NUT AND BARLEY MUFFINS

MAKES 6 BIG MUFFINS

30 G GOJI BERRIES

2 TABLESPOONS ORANGE JUICE

4 TABLESPOONS KIBBLED (CRACKED) PEARL BARLEY

1 TEASPOON GROUND CINNAMON

60 G DRIED APPLE, DICED

30 G PINE NUTS, TOASTED

300 G WHOLEMEAL FLOUR (OR A MIX OF 50 PER CENT WHOLEMEAL AND 50 PER CENT PLAIN FLOUR)

2 TEASPOONS BAKING POWDER

90 G DARK BROWN SUGAR

240 ML BUTTERMILK

65 ML EXTRA VIRGIN OLIVE OIL

1 FREE-RANGE EGG, BEATEN

EXTRA VIRGIN OLIVE OIL (EXTRA) OR BUTTER, TO SERVE

I'm not a fan of over-refined foods and sugar rushes. When I want a snack, I want something with substance and nutritional value. The wholemeal flour, barley and nuts in these muffins will give you the energy to sustain you until your next meal, rather than make you bounce off the walls for 15 minutes and then just fall asleep – a problem with a lot of sugary snack foods.

The goji berries can be replaced with any little dried berries, such as cranberries, if you prefer, but I like them because they're packed with vitamins and antioxidants. I also use sulphur-free dried apple. The colour may not be as appealing as the sulphur-dried variety, but who cares when the apples are just going to be baked?

1 Soak the goji berries in the orange juice for about 20 minutes.

2 Preheat the oven to 180°C fan-forced (200°C conventional) and line a 6-cup muffin tin with greased muffin foils or baking paper. Place the pearl barley and cinnamon in a small saucepan with about 150 ml of water. Cook over low heat for 5 minutes or until the pearl barley is tender, then drain.

3 Combine the goji berries and juice, pearl barley and all remaining ingredients gently in a large bowl. You may need to add a splash of water just to bring the ingredients together, but try not to overmix the batter as this will result in tough muffins.

4 Spoon the batter into the muffin foils or papers. Bake the muffins for 25–30 minutes or until a skewer inserted into the centre comes out clean and the tops are golden brown.

5 Serve the muffins with olive oil or butter.

LOQUAT TARTE TATIN

SERVES 6

30 LOQUATS, HALVED AND PIPS REMOVED

2 TABLESPOONS LEMON JUICE

200 G DARK BROWN SUGAR

1 TEASPOON FINELY GRATED LEMON ZEST

1 TEASPOON THYME, CHOPPED

30 G UNSALTED BUTTER, CUBED

½ CUP (140 G) GREEK-STYLE YOGURT

ROUGH PUFF PASTRY

400 G PLAIN FLOUR

1 TEASPOON FINE SALT

400 G CHILLED UNSALTED BUTTER, CUT INTO 1 CM SQUARES

220 ML REALLY COLD WATER

Spring brings the first flush of loquats, my fave granny fruit. I never really understood why loquats ended up out of favour with most cooks. It probably has something to do with the numerous (and relatively large) pips, but none the less I reckon they're worth the effort. Just about every old neighbourhood has at least one tree and it's such a shame to see the fruit falling to the ground. The fruit doesn't keep very well, so if your loquats are less then perfect-looking, this is the recipe to disguise them. I rarely peel the skins but that's more to do with laziness and I do like a bit of chewy stuff in my food.

Making your own rough puff pastry is optional. By all means buy it instead if you feel like it, but everyone should make a rough puff at least once, just to see how easy it is and how great the results are. This is a method for those of us who don't have all day and a professional pastry chef's equipment, i.e. most of us! It may not be a 'true' puff pastry but it does achieve the requisite layers and crispiness and, frankly, it gives a great result considering the time it saves. This recipe yields twice the amount of pastry you'll need for the tart, but the rest will keep in the freezer for up to 6 months, if wrapped tightly and stored in a freezer bag.

These tarts look cute in baby pans and you'll get better caramelisation compared to making one big tart. Whatever size you opt for, a cast-iron pan is non-negotiable, as you need the density of the metal to conduct enough heat to caramelise the loquat and sugars.

1 To make the rough puff, combine the flour and salt. Make a well in the centre and cut the butter into the flour using a pastry card or your fingertips. Pour in the water. Gather together, but don't knead; just pull it into a lump. Flour your benchtop and roll the dough into a rectangle about 1 cm thick. Fold in the sides to meet, then fold in half again to give you four layers. Turn a quarter, then re-roll the dough. Repeat twice more. Roll out the dough until 3–4 mm thick, lightly flour and place a sheet of baking paper on top. Roll up into a cylinder and leave in the freezer for 20 minutes.

2 Preheat the oven to 200°C fan-forced (220°C conventional). Place the loquats in a bowl, add the lemon juice and sprinkle with half the sugar.

3 Place the remaining sugar and 1 scant tablespoon of water in a medium-sized saucepan over really low heat. Once caramelised, add the lemon zest and thyme, and quickly remove the pan from the heat. Chuck in the butter and loquats, and stir to combine.

4 Divide the loquats among six little cast-iron pans (or one 20–30 cm biggy). Remove the pastry from the fridge, unroll half of it and cut six discs slightly larger than the top of the pans to allow for shrinkage. Place a pastry disc on top of each pan, gently nestling the edges of the pastry down the sides.

5 Bake the tarts for 25 minutes or until the pastry is puffed and golden. Remove the tarts from the oven and when cool enough to handle, flip them over to expose the cooked fruit. Serve them warm with yoghurt dolloped on top.

SUMMER

In summer,
the markets are amazingly
colourful and alive.

Full, fat tomatoes in an array of wonderful colours and varieties sit next to heavy, glossy eggplants. Herbs are abundant; melons, mangoes and stone fruit are everywhere.

On hot, hazy days, I want my food to be light, vibrant and easy to eat. Most importantly, I want to feel energised afterwards. For me, this means cold or spicy soups, lightning-fast stir-fries, fragrant coconut dishes, simple salads with tons of fruit, and – my obsession – chillies! The hotter the weather, the hotter I want my chilli. I love the life and zing it brings to a dish.

This is the time of year when my knife is used more than my pots and pans. It's about chopping and slicing, and then a quick saute, char-grill or plunge into hot oil. Or it's just a drizzle of the best extra virgin olive oil and no cooking at all.

WATERMELON SALAD with PISTACHIOS, BASIL and VINCOTTO

SERVES 4

8 SLICES GOLDEN MIDGET WATERMELON, CUT INTO LARGE TRIANGLES

8 SLICES RED WATERMELON, CUT INTO LARGE TRIANGLES

100 ML EXTRA VIRGIN OLIVE OIL

SALT FLAKES AND CRACKED BLACK PEPPER

2 SMALL–MEDIUM TOMATOES, ROUGHLY CHOPPED OR 8 CHERRY TOMATOES, HALVED

½ BUNCH BASIL, LEAVES PICKED

2 SPRIGS MINT, LEAVES PICKED

⅓ CUP (50 G) PISTACHIOS, ROASTED AND ROUGHLY CHOPPED

2 TABLESPOONS VINCOTTO (SEE INGREDIENTS)

PICKLED WATERMELON RINDS

½ CUP (125 ML) RICE VINEGAR (SEE INGREDIENTS)

¼ CUP (55 G) CASTER SUGAR

1 TABLESPOON FINE SALT

WATERMELON RINDS (SEE ABOVE) WITH 1–1.5 CM FLESH ATTACHED, SKINNED AND CUT INTO 3 CM LENGTHS

Golden midget watermelons are perfect for this summer salad as they're a little less sugary than other varieties. If you can't get hold of them, any watermelon will do – just avoid overripe ones. To determine ripeness, feel the weight of the melon and give it a slap. A ping means the melon is unripe, while a dull thud indicates it's overripe: you want a sound somewhere in the middle.

Chilling the sliced melon before grilling it allows you to sear the outside without the middle turning to mush. You need to use a lot of oil and salt on the grill, as this produces the smokiness that prevents the dish from tasting like dessert. The generous use of pepper also pushes everything to a savoury finish. To avoid waste, I like to pickle the watermelon rinds. They work brilliantly as a garnish for the salad or you can save them to eat as a snack. The sugar content in the pickle is on the low side, so they will only keep for a week or so and must be stored in the fridge. (You can add more sugar to make them last longer, but they'll be too sweet to use here.)

I find that many nuts taste like cardboard, mainly due to extended periods in overseas warehouse, so I always try to buy local. When you roast the pistachios for this dish, they enter a new realm of scent and flavour. Roast them as close to serving time as possible; I also recommend adding some salt flakes, and flipping the nuts over a few times as a fair bit of the flavour comes from contact with the oven tray. Little details maybe, but they will make all the difference to the final dish.

1 Chill the sliced watermelon in the fridge for 10 minutes. This will help the melon to seize up a little, which is essential if it's ripe and in danger of going cactus on a hot grill.

2 If you're making the pickled watermelon rinds, bring the vinegar, sugar, salt and 3 tablespoons of water to the boil and heat until the sugar and salt dissolve. Leave to cool. Place the watermelon rinds in a sterilised jar (see page 223), then pour the pickling liquid over the top.

3 Preheat a grill-plate to hot. Brush 20–30 ml of olive oil over both sides of the watermelon triangles and sprinkle with a pinch of salt. Grill for 2 minutes or until grill-marks appear and a little smokiness becomes evident. It's really important not to overcook the watermelon, though, or it will fall apart.

4 Lightly salt the tomato and rip up the basil leaves. Arrange the grilled watermelon on plates and add the tomato, basil, mint and pistachios. Season with black pepper and drizzle with vincotto and the remaining olive oil.

5 Serve immediately, with a roughly diced pickled watermelon rind if you like.

SNAKE BEANS WITH GARLIC AND TOMATO KUSUNDI

**SERVES 4 WITH RICE OR
6 AS PART OF A SHARED MEAL**

PEANUT OIL, FOR DEEP-FRYING

800 G YOUNG SNAKE BEANS,
TIED INTO LOOSE KNOTS

5 CLOVES GARLIC, PEELED AND
LIGHTLY BASHED

SALT FLAKES

TOMATO KUSUNDI

2 TABLESPOONS BLACK
MUSTARD SEEDS

2 CUPS (500 ML) MALT VINEGAR

250 G GINGER, ROUGHLY CHOPPED

20 CLOVES GARLIC, PEELED

2.5 KG RIPE TOMATOES

30 ML VEGETABLE OIL

2 TABLESPOONS GROUND TURMERIC

2 TABLESPOONS CHILLI POWDER

6 TABLESPOONS GROUND CUMIN

30 LONG RED CHILLIES, HALVED AND
SEEDED (OR SEEDS LEFT IN,
IF YOU ARE A CHILLI NUT LIKE ME)

1½ CUPS (330 G) WHITE SUGAR

SALT FLAKES

I seriously believe that less is often more. Sometimes your ingredients are too good to cloud with other flavours (just ask any Italian!). I love this simple dish, and every time I cook it I'm reminded of how easy it can be to prepare good food. The most complicated part of this recipe is tying the snake beans in knots. For this reason, it's important to use young, unwrinkled snake beans as they can be tied without splitting; they also have the water content to withstand the deep-frying. The trick is to loop the beans gently in a big loose knot so they will fit in the wok, but not so tight that they will bust open. If the beans crack, they will take in too much oil and will no longer taste as vibrant.

It's best to make your kusundi about a week beforehand to allow the full flavour to develop, but I've eaten it straight away and it's still a winner. I suggest you make a bucketload when tomatoes and chillies hit rock-bottom prices, and store it. The snake beans also make a good accompaniment for the Chilli, salt and pepper tofu with ginger (see page 78) or Eggplant curry with green chilli and coconut (see page 105), with or without the kusundi.

1 For the kusundi, soak the mustard seeds in the vinegar overnight. The next day, puree the mustard and vinegar mixture in a blender, then add the ginger and garlic and blend until smooth. Set aside. Blanch the tomatoes in a pan of boiling salted water for 30 seconds, then transfer to a bowl of iced water to cool. Peel off their skins, then cut them in half and remove most of their seeds (a few won't really matter). Dice the tomato flesh.

2 Heat the vegetable oil in a heavy-based saucepan or deep-sided sauteuse until smoking. Remove from the heat and leave the oil to cool slightly, then stir in the turmeric, chilli powder and cumin. Return the pan to the heat and add the mustard, garlic and ginger puree, diced tomato, chillies, sugar and salt to taste. Simmer the mixture over medium–low heat, stirring periodically to prevent sticking, for about 1 hour or until the tomato turns to pulp and a layer of oil floats on the top. This recipe yields 600 g of tomato kusundi. Set aside about 100 g for the snake beans, then pour the remaining kusundi into sterilised jars (see page 223). Leave in the fridge for at least a week (ideally) before using; it will keep for up to 6 months.

3 To deep-fry the snake beans, first cover a decent-sized tray or plate with paper towel. Gently heat the peanut oil in a wok over medium heat to reach 160°C. Don't let the oil shimmer or it will burn the garlic and overcook the outside of the beans before the centre is tender. You will need to deep-fry the beans in at least four batches to prevent overcrowding. Pop a clove or two of garlic in with every batch and fry the lot for 2–4 minutes. When they're ready, the beans should start to wilt around the knotted area and blister slightly. Remove the beans and garlic from the oil with a slotted spoon or spider and leave to drain on paper towel. Salt lightly.

4 Serve the snake beans and garlic cloves with the tomato kusundi.

HOT-AND-SOUR LEMONGRASS AND TOMATO SOUP

SERVES 6

STOCK

1 LITRE COLD WATER

1 TEASPOON FINE SALT

1 TEASPOON WHITE SUGAR

2 TABLESPOONS TAMARIND
CONCENTRATE

6 CLOVES GARLIC, PEELED
AND SMASHED

6 SMALL RED SHALLOTS, PEELED

ABOUT 800 G MAD MIX OF DIFFERENT
TOMATOES, A LITTLE OVERRIPE
(BRUISE THE BIGGER ONES, BUT
LEAVE THE LITTLE GUYS WHOLE)

4 STALKS LEMONGRASS, BRUISED
(YOU MAY NEED TO CUT THEM
IN HALF TO FIT THE PAN)

1 BUNCH CORIANDER, STEMS AND
ROOTS SCRAPED

GARNISH

6 BIRD'S EYE CHILLIES, POUNDED
USING A MORTAR AND PESTLE

1 TEASPOON CHILLI FLAKES

4 KAFFIR LIME LEAVES

2 TABLESPOONS LIME JUICE

2 TABLESPOONS THAI LIGHT
SOY SAUCE (SEE INGREDIENTS)

1 HANDFUL CORIANDER LEAVES

4 BIG PINCHES OF FRESHLY GROUND
WHITE PEPPER

GARLIC CHIPS

4 CLOVES GARLIC, VERY THINLY
SLICED LENGTHWAYS

½ CUP (125 ML) FLAVOUR-NEUTRAL OIL
(SEE INGREDIENTS)

SALT FLAKES

Hot-and-sour soup has a sullied reputation, largely caused by lazy chefs using jars of hot-and-sour paste. That may be the easy option, but there is absolutely nothing like chucking all the ingredients in a pan yourself and serving it up straight away when the lemongrass is still alive and aromatic. I know a million people have written recipes for this and I suspect you're thinking 'meh' right now, but I slipped this in because it's one of the first things I learnt how to cook properly in a Thai restaurant, and then a guest-chef stint by David Thompson at the restaurant where I was working helped me nail it.

I have an issue with dishes that overwhelm you at the first mouthful and then get cloying halfway through. You rarely finish them, and if you do, it feels like work. I like this dish to start off by punching you so hard in the face with chilli that you want to cry, while the rest of the components in the soup leave you feeling a little underwhelmed. The heat makes you want to take another mouthful because you need liquid to cool your palate. Before you know it, you are in a spooning frenzy and you just can't stop shovelling the soup down because the subtlety of the lime, tamarind and coriander slowly come to the fore. I think the only way to achieve this is to go easy on the salt and sugar to allow the rest of the flavours to sing. By the end of the bowl, you are left with a happy numbing buzz and a bizarre sense of accomplishment from withstanding the self-inflicted pain.

I use whole lemongrass (untrimmed) because there is some flavour in the tips and it seems a shame to waste them. With no fuss or straining, this soup looks a little like a witch's brew. Let your guests pick around the kaffir lime leaves and lemongrass stalks, which aren't edible. The whole shallots and coriander stems are not for everyone, but they're my favourite bits of the dish.

1 To make the garlic chips, place the garlic and oil in a small saucepan. Bring up the temperature over medium heat. The garlic will start to spit and hiss a bit. Gently remove any 'stickers' from the bottom and sides of the pan and separate the slices from each other, but try not to disturb them too much. When the garlic slices are just turning a very light golden, lift them out carefully with a spider and spread them out on a tray lined with paper towel. Lightly salt them to help them stay crispy. You'll need 2 teaspoons of garlic chips for this recipe; you can store the leftovers in an airtight container for a few months (they might just need a gentle heat in a pan or the oven to re-crisp). The garlic-flavoured oil is also handy for booting up flavour in dressings and for frying, so strain it and store it for up to 6 months.

2 To make the stock, place all of the ingredients in a large saucepan and simmer for 10 minutes over medium heat. Place all of the garnishes except for the pepper in a big bowl. Pour the stock, without straining it, over the top and give it a little stir. Hit it with the pepper and 2 teaspoons of garlic chips.

3 Plonk the soup in the middle of the table and let everyone help themselves.

ZUCCHINI, EGGPLANT AND POTATO TIMBALES WITH LIME AIOLI

SERVES 4

5 ZUCCHINI (COURGETTES),
    PLUS 1 EXTRA TO GARNISH

EXTRA VIRGIN OLIVE OIL, FOR BRUSHING

SALT FLAKES AND CRACKED
    BLACK PEPPER

650 G UNSALTED BUTTER

800 G WAXY POTATOES (SEE PAGE 117),
    PEELED AND CUT LENGTHWAYS INTO
    1 CM THICK SLICES

FINELY GRATED ZEST OF 1 LEMON

3 TABLESPOONS MARJORAM LEAVES,
    CHOPPED

3 TABLESPOONS CHOPPED BASIL,

3 TABLESPOONS CHOPPED
    FLAT-LEAF PARSLEY

HERB SPRIGS, TO GARNISH (OPTIONAL)

LIME AIOLI

2 LARGE CLOVES GARLIC, PEELED

2 EGG YOLKS

½ TEASPOON DIJON MUSTARD

FINELY GRATED ZEST AND JUICE
    OF 1 LIME

SALT FLAKES AND CRACKED
    BLACK PEPPER

4 TABLESPOONS EXTRA VIRGIN OLIVE
    OIL BLENDED WITH 3 TABLESPOONS
    FLAVOUR-NEUTRAL OIL
    (SEE INGREDIENTS)

BABA GHANOUSH

4 SMALL EGGPLANTS (AUBERGINES)

2 TABLESPOONS UNHULLED TAHINI

JUICE OF ½ LEMON

2 TABLESPOONS GREEK-STYLE YOGHURT

1 TEASPOON SALT FLAKES

All those years of hotel training are hard to let go of, and I sometimes get uncontrollable urges to make food that looks like it's been created by an uptight chef obsessed with precise geometric shapes. Despite the fancy appearance of these timbales, however, there is a little logic involved: you can prepare them in advance, which is perfect if you're having a dinner party and actually want to spend time with your guests instead of running around the kitchen like a maniac.

I like to make this with different-coloured zucchini when they're available. Young zucchini are best here. Avoid older ones with telltale wrinkles, as they tend to break around the seeds during cooking, and in this dish you need a solid wall to hold the baba ghanoush in place. It's also important that the grilled zucchini are soft all the way through; otherwise the flavour of the final dish will fall short. Marjoram, basil and parsley is a winning herb combination. I use young marjoram tips because they have a subtle fragrance and superior texture compared to the larger, more robust leaves, which can be a little furry.

1 To make the baba ghanoush, place the eggplants on a hot grill-plate. Cook until the skin is well blackened and the flesh is super-soft, turning to grill all sides. Transfer the eggplants to a bowl, cover with plastic film and leave to cool. Peel the skins off the eggplants and mash the flesh with a fork. Add the remaining ingredients and mash to combine. Set the baba ghanoush aside.

2 Slice the zucchini lengthways into strips 2–3 mm thick. Soak them in water for 20 minutes (this is not essential, but it will prevent the zucchini absorbing so much oil when they are grilled), then drain and dry with a tea towel. Brush the zucchini with olive oil and season with salt and pepper, then cook them in batches in a hot char-grill pan for a few minutes on both sides to colour. The zucchini should be soft but not falling apart. Set aside.

3 Melt the butter in a large saucepan over low heat. Add the potato slices and salt to taste. The potato should be immersed in the melted butter, and the butter should be just gently bubbling away rather than boiling. Cook the potato for 15–20 minutes until softened. Partially cover the pan with a plate and tip off most of the butter. (You can chuck the butter in the fridge and use it again; it will be especially good for making soups or bechamel as it will contain some starch from the potato.) Set the potato aside; a little butter sitting around it at this stage is nice.

ZUCCHINI, EGGPLANT AND POTATO TIMBALES WITH LIME AIOLI (CONT.)

4 Line four individual 1 cup (250 ml) capacity moulds (a Chinese soup bowl is a good size) with plastic film and grease with butter. Line the inside of each with the zucchini slices, overlapping them slightly and leaving the ends overhanging. Coat with lemon zest, then add a layer of potato, then some baba ghanoush. Season with salt and pepper and sprinkle with herbs. Repeat, finishing with potato on the top layer to give a solid base when the mould is inverted to serve. Fold over the overhanging zucchini, squeeze up the plastic film and press down with a light weight on top of each bowl (a saucer with a small can on top is a good option). Leave the timbales to set at room temperature for a couple of hours, or pop them in the fridge to speed the process up. If you want to serve the timbales warm, heat them only slightly – they taste best anywhere from room temperature to just warm. (And remember to remove the plastic film beforehand!)

5 Meanwhile, to make the lime aioli, blanch the garlic in salted boiling water for 2 minutes. Crush the garlic and place it in a bowl with the egg yolks, mustard, lime zest and juice, ½ teaspoon of salt and pepper. Slowly whisk in the oil in a very slow, steady stream, whisking continuously to incorporate. (You can add up to 1 tablespoon of hot water if the mayo shows signs of splitting.) Keep adding oil until you have a thick mayonnaise. Store leftover aioli in a clean airtight container and refrigerate it immediately. Use it within 3–4 days.

6 For the garnish, slice the extra zucchini into long thin ribbons using a mandoline. Blanch until tender in salted simmering water, then drain.

7 To serve, unwrap the plastic film at the bottom of each mould and turn the timbales out onto serving plates (they might need a few taps). Peel away the remaining plastic film. Brush each timbale with olive oil, garnish with herb sprigs, if you like, and season with black pepper. Serve with the zucchini ribbons and lime aioli alongside.

SALTBUSH, ORANGE AND QUANDONG SALAD

SERVES 4 AS A SIDE

8 VALENCIA ORANGES

½ CUP (40 G) DRIED QUANDONGS

1 STAR ANISE

1 STICK CINNAMON

1 TEASPOON SUGAR

150 G SALTBUSH LEAVES

2 EGG WHITES, WHISKED WITH
   A CUBE OF ICE FOR 20 SECONDS

½ CUP (75 G) WHEAT STARCH
   OR CORNFLOUR

FLAVOUR-NEUTRAL OIL (SEE
   INGREDIENTS), FOR DEEP-FRYING

3 TABLESPOONS EXTRA VIRGIN
   OLIVE OIL

JUICE OF 1 LEMON

1 HANDFUL MINT LEAVES

CRACKED BLACK PEPPER

Old man saltbush is a hugely underrated native plant. While many people have less than enthusiastic memories of eating it, I reckon success is just a matter of sourcing fresh leaves from a decent bush-food supplier or chucking a plant of your own in your garden. It's also about balancing the finished dish correctly. In this recipe, the plant's natural saltiness marries well with the sweet valencia oranges, the tart lemon and the tangy quandongs.

Quandongs are available in fresh, dried or frozen form. The vibrant red of the fresh fruit turns to a rich deep hue when dried, bringing a striking colour to this salad. To make a meal, I often serve this with a little steamed couscous underneath. It also goes sensationally with the Warrigal green and desert lime pesto with wholemeal pasta on page 100. See Ingredients for more info on native Australian foods.

1 Segment 3 of the oranges and set them aside, reserving the cores. Juice the remaining 5 oranges and squeeze any residual juice from the cores. (I rarely strain juice and prefer just to pick out any stray pips as a lot of flavour is lost in the straining.) Soak the quandongs in a bowl with the orange juice for 2 hours, adding ½ cup (125 ml) of water if the quandongs start to look too thirsty. They should be almost rehydrated after a couple of hours, but still retain some bite. There should be about a ½ cup (125 ml) of juice left in the bowl; if not, top up the juice with water (or orange juice, if you have it). Transfer the quandongs and orange juice to a small saucepan over medium heat and add the star anise and cinnamon. Add the sugar and reduce for about 5 minutes, until the quandongs are soft and the juice is thick and syrupy. Remove the star anise and cinnamon and set the quandongs and syrup aside.

2 Pick out a good handful of the smallest saltbush leaves and coat them with the egg white. Dust them with wheat starch or cornflour, shaking off any excess. Heat the oil for deep-frying in a small wok or deep saucepan until just shimmering (about 180°C). Deep-fry the saltbush leaves for 30 seconds or so on each side, until the batter firms up. Remove the leaves from the oil and spread them out on paper towel. The batter will continue to crisp up over a few minutes as it cools. If it doesn't, just return the leaves to the hot oil for a quick re-fry. You can fry the saltbush hours in advance and the batter will stay crisp, as long as you don't refrigerate them or leave them in a humid spot.

3 Warm the olive oil in a heavy-based frying pan over medium heat. Add the remaining saltbush leaves and toss them lightly in the pan, then add the lemon juice. The saltbush will retain its structure, rather than wilting like spinach; you are just warming it through. Fold in the orange segments and the quandongs and orange syrup and toss the pan a few times to ensure everything is coated evenly. Check the seasoning: if it's too sweet, add a little more lemon juice; salt should not be needed. Turn out the saltbush, oranges and quandongs onto a serving plate and top with the crispy saltbush. Garnish with mint leaves and season with black pepper.

MINT, CORIANDER AND PARSLEY FALAFELS WITH YOGHURT

MAKES ABOUT 16

- 1 CUP (200 G) DRIED KABULI CHICKPEAS (SEE INGREDIENTS), SOAKED OVERNIGHT IN COLD WATER
- 1 LARGE ONION, CHOPPED
- 2 CLOVES GARLIC, CHOPPED
- 1 TEASPOON GROUND CORIANDER
- 1 TEASPOON GROUND CUMIN
- 2 LONG GREEN CHILLIES, SEEDED AND CHOPPED
- ½ TEASPOON BAKING POWDER
- SALT FLAKES AND CRACKED BLACK PEPPER
- 5 TABLESPOONS ROUGHLY CHOPPED FLAT-LEAF PARSLEY
- 3 TABLESPOONS CHOPPED CORIANDER
- 2 TABLESPOONS CHOPPED MINT
- 3 TABLESPOONS PLAIN FLOUR, IF NEEDED
- 2 CUPS (500 ML) FLAVOUR-NEUTRAL OIL (SEE INGREDIENTS)
- ½ CUP (70 G) SESAME SEEDS (OPTIONAL)

YOGHURT SAUCE

- 150 G NATURAL YOGHURT
- 1 TABLESPOON UNHULLED TAHINI
- 1 CLOVE GARLIC, CRUSHED WITH A LITTLE SALT
- GRATED ZEST AND JUICE OF 1 LEMON
- CRACKED BLACK PEPPER
- BIG PINCH OF SMOKED PAPRIKA OR SUMAC, TO GARNISH (OPTIONAL)
- CHOPPED PARSLEY, CORIANDER AND MINT, TO SERVE (OPTIONAL)
- EXTRA VIRGIN OLIVE OIL, FOR DRIZZLING

The first time I had falafels, they reminded me of greasy fried cardboard, but then a cooky mate of mine, Stephy, made these and I was converted. The falafels are packed full of herbs, which lighten up the mealiness of the chickpeas. You know you have enough herbs in there if your falafels are green and not the traditional brown I associate with packet mix. You may not need the flour as sometimes the mixture binds up without it. It depends on the moisture and starch present in the chickpeas. Local ones from this season's harvest will always be higher on both counts. Just play around and see how wet and sticky the falafel mixture feels when you ball it up.

1 Drain the chickpeas, discarding the soaking water. Place the chickpeas, onion, garlic, ground coriander, cumin, chilli, baking powder and salt and pepper in a food processor. Pulse until the mixture starts to climb the sides of the bowl instead of just spinning around the bottom – this indicates that it's starting to bind together. Add most of the parsley, coriander and mint, reserving a little of each herb for the sauce, and pulse to mix through.

2 Grab a golfball-sized amount of falafel mixture and see if you can form a ball. If the mixture is sticky, this is a good sign there is sufficient binding. If the mix is either too wet or too crumbly, add about 1½ tablespoons of the flour, mix through and check again; you may need to add the full 3 tablespoons. If the mixture is still too crumbly, add a tablespoon or so of boiling water.

3 Preheat the oven to 180°C fan-forced (200°C conventional). Heat the flavour-neutral oil in a large, deep saucepan until just shimmering (about 180°C) and trial a falafel to check that it doesn't fall apart in the oil. This will happen if there are cracks in the mixture or the oil is not hot enough. Shape the remaining falafel mixture into golfball-sized balls, then form them into ovals and coat with sesame seeds, if you like. Working in batches, fry the falafels for 3–4 minutes until golden brown. Drain on paper towel, then transfer to a baking tray and finish in the oven for 5–7 minutes. (Alternatively, you can just flatten the balls into thin discs and they will cook through sufficiently in the oil without the need to finish them in the oven.)

4 While the falafels are cooking, make the yoghurt sauce. Whisk the yoghurt, tahini, garlic, lemon zest and juice and pepper until smooth. Check the seasoning. Place the yoghurt sauce in a small bowl and sprinkle with a little smoked paprika or sumac, if using. Finally, top with chopped herbs, if you like, then add a drizzle of olive oil. Serve the falafels with the yoghurt sauce.

CUCUMBER AND GIN SOUP WITH TOMATO AND AVOCADO

SERVES 4

6 LONG CUCUMBERS
(USE A THICK-SKINNED VARIETY
FOR A MORE VIBRANT COLOUR)

30–40 ML GIN OR PIMM'S NO. 1 CUP

SALT FLAKES AND CRACKED
BLACK PEPPER

4 BLACK RUSSIAN OR OXHEART
TOMATOES, AT ROOM TEMPERATURE

4 TABLESPOONS EXTRA VIRGIN
OLIVE OIL

1 AVOCADO, AT ROOM TEMPERATURE

JUICE OF 1 LEMON

FINELY GRATED ZEST OF ¼ LEMON

1 HANDFUL MINT SPRIGS, BABY LEAVES
LEFT WHOLE, OLDER LEAVES TORN

This soup shouts summer lunch: light and refreshing, lazy and a little indulgent. It's one of those simple dishes that punches way above its weight because all the key ingredients sing at the same time of the year.

I'm not being precious about the black russians, but they really are the king of tomatoes. They're the sexiest thing to look at and the taste is both sweet and smoky, but if you can't get them, grab oxhearts instead and the dish will taste just as nice. Whichever variety you use, just make sure the tomatoes have enough flavour to keep up with the gin. Pimm's No. 1 Cup works brilliantly, as it's a perfect partner for the cucumber.

To allow all the different flavours to open up, it's best to serve the soup chilled and the avocado and tomato at room temperature. Remove the cucumber juice from the fridge about 30 minutes before serving. You want a soup that is cold, but not so cold it bites.

1 Blanch the whole cucumbers for 2 minutes in a large saucepan of salted boiling water (cut the cucumbers in half if you don't have a large enough pan). Refresh in iced water, then drain. Use a lemon zester to peel long fine ribbons from the skin of one cucumber; this will be the garnish for the soup. Roughly chop the cucumbers and place them in a blender – you may have to do this in a few batches – and blend and blend and blend! You want the soup to be super-smooth.

2 Wrap the pureed cucumber in muslin and squeeze the living daylights out of it, capturing the juice in a bowl. If you like, you can strain the puree through a coarse sieve first to make the job easier, but make sure you push it through with the back of a ladle to extract every drop. You should end up with at least 1 litre of cucumber juice if you blend and squeeze with gusto! Place the strained cucumber juice in the fridge to cool.

3 Half an hour before serving, remove the cucumber juice from the fridge and add the gin or Pimm's, a little at a time, until there's just a hint of fruity gin. Season really well with salt (about a tablespoon), then taste and adjust.

4 Cut the tomatoes into random-sized wedges, lightly season them with salt and pepper, and splash over 10 ml or so of olive oil. Mash the avocado flesh in a bowl with a fork, then add the lemon juice, season with salt and fold in the zest. Arrange the avocado and the tomato wedges in shallow soup bowls.

5 To serve, pour the cucumber soup around the avocado and tomato. Garnish with the cucumber ribbons and mint, drizzle over the remaining olive oil and season with black pepper.

CHILLI, SALT AND PEPPER TOFU WITH GINGER

SERVES 4–6

1 KG SILKEN FIRM TOFU, CUT INTO 4 CM × 3 CM × 2 CM PIECES

½ CUP (75 G) SELF-RAISING FLOUR

2 TABLESPOONS FLAVOUR-NEUTRAL OIL (SEE INGREDIENTS), PLUS EXTRA, FOR DEEP-FRYING

1 CUP (150 G) CORNFLOUR

4 SPRING ONIONS, FINELY CHOPPED, WHITE AND GREEN PARTS SEPARATED

4 CLOVES GARLIC, CHOPPED

2 SMALL RED CHILLIES, SEEDED AND CHOPPED (OR SEEDS LEFT IN IF YOU PREFER)

3 CM PIECE GINGER, PEELED AND CUT INTO MATCHSTICKS

4 CORIANDER ROOTS, SCRAPED AND CHOPPED

100 ML SHAOHSING (SEE INGREDIENTS)

STEAMED JASMINE RICE, TO SERVE

LEMON HALVES, TO SERVE

SPICE MIX

1½ TABLESPOONS GROUND GINGER

½ TEASPOON FRESHLY GROUND WHITE PEPPER

2 TABLESPOONS SALT FLAKES

1½ TEASPOONS FIVE-SPICE POWDER

This is one of my favourite tofu dishes, if executed correctly. The technique produces a crisp batter, which means the tofu can be picked up easily while retaining its soft centre. It's important not to salt the batter as this will draw out liquid from the tofu, resulting in soggy batter. The salt is instead added during the dry-fry (in the spice mix), where it works to extract moisture from the batter, giving double protection against sogginess.

The recipe calls for less than half of the spice mix, but the amount you use in the final dish is entirely up to you. I often put a little of the mix on the table and let people help themselves. (I usually add double to mine, then soak it up with lots of rice and beer!) If you have no takers, store the mix in an airtight container for the next time you make the dish.

1 To make the spice mix, combine all ingredients and set aside. Drain the tofu well by wrapping it in a clean tea towel for 30 minutes.

2 Mix together the self-raising flour, 2 tablespoons of flavour-neutral oil and ½ cup (125 ml) of lukewarm water to make a slightly thick pancake-like batter. Add a couple more tablespoons of water if you need to. Place the cornflour in a separate bowl. Slide the tofu gently into the batter and coat it well by carefully turning it with a slotted spoon. Hold the tofu briefly over the bowl to allow the excess batter to drip away, then toss it in cornflour to lightly coat. (Handle it like a baby!)

3 Heat the oil for deep-frying in a wok over medium heat until it reaches a smidge under a shimmer (about 170°C). Drop small batches of tofu into the oil, adding just four or five at a time – do not overcrowd the wok. Cook the tofu until it's golden and crisp, about 1 minute on one side and 45 seconds on the other. Carefully lift it out with a slotted spoon or spider and spread out on paper towel to drain. (If the tofu has not firmed up, just re-fry it briefly. The batter should not colour past golden; if it does, your wok is too hot or your cooking time too long.)

4 Carefully pour the oil out of the wok and wipe clean. Heat over low–medium heat and add the white spring onion, garlic, chilli, ginger and coriander roots. Dry-fry for a few seconds, stirring continuously as the mixture will burn quickly. When it becomes highly aromatic, immediately add the drained tofu and 2–3 teaspoons of the spice mix (or more if you like it lively). Gently slide the tofu up the sides of the wok and slowly rain in the shaohsing, being careful not to steam the tofu. Add the green spring onion and allow the shaohsing to sizzle with the spices and begin to evaporate before letting the tofu slide back down. The shaohsing will glue all the flavours together, and the herbs, spices and spring onion should stick lightly to the tofu. Toss a few times to combine.

5 To serve, spread the tofu out on a platter. (Don't pile it up or it will sweat.) Serve immediately with bowls of steamed jasmine rice, lemon halves and the remaining spice mix on the side.

BAKED EGGPLANT with CHERRY TOMATO and BUFFALO MOZZARELLA

SERVES 2

2 FIST-SIZED EGGPLANTS (AUBERGINES)

JUICE OF 2 LEMONS

SALT FLAKES AND CRACKED
BLACK PEPPER

10 CLOVES GARLIC, 6 UNPEELED AND
BRUISED LIGHTLY WITH BACK OF
KNIFE, 4 CRUSHED

3 GOLDEN SHALLOTS, DICED

100 ML EXTRA VIRGIN OLIVE OIL, PLUS
A LITTLE EXTRA FOR DRIZZLING

1 × 250 G PUNNET CHERRY TOMATOES
(OR JAZZ IT UP BY USING A
COMBINATION OF BABY TOMATOES,
SUCH AS YELLOW CURRANTS AND
RED FIGS)

4 TABLESPOONS AGED SWEET
RED VINEGAR (SEE INGREDIENTS)
OR BALSAMIC VINEGAR

250 G BUFFALO MOZZARELLA (OR
GOOD-QUALITY COW MOZZARELLA),
SLICED INTO 1 CM DISCS

FINELY GRATED ZEST OF 1 LEMON

80 G PARMESAN, SHAVED

1 BIG HANDFUL BASIL LEAVES
(TORN IF LARGE)

1 HANDFUL ROCKET LEAVES

This recipe came about one summer when I had a garden bursting with basil, tomato and eggplant. I'd been reading about the history of melanzane alla parmigiano and I was taken by the theory that the name was derived from the Sicilian-dialect word 'parmiciana', referring to the slats in a louvred window shutter. So, inspired, I ran with the shutters idea . . .

Select fist-sized eggplants that are heavy and shiny for this. The eggplant should offer some resistance when you give it a squeeze: too firm means it's not quite ready; too soft (or too dull) and it's been hanging around too long since it was picked. Don't be too light-handed when seasoning the eggplants with salt or they will end up tasting bland – a common mistake. When it comes to choosing tomatoes, I always give them a sniff first because I reckon their smell is a good reflection of how they'll taste. Popping the tomato skins in the pan is important as it allows the flavour to bust out, so go hard with the heat for this part.

I always add a dash of olive oil to a finished dish that has been baked using the same oil. Straight from the bottle, the flavour of the oil is completely different and it brings a nice peppery-grassy dimension into play.

1 Preheat the oven to 200°C fan-forced (220°C conventional). Make lengthways slits along the eggplants, about 1 cm apart, starting from the fat base and cutting up to the stem end. You will need to leave about 4 cm of the stem end uncut to hold the eggplant together but still enable you to fan it apart for stuffing. Place each eggplant on a well-greased 30 cm square of foil. Douse the eggplant slits with lemon juice and season with lots of salt (almost ½ teaspoon per eggplant) and pepper. Throw 3 of the bruised whole garlic cloves around each eggplant, then wrap up the foil and bake the eggplant and garlic for 20 minutes.

2 Meanwhile, over medium heat in a small heavy-based frying pan, saute the shallot and crushed garlic in half of the olive oil until translucent and soft. Turn the heat up to high. Add the tomatoes and a good pinch of salt and pepper, and stir until the tomato skins just start to pop and burst. Add 3 tablespoons of vinegar. Remove the pan from the heat and set aside.

3 Remove the eggplants from the oven and allow them to cool slightly so you can handle them. Stuff the slits with the tomato mixture, then the mozzarella slices. Pour the remaining oil and vinegar over the eggplants and season them heavily with 2 large pinches of salt and pepper and the lemon zest. Reseal the foil packages and bake for another 20 minutes or until the eggplant flesh is silky. (If the garlic cloves are still too firm, just re-foil them on their own and return them to the oven briefly to finish cooking.)

4 Place an eggplant package on each plate and unwrap it carefully, ensuring all the juices and any tasty bits stuck to the foil are transferred to the plate. Top with parmesan, basil, salt and pepper. Tuck a little rocket around the eggplant, drizzle over a few more drops of olive oil and serve.

SUGAR SNAPS AND CAPSICUM WITH BURNT CHILLI SAMBAL AND BASIL

**SERVES 4 WITH RICE OR
6 AS PART OF A SHARED MEAL**

400 G SUGAR SNAPS

6 BANANA CAPSICUMS (PEPPERS)

3 TABLESPOONS FLAVOUR-NEUTRAL OIL
(SEE INGREDIENTS)

2 LONG RED CHILLIES, SEEDED
AND ROUGHLY CHOPPED

¼ TEASPOON SALT FLAKES

4 TABLESPOONS BURNT CHILLI SAMBAL
(SEE BASIC RECIPES)

1 TABLESPOON TAMARIND CONCENTRATE

1 TABLESPOON LIGHT SOY SAUCE
(SEE INGREDIENTS)

1 BUNCH THAI BASIL, LEAVES PICKED

SOFT NOODLES, STEAMED JASMINE
RICE OR CHILLI, SALT AND PEPPER
TOFU WITH GINGER (SEE PAGE 78),
TO SERVE

I love overcooked good old garden-variety peas – my people come from England and it's a weakness we have, so please don't judge me too harshly. I love properly cooked al dente peas too, but now and again I just can't help myself. This dish is my Asian-restaurant-trained chef ('Keep the sugar snaps fresh and vibrant in the wok!') fighting with that English upbringing ('Kill the peas!'). I guess everyone's a winner here, because I get to murder the outside of the peas and yet they're still fresh and vibrant on the inside.

The trick is to keep the sugar snaps and capsicum moving (either tossing or using a wok spoon), so that the skins blister but the insides never get a chance to turn to mush. It's a fine balance but the result is an incredible blend of tastes and textures. Banana capsicums are best for this, because the outsides can be blistered without killing the inside flesh. It's not a total deal-breaker to use normal capsicum, but it will alter the outcome considerably. The roll-cut technique makes random-shaped darts of capsicum that look more organic and casual than uniform angled slices and complement the natural shape of the uncut sugar snaps. It's a little ironic that sometimes it takes more effort to make your cooking look nonchalant.

1 Clean the sugar snaps by ripping the vine-end away from the pod, but leave them whole. Roll-cut the capsicums into 4 cm lengths: place the capsicum on a chopping board and cut it at a sharp angle, then roll it a quarter of a turn and cut again. Discard the seeds and core from the larger pieces of capsicum.

2 If you don't have a wok burner, cook this in two batches. Heat the oil in a wok over high heat until just shimmering (about 180°C). Chuck in the sugar snaps, capsicum, chilli and salt and allow the skins to just blister. Add the Burnt chilli sambal, then immediately remove the wok from the heat and deglaze with 4 tablespoons of water. Fold in the tamarind, soy sauce and basil leaves and allow the residual heat to penetrate the basil. Turn the sugar snaps out onto a platter.

3 Serve with soft noodles or steamed jasmine rice, or as an ideal accompaniment to Chilli, salt and pepper tofu with ginger.

GREEN MANGO AND PINEAPPLE SALAD WITH TOFU WONTONS AND PEANUTS

SERVES 6 AS A MAIN

⅔ CUP (100 G) UNSALTED PEANUTS

FLAVOUR-NEUTRAL OIL (SEE INGREDIENTS), FOR DEEP-FRYING

SALT FLAKES

2 TABLESPOONS GRATED COCONUT PALM SUGAR (SEE PAGE 52)

¼ LARGE OR ½ SMALL PINEAPPLE, PEELED, CORED AND CUT INTO WEDGES

1 GREEN MANGO, PEELED AND CUT INTO LONG MATCHSTICKS

1 BUNCH CORIANDER, LEAVES PICKED

½ BUNCH VIETNAMESE MINT, LEAVES PICKED

½ BUNCH THAI BASIL, LEAVES PICKED

1 CUP (80 G) BEAN SPROUTS

BURNT CHILLI SAMBAL (SEE BASIC RECIPES), TO SERVE

TOFU WONTONS

½ TEASPOON BLACK SESAME SEEDS

250 G FIRM TOFU

2 EGG WHITES

2 TABLESPOONS FINELY CHOPPED GINGER

2 CLOVES GARLIC, FINELY CHOPPED

2 SPRING ONIONS, FINELY SLICED, WHITE AND GREEN PARTS SEPARATED

3 TABLESPOONS THAI LIGHT SOY SAUCE (SEE INGREDIENTS)

1 TABLESPOON VEGETARIAN OYSTER SAUCE (SEE INGREDIENTS)

2 TEASPOONS TOASTED SESAME OIL

GOOD PINCH OF FINE SALT

¾ TEASPOON GROUND WHITE PEPPER

1 TEASPOON CORNFLOUR

30 OR SO WONTON WRAPPERS

FLAVOUR-NEUTRAL OIL (SEE INGREDIENTS), FOR DEEP-FRYING

DRESSING

3 TABLESPOONS GRATED COCONUT PALM SUGAR (SEE PAGE 52)

3 TABLESPOONS LIME JUICE

3 CLOVES GARLIC, CRUSHED

3 TABLESPOONS THAI LIGHT SOY SAUCE (SEE INGREDIENTS)

Not all mangoes are palatable when green. If you are unsure about which varieties are good to use, a safe bet is to shop at an Asian grocer because they will most likely have the ones you are looking for. Handle them to ensure they're not too ripe; a little thumb press will alert you to this. The addition of peanut and tofu to this salad makes it a great source of protein. Pineapple has an enzyme in its flesh that helps with the absorption of protein, so if you are vegetarian and a little low on protein intake, this is a perfect dish.

The super-crunchy peanuts are prepared in a similar way to good old-fashioned chips. They're simmered in water first, so that when they're fried they crisp up really well without burning. You could just roast some raw peanuts, but believe me the result is just not the same. If Thai basil is unavailable, use double the amount of sweet basil and add a few sprigs of garden-variety mint to approximate the slightly minty flavour of Thai basil.

1 For the dressing, gently heat the palm sugar in the lime juice until dissolved; do not boil. Leave to cool, then fold in the garlic and soy sauce.

2 Place the peanuts in a saucepan with 3 cups (750 ml) of cold water. Simmer for 30 minutes until the peanuts are soft (the water will look all cloudy). Drain well, then spread out on a tea towel for 1 hour or so. The longer you leave the peanuts to drain, the safer the next stage will be.

3 Place the oil for deep-frying and the peanuts in a wok over medium heat, making sure the oil does not rise higher than halfway up the sides of the wok; you may need to do the peanuts in two batches. Bring the oil up to just shimmering (about 180°C), using caution as the peanuts will spit a bit due to the water content. You will notice that the soaked peanuts take a lot longer to crisp and colour than dry nuts, about 5–10 minutes. Lift them out using a spider or slotted spoon and leave them to drain on paper towel, salting them lightly before they cool.

4 Place the palm sugar on a plate and press the pineapple wedges into it to coat. Preheat a grill-plate to low, then add the pineapple. It will caramelise very quickly, so turn it over as soon as slightly blackened grill marks appear and grill the other side. Set aside to cool, then cut into chunks.

5 To make the tofu wontons, first toast the sesame seeds in a dry frying pan. Wrap the tofu in a clean tea towel and squeeze to extract water. Crumble the tofu and place it in a food processor along with 1 egg white and the toasted sesame seeds, ginger, garlic, white spring onion, soy sauce, oyster sauce, sesame oil, salt and white pepper. Sprinkle in the cornflour and pulse until the ingredients just come together. Do not puree the mix, as you want the tofu to retain some texture. If the mix is very dry and crumbly, add the other egg white; if it's too wet, add a little extra cornflour. It should just hold together when lightly squeezed.

GREEN MANGO AND PINEAPPLE SALAD WITH TOFU WONTONS AND PEANUTS
(CONT.)

6 Transfer the mixture to a bowl and add a couple of tablespoons of green spring onion. Spoon about 1 heaped teaspoon of filling into the centre of each wonton wrapper. Dip your finger in a little water and rub around the outer rim of the wrapper, then gather it up and squeeze to form a 'money bag'. If there is extra liquid in the filling mixture at the bottom of the bowl, avoid scooping it up when you fill the dumplings as it will make the finished wontons soggy.

7 Preheat oil for deep-frying in a wok over medium heat until just shimmering (about 180°C). Pop in the wontons a few at a time and fry until golden and crispy. The wontons will float and have small blisters on the surface when they're ready, but they may need to be turned or even pushed down with a slotted spoon if raw dough patches are floating above the oil level. Remove the cooked wontons and leave them to drain on paper towel.

8 To assemble the salad, mix together the pineapple, mango, herbs and bean sprouts in a large bowl. Add a few spoonfuls of the dressing to the salad until it's just coating everything. Divide the salad among plates and arrange the wontons on top. Drizzle about 1 tablespoon of sambal around each plate, or serve it in a small bowl to the side. Finally, scatter the peanuts over the top.

BANANA POORIS

MAKES 8

280 G ATTA FLOUR (SEE INGREDIENTS)

LARGE PINCH OF SALT FLAKES

2 TABLESPOONS FLAVOUR-NEUTRAL OIL OR GHEE (SEE INGREDIENTS)

160 G BANANA PUREE (FROM ABOUT 2 LARGE BANANAS, BLENDED TO A PULP)

FLAVOUR-NEUTRAL OIL (EXTRA), FOR FRYING

ICING SUGAR, FOR DUSTING (IF YOU ARE MAKING THE SWEET VERSION)

Pooris are deep-fried flatbreads popular in India and Pakistan. This recipe is for those of us who always have a fruit bowl full of mad, bad brown bananas bought on over-excited shopping trips, but can't be stuffed baking yet another banana cake. I'm always using dessert ingredients in my savoury cooking as I'm not a great pastry chef but I absolutely love cooking with fruit. You can serve these with a savoury dish such as the Mushroom dal on page 141, or as a sweet snack sprinkled with icing sugar.

1 Sift the flour into a bowl, add the salt and oil or ghee, and rub together until the mixture resembles coarse breadcrumbs. Add the banana puree and 2 tablespoons of room-temperature water and combine to form a ball. Knead the dough for about 10 minutes until elastic, then shape it into a ball. Let the dough rest in an oiled bowl covered with plastic film for at least 1 hour.

2 Divide the dough into eight and roll each piece into a ball. Sprinkle the benchtop with a little flour and roll out each ball into a very thin 10 cm round. In a small wok over medium heat, add enough oil for one poori to be submerged and heat until just shimmering (about 180°C). Fry the poori in the hot oil, one at a time. The poori should puff up immediately on one side; working quickly, turn it over using tongs and cook the other side, about 15 seconds per side. (If the outside of the poori becomes really dark but the centre is still doughy, you have not rolled it flat enough.) Gently remove the poori from the oil, holding it vertically and carefully shaking off the excess oil. Drain the poori on paper towel, turning it over after a minute or two to prevent any ponding of oil on the top side. If you are not using the pooris immediately, wrap them loosely in a tea towel or napkin to keep them warm.

3 Serve the pooris hot as an accompaniment to savoury Indian dishes, or dust with icing sugar for a sweet version.

PAPAYA AND POUNDED BEAN SALAD

SERVES 4 AS A SIDE

4 CLOVES GARLIC, PEELED

PINCH OF SALT FLAKES

4 BIRD'S EYE CHILLIES, CHOPPED, SEEDS AND ALL

2 TABLESPOONS SALTED PRESERVED TURNIP SLIVERS

40–50 G SNAKE BEANS OR GREEN BEANS, CUT INTO 2 CM LENGTHS

1 CARROT, PEELED AND CUT INTO THIN MATCHSTICKS

1 SMALL GREEN PAPAYA, PEELED AND SEEDS SCRAPED, FLESH CUT INTO MATCHSTICKS

1–1½ GREEN MANGO, PEELED AND CUT INTO MATCHSTICKS

8 CHERRY TOMATOES, HALVED

3 TABLESPOONS CHOPPED ROASTED UNSALTED PEANUTS

DRESSING

1 TABLESPOON TAMARIND CONCENTRATE

JUICE OF 2 LIMES

2 TABLESPOONS THAI LIGHT SOY SAUCE (SEE INGREDIENTS)

2 TABLESPOONS GRATED COCONUT PALM SUGAR (SEE PAGE 52)

Plenty of farmers' markets and some supermarkets sell ripe papaya (also called pawpaw), and I do love a juicy ripe one for a dessert dish or a fruit plate. However, for this classic Thai salad, known as som tam, you'll need an unripe green papaya, so a trip to the Asian grocer might be in order. A ripe papaya will have a yellow brown skin and will bruise as easily as a ripe peach. A good green papaya will have a teeny amount of give when pressed; no give and it will be too unripe (it will also probably feel really heavy in your hand). To make this dish without the usual dried shrimp and fish sauce and still get a great result is not hard, as salted preserved turnip slivers (widely available in Asian grocers) give a little hit of the same flavour and slightly chewy texture. The best way to achieve the matchstick cut of the vegetables is to use a mandoline.

When I'm in Darwin, I love watching the women at the Rapid Creek markets making this salad with their mortars and pestles. Everyone has a different approach. The ingredients remain pretty similar across recipes, but arguments never end about which ingredient should be pounded the most. When we were shooting this recipe for the book, my long-time assistant, Carolyn, took control of the pounding, so the method given here is hers – and I've again changed my mind (for the better) regarding how it should be done. I love this about cooking: it's a journey of refinement that never ends. On my headstone I would like, 'He is still trying to improve his som tam.'

1 Pound the garlic, salt and chilli to a fine paste using a mortar and pestle. Add the turnip and three-quarters of the beans and pound gently to bruise. Follow with half the carrot and half the papaya and lightly pound until all the ingredients are well-bruised, so that they absorb the heat and flavour of the chilli and garlic but do not turn to mush. Add half the mango and bruise lightly.

2 For the dressing, combine most of the tamarind, lime juice, soy sauce and palm sugar in a bowl. It's good to hold back a little of each so you can rebalance the final flavours to your preference. Gradually add the dressing to the salad and mix together, gently pounding to blend the fruit and vegetables with the seasoning. Taste and adjust the flavours to the desired combination of hot, sour, sweet and salty, adding more dressing (or just tamarind, lime, soy sauce or palm sugar) as required.

3 Add the tomatoes and the remaining carrot, papaya and green mango to the salad, then the remaining beans. Mix together well. Note that these ingredients are not pounded up but just folded through, adding another texture and a few crunchy bits to the finished salad. Lastly, add the peanuts and serve.

BERRY AND MINT SALAD WITH FETA

SERVES 4

1 HANDFUL ALMONDS

4 TABLESPOONS EXTRA VIRGIN
OLIVE OIL

200 G FETA, DRAINED AND BROKEN
INTO SMALL CHUNKS

600–700 G BERRIES (WHATEVER TYPE
YOU LIKE), AT ROOM TEMPERATURE

1 BUNCH MINT, LEAVES PICKED

1 BUNCH CORIANDER, LEAVES PICKED
WITH 3–4 CM STEM

½ BUNCH FLAT-LEAF PARSLEY,
LEAVES PICKED

1 TABLESPOON AGED SWEET RED
VINEGAR (SEE INGREDIENTS)
OR BALSAMIC VINEGAR

2 THICK SLICES GOOD WHOLEMEAL,
SPELT OR SOURDOUGH BREAD,
RIPPED INTO SMALL PIECES,
CRUST ON

SALT FLAKES AND CRACKED
BLACK PEPPER

I owe this recipe to my friends Jordie and Stephy, who served up a berry salad in their waterside cafe one sunny Saturday. I think a perfect day makes your meal-memory crystal clear and the combination of the salty feta, sweet–acid mulberries and palate-cleansing mint proved unforgettable . . .

Choose any berries you like for this: raspberries, silvanberries, mulberries, blackberries and gooseberries are my favourites. My advice is to hit the market without a shopping list and see which berries taste best. It doesn't matter how many different types you include as long as they're good. I'm spoilt because a number of local berry-growers ring me when their trees are busting. One couple has a 100-year-old mulberry tree in the Adelaide Foothills and I'm always left speechless by the flavour of their produce. Oh, and a lesson learnt from Maggie Beer – don't refrigerate the berries! They're most flavoursome when they're just above room temperature. I love berries picked up off the ground in the garden for this very reason. Ice-cold berries (and feta) are always underwhelming. A mild, creamy, less briny feta works best here. If you are using brined feta, wash it well.

1 Preheat the oven to 180°C fan-forced (200°C conventional). Place the almonds on a baking tray and roast them for 8–10 minutes. Remove from the oven and as the almonds are cooling, splash about a teaspoon of olive oil over them. Bash the almonds into small pieces and keep them warm by returning them to the oven with the heat turned off and the door ajar.

2 Chuck the feta, berries and herbs together in a bowl. Add the remaining olive oil and the vinegar and toss lightly.

3 Transfer the dressed salad to serving plates and sprinkle with warm almonds and bread. Season with salt – you'll need a fair bit to push the sweet flavours into a savoury dimension – and a good grinding of black pepper. Serve immediately.

GRILLED ASPARAGUS WITH HOLLANDAISE AND BAKED BEANS

SERVES 4

12 ASPARAGUS SPEARS

30 ML EXTRA VIRGIN OLIVE OIL

¼ TEASPOON SALT FLAKES

CRACKED BLACK PEPPER

GOOD CRUSTY BREAD, TOASTED,
    TO SERVE

POACHED FREE-RANGE EGGS,
    TO SERVE (OPTIONAL)

BAKED BEANS

250 G DRIED CANNELLINI BEANS,
    SOAKED OVERNIGHT IN COLD WATER

2 TABLESPOONS EXTRA VIRGIN
    OLIVE OIL

1 SMALL ONION, CHOPPED

2 CLOVES GARLIC, CRUSHED

400 G REALLY RIPE TOMATOES,
    CHOPPED (SEEDS AND SKINS OKAY)

2 TABLESPOONS MAPLE SYRUP

1 BAY LEAF

2 TABLESPOONS DIJON MUSTARD

SALT FLAKES AND CRACKED
    BLACK PEPPER

10 BASIL LEAVES, RIPPED

HOLLANDAISE

50 ML WHITE-WINE VINEGAR

8 WHITE PEPPERCORNS, CRUSHED

1 BAY LEAF

300 G UNSALTED BUTTER

3 FREE-RANGE EGG YOLKS,
    AT ROOM TEMPERATURE

1 TEASPOON BOILING WATER

½ TEASPOON SALT FLAKES

JUICE OF ½ LEMON

The last of the local asparagus in summer is great to chuck on a char-grill (something I wouldn't usually do with tender, new-season produce). It doesn't matter if the stems are a little dry or woody, as the intense heat softens them up nicely and the small black blisters add a great flavour. Coat the asparagus with plenty of olive oil and be generous with the salt. If you want to preserve the gentle tips, just hang them off the side of the grill and just concentrate the heat on the stems.

I always find it ironic that commercially made, pre-prepared foods, such as apple pie, chips and mashed potato, were created because people loved the original dishes so much, but inevitably the essence of the food disappears in the production process. I've rarely tasted a commercial baked bean that actually tastes baked. Overnight soaking aside, it really doesn't take long to knock up a batch of these homemade beans. This recipe is a bit of a cheat because you quickly boil the white beans to give them a kick start, so the baking time is reduced.

This version of hollandaise is a sure-fire, idiot-proof, no-whisk version. It works on the principle that if you heat the butter and blend it with room-temperature yolks, it will be warm enough to coagulate the yolks but not so hot as to curdle them. Heating it to the right temperature kills off any harmful bacteria – a cheap milk thermometer will do for this. The vinegar also renders the sauce a little hostile to nasties, but it's always wise to use your hollandaise immediately and discard any leftovers.

1 For the baked beans, drain the cannellini beans and rinse them well, discarding the soaking water. Place the beans and 1 cup (250 ml) of cold water in a heavy-based saucepan over medium heat and bring to a rapid simmer for 20 minutes, with the lid on. Remove from the heat and set aside.

2 Preheat the oven to 180°C fan-forced (200°C conventional). Place a large heavy-based ovenproof saucepan (or cast-iron casserole) with a tight-fitting lid over medium heat. When hot, add the olive oil and saute the onion until translucent. Add the garlic and continue to sweat, then add the tomatoes (including their juices) and maple syrup. Add the par-cooked beans along with their cooking water, and the bay leaf. Stir, then place the lid on the pan and transfer it to the oven to bake for about 1½–2 hours until the beans are soft. Top up the pan with a little extra water if the beans are becoming dry (but not too much, because you want a thick, rich sauce).

3 To make the hollandaise, place the vinegar, peppercorns and bay leaf in a teeny pan over medium heat and reduce by half. Strain, discarding the peppercorns and bay leaf, and set aside. Place the butter in a medium-sized heatproof bowl that will sit over a saucepan without touching the base of the pan. Cover the bowl with plastic film and set over a saucepan filled with 5–7 cm of water. Place over low heat for 20–30 minutes until the white

solids fall to the bottom. Tip the clarified butter into a clean, small heavy-based saucepan, leaving the white solids in the bottom of the bowl. Place the clarified butter over low heat and take the temperature up to 80°C. Place the warm vinegar reduction and the egg yolks in a small heatproof jug and blend using a stick blender. Carefully pour the clarified butter into the jug while blending. Start slowly with a teeny drizzle; once halfway through, you can get a little more cavalier with your pouring. Whisk in the boiling water to lighten and stabilise the sauce, then add the salt and lemon juice. Keep the hollandaise in a warm place and use it within an hour.

4 For the asparagus, preheat a grill-plate or char-grill pan to high. Toss the asparagus in the olive oil, salt and pepper. Grill both sides of the asparagus until it's wilted and a little blackened on the stems.

5 When you're ready to serve, remove the beans from the oven. Add the mustard, ½ teaspoon of salt and pepper and stir through. Check the seasoning, then add the basil. Serve the beans on good crusty toast. Place the grilled asparagus to the side and top with hollandaise. This is especially nice with a poached free-range egg on top.

PEACH AND HAZELNUT SALAD WITH ROCKET

**SERVES 4 AS A STARTER
OR A SIDE SALAD**

100 G UNSALTED BUTTER

JUICE OF 1 LEMON

SALT FLAKES

3 RIPE PEACHES, AT ROOM TEMPERATURE

2 HANDFULS BABY ROCKET

1 HANDFUL WATERCRESS

NUT SPICE BLEND

2 TEASPOONS CORIANDER SEEDS

1 TEASPOON LEMON MYRTLE

½ TEASPOON ANISEED MYRTLE

1 TEASPOON MOUNTAIN PEPPER

1 TEASPOON GROUND BUSH TOMATO

100 G HAZELNUTS (OR MACADAMIAS),
CRUSHED

When stone fruit hits the market and the days are hot, I make a lot of salads like this. They're perfect for lunch. A combination of white and yellow peaches looks nice for this, but that's just a bonus and certainly not essential.

The nut spice blend exudes a bouquet that is boldly aromatic and uniquely Australian. Lemon myrtle, aniseed myrtle, mountain pepper and ground bush tomato are available from Outback Pride (see Ingredients for more info). Spices can vary in intensity from crop to crop, so hold back a little of the blend as you add it to the dressing, then check the balance and adjust as you go.

I always advise young chefs to taste a dressing and consider how it will work with the other ingredients, in this case the peaches and rocket. If I notice the chef has snuck a taste of the peaches for sweetness, popped a bit of the rocket in their mouth to check for pepperiness and then closed their eyes when tasting the dressing, I know they're concentrating on bringing all the ingredients together in their mind and they have a chance of a big future in this industry.

1 For the nut spice blend, finely grind all the spices and then fold in the crushed nuts.

2 To make a dressing, melt the butter in a frying pan over medium heat until it froths and turns nut-brown. Remove the pan from the heat and add the lemon juice, then gradually add 1½ teaspoons of the nut spice blend, tasting as you go. Season with salt to taste.

3 Halve the peaches and take out the stones, then cut them into quarters. Combine the peach quarters with the rocket and watercress, pile the salad onto a plate and pour over the hot dressing. Sprinkle another teaspoon of nut spice blend over the top. (Leftovers can be stored in an airtight container in the pantry for up to 6 months.)

4 Serve the salad in a big bowl as a shared side dish, or divide among individual plates to serve as a starter.

GREEN TOMATO AND MUSHROOM BRUSCHETTA WITH BASIL AND WATERCRESS

SERVES 4

8 SLICES CIABATTA, TOASTED

6 GREEN ZEBRA TOMATOES OR RIPE RED HEIRLOOM TOMATOES

½ BUNCH BASIL, LEAVES PICKED AND RIPPED

1 SMALL BUNCH WATERCRESS, LEAVES PICKED WITH 3–4 CM STEM

1 TABLESPOON LEMON JUICE

3 TABLESPOONS EXTRA VIRGIN OLIVE OIL

SALT FLAKES AND CRACKED BLACK PEPPER

80 G PARMESAN, SHAVED

MUSHROOM PASTE

1 CUP (40 G) DRIED PORCINI

100 ML EXTRA VIRGIN OLIVE OIL, PLUS EXTRA TO COVER

4 GOLDEN SHALLOTS, DICED

3 SPRIGS OREGANO, LEAVES PICKED

3 SPRIGS THYME, LEAVES PICKED

4 CLOVES GARLIC, FINELY CHOPPED

4 PORTOBELLO MUSHROOMS, TRIMMED AND VERY FINELY DICED

6 FRESH SHIITAKE MUSHROOMS, TRIMMED AND VERY FINELY DICED

6 BUTTON MUSHROOMS, STEMS REMOVED, CAPS VERY FINELY DICED

4 SWISS BROWN MUSHROOMS, TRIMMED AND VERY FINELY DICED

1 TABLESPOON FINE SALT

½ CUP (125 ML) DRY WHITE WINE

50 ML RED-WINE VINEGAR

The green zebra tomato has pretty much all the properties of a ripe red tomato; it's fun to eat a raw green tomato that is surprisingly sweet and juicy. They're popping up in markets more and more these days, and their stripes look stunning in this salad. However, they're not essential here and you can substitute any good heirloom tomato if you are struggling to find them.

The mushroom paste is absolutely magic. As well as being a delicious bruschetta topping, it makes a sensational pasta sauce or pizza base and is also great tossed through warm potatoes. Mushrooms require lots of salt so season well; this will also help to preserve the paste. This recipe makes 450 g of mushroom paste. Leftovers will keep for about 3 months in the fridge.

1 To make the mushroom paste, place the porcini in a bowl and pour over warm water until the porcini are just covered. (Make sure you use only the minimum amount of water required to cover, otherwise you'll be reducing the paste for a long time later in the recipe!) Soak the porcini for 20 minutes or until soft, then strain them through a fine sieve, squeezing the juice from the porcini and reserving the soaking liquid. Finely chop the porcini.

2 In a large sauteuse or frying pan, heat the olive oil over medium heat, then add the shallot and fry until fragrant. Add the chopped porcini and stir. Add the herbs and garlic, continuing to stir. Add all the mushrooms and saute for about 10–15 minutes – it can take quite a lot of time for the mushrooms to really cook out. A good indicator is the oil in the pan: at first the mushrooms act like sponges and suck up all the oil, but once they're cooked, they start to give the oil back. They also become highly aromatic. When the mushrooms are cooked, add the salt. Deglaze the pan with the wine and then the vinegar and continue to cook until the liquid has evaporated. Add the reserved porcini liquid and simmer until it has evaporated.

3 Remove the pan from the heat and blend the mushroom mixture with a stick blender; you want it to retain a little texture, a bit like crunchy peanut butter. Pour the mushroom paste into sterilised jars (see page 223). Let it settle to remove any air pockets (tap the jar gently on the bench to help it along), then cover with olive oil to make an airtight barrier.

4 To assemble the bruschetta, spread a layer of mushroom paste over the toasted ciabatta. Slice 3 tomatoes and cut the remaining 3 into quarters. Toss the tomatoes with the basil, watercress, lemon juice and olive oil and season well with salt and pepper. Pile the tomatoes on the toast and top with parmesan and extra salt and pepper. Serve with a small bowl of mushroom paste on the side.

CORN SHORT SOUP
with SILKEN TOFU and EGG THREADS

**SERVES 8 AS A STARTER
OR 4 AS A MAIN**

50 ML FLAVOUR-NEUTRAL OIL
(SEE INGREDIENTS)

½ ONION, DICED

2 SPRING ONIONS, SLICED, WHITE
AND GREEN PARTS SEPARATED

2.5 CM PIECE GINGER, CHOPPED

4 CLOVES GARLIC, CHOPPED

SALT FLAKES AND FRESHLY GROUND
WHITE PEPPER

½ CUP (ABOUT 75 G) COOKED SHIITAKE
MUSHROOMS, STEMS DISCARDED,
THINLY SLICED

12 BABY CORN, SLICED

1 CUP (120 G) FROZEN SHELLED
SOYBEANS (SEE PAGE 28) OR
BABY PEAS OR 1 CUP (160 G)
FRESH BABY PEAS

3 TABLESPOONS SHAOHSING
(SEE INGREDIENTS)

1 LITRE SHIITAKE STOCK
(SEE BASIC RECIPES)

2 TABLESPOONS LIGHT SOY SAUCE
(SEE INGREDIENTS)

3 TABLESPOONS CORNFLOUR,
MIXED WITH A LITTLE WATER TO
MAKE A SMOOTH PASTE

100 G SILKEN TOFU, CUT INTO SQUARES

2 FREE-RANGE EGG WHITES,
AT ROOM TEMPERATURE, LIGHTLY
BEATEN WITH A LITTLE SALT

½ TEASPOON SESAME OIL

Texture is underrated in cooking. We're so obsessed with flavour, it falls off the radar. In this dish, a rough version of a Chinese short soup, the silken tofu contrasts beautifully with the crunchy corn and the chewy shiitakes. Temperature also plays a critical role here. To achieve the perfect serving temperature, the bowls of cold tofu are flashed in the oven. This takes the chill off the tofu, but more importantly the simmering soup and the warmish bowl combine to produce the ideal temperature for optimum flavour.

To get the egg threads right, I use a squeezy bottle or plastic bag with a small hole in the corner to achieve a steady stream arcing into the swirling pot of soup. Chicken stock is often the base of this dish, but a light clean shiitake stock is such a great background note to the sweetness of the corn. Buy the best dried shiitakes you can find; they should smell all sunny and earthy, not dusty or musty.

White pepper is the underdog of the spice world. I use loads in this dish, as it's the perfect partner to spring onion and shaohsing. I never tire of these three flavours together. Don't use the talcum-powder supermarket stuff: go to a good spice merchant instead and pound your own peppercorns, just before serving. Do this and you will rediscover the magic of this humble spice.

1 Heat the flavour-neutral oil in a heavy-based frying pan over medium–high heat and saute the onion, white spring onion and ginger. Get a little colour on the ginger, then add the garlic and continue to fry. Add a pinch of salt and the sliced shiitakes and turn up the heat. You may need a little more oil at this stage because the mushrooms are like little sponges! Once they're a little crispy around the edges, add the corn and continue to fry over high heat, stirring frequently. Fold in the soybeans or peas and fry for another minute or two. Deglaze with the shaohsing, then remove the vegies from the pan and set them aside.

2 Add the Shiitake stock to the pan and bring to a simmer over medium heat. Add the soy sauce, and salt to taste, then remove the pan from the heat. Add the cornflour paste in a smooth stream, stirring constantly until the soup achieves a thick but not gluggy consistency. Return the pan to the heat to cook out the cornflour for a minute, then return the vegies to the pan and bring back to a simmer.

3 Meanwhile, preheat the oven to 150°C fan-forced (170°C conventional). Divide the tofu among ovenproof Chinese soup bowls and place them in the oven for 5 minutes to warm.

4 Remove the pan from the heat and make a little whirlpool by stirring a large wooden spoon around the pan in one direction. Immediately pour in the beaten egg whites in a thin stream. The residual heat will cause egg threads to form; don't disturb the soup while it's setting or you'll create a mess.

5 Ladle the soup over the tofu in the warmed bowls. Finish with sliced green spring onion, a few drops of sesame oil and a big pinch of white pepper.

WARRIGAL GREEN AND DESERT LIME PESTO WITH WHOLEMEAL PASTA

SERVES 4

500 G WHOLEMEAL OR SPELT PASTA

EXTRA VIRGIN OLIVE OIL,
   FOR DRIZZLING

SALT FLAKES AND CRACKED
   BLACK PEPPER

SHAVED PARMESAN, TO SERVE

**WARRIGAL GREEN AND
DESERT LIME PESTO**

250 G WARRIGAL GREENS, LEAVES
   PICKED, BABY LEAVES RESERVED
   TO GARNISH

1 LARGE HANDFUL SEA PARSLEY
   LEAVES AND STALKS, ROUGHLY
   CHOPPED, A FEW LEAVES RESERVED
   TO GARNISH

JUICE OF 3 LEMONS

1 CUP (250 ML) EXTRA VIRGIN OLIVE
   OIL, PLUS EXTRA TO COVER

200 G MACADAMIAS

ABOUT 30 DESERT LIMES, PLUS A FEW
   HALVED LIMES TO GARNISH

4 CLOVES GARLIC, PEELED

SALT FLAKES AND CRACKED
   BLACK PEPPER

¾ CUP (60 G) GRATED PARMESAN

A little practice cooking with native Australian ingredients will bring great rewards. This recipe features a few harder-to-get ingredients, but I say get used to eating them – they're the future! The beauty of the native ingredients in this dish is that they stand up to the robust wholemeal pasta, which can sometimes overpower pasta sauces with its earthiness.

Warrigal greens are a leafy vegetable similar to spinach. As an alternative, good old English spinach would suffice. Some caution should be taken with warrigal greens as the leaves contain toxic oxalic acid (also found in rhubarb leaves), which can be harmful for some people if consumed in large quantities. To remove the oxalic acid, it's a good idea to blanch the leaves first. Sea parsley is a bit like parsley on steroids. (You can substitute dark-green, hardy flat-leaf parsley, but you will need to use double the quantity.) Desert limes are punchier and sourer than regular tahitians, so my substitute would be a small preserved lemon. These native limes freeze really well, so grab a bunch if you see them (they also make the greatest addition to vodka and tonic, so they won't go to waste). I seem unable to kill my warrigal greens and sea parsley no matter how much love I don't give them. The seedlings are available from good nurseries, but if you just want to buy some to try, get Googling (see Ingredients).

1 To make the pesto, first blanch the warrigal greens in a large saucepan of boiling water for 1 minute, then rinse them in cold water. Drain well and squeeze out excess liquid. Roughly chop the blanched greens and the sea parsley and place them in a food processor with the lemon juice and a little olive oil. Blend until the greens are roughly pureed. Add the macadamias, limes and garlic and continue to blend until the mixture looks like crunchy peanut butter. Continue blending slowly while drizzling in the remaining olive oil until you have a coarse pesto, then season to taste with salt and pepper. Add the parmesan and pulse to blend through, then check the seasoning. Transfer the pesto to sterilised jars (see page 223). Let it settle to remove any air bubbles, then cover with olive oil. This makes about 750 g of pesto. Store it in the fridge for up to 3 months. If you want to eat the pesto as a dip, add a little more oil to thin it down.

2 Cook the pasta in boiling salted water until al dente, then toss it in a little olive oil to prevent it from clumping together. Fold in 100 g of pesto per serve, drizzle with olive oil and season with black pepper.

3 Make a salad of the reserved warrigal green baby leaves, sea parsley and desert limes. Season with salt to taste, then add a little olive oil and pepper.

4 Divide the pasta among bowls and garnish with the salad. Serve with shaved parmesan and a small bowl of extra pesto to the side, if you like.

TOMATO SINGAPORE NOODLES WITH FRIED TOFU

SERVES 2

½ PACKET (75–100 G)
RICE VERMICELLI NOODLES

50 ML FLAVOUR-NEUTRAL OIL
(SEE INGREDIENTS)

2 FREE-RANGE EGGS, CRACKED INTO
SEPARATE SHALLOW BOWLS

2 ONIONS, SLICED LENGTHWAYS

¼ TEASPOON SUGAR

1½ TABLESPOONS MADRAS
CURRY POWDER

2 RIPE TOMATOES, DICED

½ CUP (40 G) BEAN SPROUTS

2 TABLESPOONS LIGHT SOY SAUCE
(SEE INGREDIENTS)

JUICE OF ½ LEMON

10 GARLIC CHIVES, CUT INTO
3 CM LENGTHS

¼ TEASPOON FRESHLY GROUND
WHITE PEPPER

FRIED TOFU

125 G SILKEN FIRM TOFU, DRAINED

100 ML FLAVOUR-NEUTRAL OIL
(SEE INGREDIENTS)

1 TABLESPOON THAI LIGHT
SOY SAUCE (SEE INGREDIENTS)

BIG PINCH OF FRESHLY GROUND
WHITE PEPPER

This is a nice light meal for those summer nights when it seems just too hot to eat. I like the noodles on the plain side, but feel free to bump up the curry powder. Some Indian grocers sell their own homemade blends, which I find far superior to many prepared mixes. You might want to add a fresh sambal on the side – simply blitz some fresh red chilli with a smidge of rice vinegar.

Have a little patience with this. The reason why home cooks fail with wok dishes is about more than just technique and experience. I spent three years using professional wok burners and I still struggle at home, even though I've got a pretty good cook-top. Your local Asian restaurant will have wok burners with about five times the gas pressure that domestic supply delivers. So while you can get your wok up to a really high heat before adding the oil, as the volume of ingredients builds up your wok simply can't recover the temperature. My advice is to buy a small (35 cm) wok – monster woks look impressive but you will just not get the side-heat happening – and never do more than two serves at a time. As they say, it's not the size that matters!

Correct soaking of the vermicelli is also important. I use tepid water: too cold takes too long; too hot turns the noodles to mush. Have a little bite every now and then; you want the texture of slightly under al dente pasta. If you're short of time, you can use warmer water but make sure you check the noodles frequently. Drain the noodles really well before frying them – wet noodles will steam the wok up and produce a lame result.

If this all sounds too boring, don't worry. I assure you good cooking has something to do with a reasonable recipe, but it's mostly a combination of alchemy and practice – plus a little love and luck, of course.

1 Soak the vermicelli noodles in tepid water for 1 hour or so, then drain them very well and place on a tea towel to dry.

2 For the fried tofu, wrap the drained tofu in a clean tea towel and place it on a draining board. Press it with a 1 kg weight for an hour (a couple of canned food tins are good for this). Unwrap the pressed tofu and slice it into rectangles about 4 cm × 10 cm. Preheat a wok over high heat and heat the oil until slightly hazy. Add the tofu and deep-fry it for about a minute, then flip it over and fry it for another minute or until golden and crispy. Drain the tofu on paper towel, then cut it into 8 mm-thick slices. Transfer the tofu pieces to a small bowl, pour in the soy sauce and toss rapidly. The inside of the tofu will immediately reclaim its lost moisture from the pressing process by sucking up the sauce. The outside should remain crispy; if not, you have used too much soy. Hit the tofu with a big pinch of pepper and set aside.

TOMATO SINGAPORE NOODLES
WITH FRIED TOFU (CONT.)

3 Get all the ingredients near your work area – you need everything on standby so that you can keep your head over the wok for this dish. Preheat a small heavy-based frying pan over absolutely the lowest heat for 2 minutes. Add a smidge of oil and coat the pan, then slide the eggs in very carefully and immediately put the lid on the pan. Turn the heat off after 3 minutes and leave the residual heat to cook the egg through gently for a further 5 minutes. Slow-frying the eggs this way, with absolutely no bubbling or splattering occurring in the pan, will ensure that the egg whites stay silky and the yolks remain runny.

4 Meanwhile, place a wok over medium–high heat and add the remaining oil. After a brief pause, add the onion and fry, stirring continuously. Add the sugar after a minute or so to facilitate caramelisation. When the onion is really soft and sweet-smelling, add the curry powder and fry for a minute or so, stirring continuously until the pungent raw spice notes disappear (you will notice that the aroma drops down a notch). Turn up the heat to the highest setting and fold in the tomato. Cook until it's soft and has broken down – you now basically have spicy tomato ketchup. Fold in the bean sprouts and soy sauce, stir once or twice, then add the drained vermicelli noodles. Cook for a minute or two while constantly tossing the wok so as to coat noodles with the spices and seasonings. Be careful not to overcook the noodles, as they will become 'jelly' very quickly. Splash in the lemon juice, then immediately transfer the noodles to two pre-warmed bowls and throw in the tofu and garlic chives.

5 By now, the egg whites should be just set and the yolks cooked but runny. Shake the pan to check that no egg white is still translucent; replace the lid and continue cooking if it is. Slide an egg onto each serve of noodles, add a big pinch of white pepper and serve.

EGGPLANT CURRY WITH GREEN CHILLI AND COCONUT

SERVES 4 AS PART OF A SHARED MEAL

3–4 TABLESPOONS VIRGIN COCONUT
   OIL (SEE INGREDIENTS)

2 TABLESPOONS THAI LIGHT
   SOY SAUCE (SEE INGREDIENTS)

8 APPLE EGGPLANTS, QUARTERED

½ CUP (80 G) PEA EGGPLANTS

8 FRESH KAFFIR LIME LEAVES

50 G SNAKE BEANS, CUT INTO
   2.5 CM LENGTHS

3 TABLESPOONS GREEN PEPPERCORNS

12 BABY CORN, SLICED

JUICE OF 1 LIME

3 TABLESPOONS TAMARIND
   CONCENTRATE

½ BUNCH THAI BASIL, LEAVES PICKED

3 TABLESPOONS CRISPY SHALLOT
   CHIPS (SEE BASIC RECIPES)

STEAMED JASMINE RICE, TO SERVE

CHILLI AND GARLIC PASTE

1 CLOVE GARLIC, PEELED

PINCH OF SALT FLAKES

3 BIRD'S EYE CHILLIES

GREEN CURRY PASTE

10 LONG GREEN CHILLIES, CHOPPED

4 RED SHALLOTS, CHOPPED

1 TABLESPOON CHOPPED GALANGAL

1 TABLESPOON CHOPPED GINGER

2 TABLESPOONS CHOPPED
   LEMONGRASS, WHITE PART ONLY

3 TABLESPOONS CHOPPED GARLIC

1 TEASPOON VEGETARIAN BELACAN
   (SEE INGREDIENTS)

1 TEASPOON FRESHLY GROUND
   WHITE PEPPER

BIG PINCH OF SALT FLAKES

I love this curry like no other. Pea and golfball eggplants are mainstays in our Asian groceries these days and in this dish they create a lovely combination of textures: the golfball eggplants have a great squeakiness to them and the pea eggplants deliver a little seedy crunch. If you have trouble finding them, you can always throw in sliced regular eggplant as a substitute. The virgin coconut oil carries the flavour of the dish to a level that other vegie oils struggle to achieve, and it also buffers and balances the chilli. If you have no luck finding the vegie belacan for the green curry paste, you can just omit it, bump up the soy sauce and add a touch more salt to the final dish. There's enough going on here to keep your palate happy without it.

When you taste the curry on completion, you may feel that it's too hot and salty but remember the accompanying jasmine rice is neutral, and that in essence the curry should simply season the rice. This is why the ideal way to serve such dishes is to plonk separate bowls of rice and curry on the table (I like twice the amount of rice to curry). That way, everyone can tweak the overall flavour of their dish by adjusting the amount of rice they put in their bowl. This one also goes well with Papaya and pounded bean salad on page 89.

I To make the chilli and garlic paste, pound the ingredients together using a mortar and pestle. To make the green curry paste, pound all the ingredients using a mortar and pestle to form a smooth paste.

2 In a wide shallow saucepan, heat 1 tablespoon of coconut oil until it is really hot, then fry the chilli and garlic paste over high heat until it turns golden. Turn the heat down to medium and add the green curry paste. Fry the paste, adding extra coconut oil as the paste sticks to the pan (doing this gradually will ensure you fry, rather than steam, the paste). If the mixture is sticking after you have added all the oil, you can periodically add a little water (1 tablespoon at a time). You want the mixture to glisten and not look too dry.

3 Add the soy sauce to the pan along with 3 cups (750 ml) of water and simmer for 5–10 minutes until the oil is floating on top. Add the eggplants and kaffir lime leaves and cook for about 6 minutes. Add the snake beans, peppercorns and corn and cook for a further 4 minutes until the vegetables are just cooked through. Remove the pan from the heat and hit the curry with the lime juice, tamarind, basil and shallot chips – it should be salty, hot and pungent.

4 Serve the curry in a big bowl to share, with lots of steamed jasmine rice.

FIG, BLUE CHEESE AND WITLOF SALAD

SERVES 4

40 G UNSALTED BUTTER

½ CUP (35 G) FRESH BREADCRUMBS

SALT FLAKES AND CRACKED
    BLACK PEPPER

12 PERFECTLY RIPE FIGS

150 G BLUE CHEESE

1 HEAD OF WITLOF (CHICORY/ENDIVE),
    LEAVES TRIMMED

90 ML EXTRA VIRGIN OLIVE OIL

1 TABLESPOON AGED SWEET RED
    VINEGAR OR VINCOTTO
    (SEE INGREDIENTS)

The great thing about figs is that you really don't need to do much to be blown away by a dish with them in. My favourite variety for this salad is the white adriatic fig, the variety I grow at home. It's the surprise package of the fig world: boring on the outside but with amazing strawberry-coloured flesh on the inside. However, you can use any variety as long as the figs are not bruised, have not seen a fridge, and are perfectly ripe; look for a tiny bit of sap popping out of the bottom as an indicator of a ripe fig. When these figs are baked and squishy, and served with gooey cheese, the aromas and flavours just explode. You could throw in a few hazelnuts if you like, but I honestly can't think of a better late-summer first course than this salad served just as it is.

1 Rub the butter into the breadcrumbs and season with salt and pepper. Cut each fig almost into quarters by making two incisions downwards from the stem and stopping 1 cm short of the bottom. Open up the figs slightly. Crumble in the blue cheese and chuck the breadcrumb mixture loosely over the top. Place the figs on a baking tray and grill them under high heat until the breadcrumb topping just browns up and the cheese is starting to slide around inside the fig.

2 If you are making individual servings, arrange a few leaves of witlof on each plate and top with 3 hot figs. Douse them with olive oil, then vinegar or vincotto, and season with salt and pepper. Alternatively, just combine everything in a bowl and serve as a side salad, or arrange half-figs on witlof leaves for a pre-dinner canape.

BANANAS WITH RUM AND COCONUT PALM SUGAR AND CHILLI SORBET

SERVES 6

6 LARGE BANANAS

60 G GRATED COCONUT PALM SUGAR (SEE PAGE 52)

70 G UNSALTED BUTTER

100 ML DARK RUM

FINELY GRATED ZEST AND JUICE OF 1 LIME OR LEMON

20 MINT LEAVES, SHREDDED

CHILLI SORBET

1 CUP (220 G) WHITE SUGAR

JUICE OF 4 LIMES OR LEMONS

FINELY GRATED ZEST OF 1 LIME OR LEMON

4–5 LONG RED CHILLIES, FINELY DICED

This whole dish came about because I don't like dessert! I was trying to come up with a sweet dish for a cooking class, so I just grabbed a few of my favourite sweet things (coconut palm sugar and bananas) and a few of my favourite not-so-sweet things (limes and chillies) and this is what happened.

Sorbet recipes can be a little intimidating, with all sorts of jargon that is hard to understand – to my mind, Baume scales and crack stages belong in the realm of the professional pastry chef. This, I promise, is an idiot-proof recipe. You don't even need a sugar thermometer. You do need an ice-cream machine, but there are some cheap little machines out there that work fantastically.

When it comes to chillies, generally the bigger they are, the milder they are, but I always have a little taste first. If you are a 'heat fairy' – my affectionate term for the wonderful Maggie Beer: she is a sensitive and delicate type! – it's worth remembering that most of the heat is in the membrane holding the seeds, so try a little of the cleaned skin and if it really bites, scale back the amount. For a hotter sorbet, add the chilli to the sugar syrup as it cools before churning.

1 To make the sorbet, combine the sugar with 1 cup (250 ml) of water in a small heavy-based saucepan. Place over medium–high heat and stir for 30 seconds, to lift the sugar from the bottom of the pan, then increase the heat and wait for the syrup to boil. Allow to boil for 1 minute, then remove the pan from the heat and add the lime or lemon juice. Top up the mixture with cold water to make 3½ cups (875 ml) in total.

2 Transfer the sorbet mixture to a wide bowl to facilitate quicker cooling and leave it to cool in the fridge or freezer. For best results, the mixture should be below 10°C before churning. (This is about the temperature of a beer in a good pub, i.e. cold but not freezing!) Add the zest, then transfer the mixture to an ice-cream machine and churn until firm, according to the manufacturer's instructions. Add the chilli and churn the sorbet again for 1 minute. Freeze the sorbet until you are ready to serve.

3 Cut the bananas in half on a 45-degree diagonal to create a dart shape. Place the palm sugar on a plate and roll the bananas in the sugar to coat. (Reserve the palm sugar on the plate.) Place a large heavy-based frying pan over medium heat. When hot, add half the butter, then pop the bananas in and cook for about 3 minutes until caramelised and coloured, turning to cook all sides. Carefully slide 2 tablespoons of the rum into the pan, then step back and shake the pan: it should flame up. (If not, don't worry. The alcohol will still evaporate; it just won't look as dramatic without the flame.) Lift out the bananas with a spatula and place them on a cold serving plate.

4 Add the remaining butter and rum to the pan, along with the reserved palm sugar and the zest and juice and cook over medium heat until the sugar has dissolved. Remove the pan from the heat and allow the syrup to cool slightly.

5 To serve, place a big scoop of sorbet and a couple of banana halves on each plate, and coat the bananas with the rum syrup. Garnish with shredded mint.

COCOA AND CHERRY WHOLEMEAL COOKIES

MAKES 10 BIG COOKIES

190 G PLAIN FLOUR

1 SCANT TEASPOON BICARB SODA

100 G WHOLEMEAL FLOUR

1 TEASPOON SALT FLAKES

1 TABLESPOON COCOA POWDER

250 G UNSALTED BUTTER

160 G SOFT DARK BROWN SUGAR

20 G HONEY

140 G DRIED CHERRIES, PITTED AND ROUGHLY CHOPPED

COOKING OIL SPRAY, FOR GREASING

Before the end of summer, a few of our cherry growers get busy and inventive with the last of their crop. I love the little dried cherries that usually appear at the end of February – they have a great chewy texture and intense flavour. I always struggle to like fluffy all-white flour and sugar cookies with no real substance, so these are my kind of biscuit. Wholemeal flour and bitter cocoa make these cookies a grown-up treat. Use a dark, robust honey so it doesn't get lost behind the other flavours (gum or mallee styles work well). If you're after a really quick and easy dessert, smash the cookies through a good-quality vanilla bean ice cream.

1 Sift the plain flour with the bicarb into a large bowl, then add the wholemeal flour, salt and cocoa.

2 Using an electric mixer, cream the butter, sugar and honey until pale and fluffy. Add this to the dry ingredients. Mix just enough to combine the ingredients and form a crumbly mixture. Fold in the cherries.

3 Place a 30 cm × 30 cm piece of foil on your benchtop, then place a piece of baking paper the same size on top and spray with oil. Place the cookie dough on the baking paper and wrap it up into a 10 cm-diameter log. This saves a heap of mucking around shaping the cookies. Leave the log in the freezer for 1 hour.

4 Preheat the oven to 180°C fan-forced (200°C conventional) and line two baking trays with baking paper. Remove the log from the freezer. Unwrap it and slice the dough into 1.5 cm-thick rounds. Place the cookies on the prepared trays, spacing them well so they have room to spread. Bake the cookies for 15 minutes or until firm. Remove from the oven and leave the cookies on the baking trays for 5 minutes, then transfer them to wire racks to cool for 30 minutes before serving.

AUTUMN

Autumn is
my favourite season.

I love its muted colours, and the shadows created by the gentle sunlight: the world looks softer, yet somehow more dramatic at the same time. Stunning wild mushrooms pop up overnight, and the flavours and colours of the earth return to the markets, providing a palette of natural paints for your plate: striking red beets, pomegranates and tamarillos; dark, leafy greens; and mountains of tawny spuds. Crisp apples and soft pears are piled high, and tiny root vegies snuggle against each other. Local garlic hits the stalls, and I use it in nearly everything.

This is the season to bust out the baking trays and soup pots. As the nights lengthen, take some time to enjoy and get creative with your cooking: roll your own pasta, bake souffles, and play around making dumplings, calzone and samosas.

BEETROOT CARPACCIO WITH PORCINI PUREE

**SERVES 4 AS A STARTER
OR A LIGHT LUNCH**

10 G DRIED PORCINI

1 BUNCH CYLINDRA BEETROOT,
PEELED, LEAVES RESERVED

1 BUNCH GOLDEN BEETROOT,
PEELED, LEAVES RESERVED

1 BUNCH BULLSEYE BEETROOT,
PEELED, LEAVES RESERVED

3 TABLESPOONS EXTRA VIRGIN
OLIVE OIL

½ GOLDEN SHALLOT, ROUGHLY CHOPPED

½ CLOVE GARLIC, BRUISED

1 SPRIG THYME, LEAVES PICKED

SALT FLAKES AND CRACKED
BLACK PEPPER

This recipe came about after I read about the history of carpaccio in *The Harry's Bar Cookbook*. The owner of Harry's Bar, Giuseppe Cipriani, invented the eponymous shaved raw beef dish in 1950, naming it after the Venetian painter Carpaccio, whose paintings were noted for their striking shades of red. Inspired, I created this vegie option using thinly sliced beetroot instead of beef. I love this dish for so many reasons; the vibrant colour and crunchy texture of the thinly sliced beets is only the beginning. The bold flavour of the porcini brings an earthiness to the dish that's perfect for chilly days.

I started planting slender cylindra beets because I have a small vegie patch, and their slim shape makes them great to grow where space is an issue. Sliced into ovals, the beets bring an interesting look to the plate. The red-and-white stripes of the bullseye beets are visually stunning too, and they have a lovely sweetness that combines nicely with the more peppery golden beets. Even if this assortment is not available at your market, you should still have a crack at the recipe. Any good beets will do, as long as they are well-watered and not too old (or they will be woody and lack sweetness). If there are no leaves attached to your beets, add a handful of young ruby chard to your shopping list.

1 Place the porcini and 1 cup (250 ml) of warm water in a saucepan and leave to soak for an hour or so. Place the pan over high heat and simmer the porcini in their soaking liquid for 1 minute, then drain, reserving the liquid, and set the porcini aside. Strain the liquid through a muslin-lined sieve to remove any grit and set this aside too. You should have about 100 ml; if there is insufficient liquid, just top up with a little more boiling water to achieve this amount.

2 Very finely slice all the beetroots using a mandoline. If you want a more oval shape, simply angle the beet so that it's at 45 degrees to the mandoline blade, instead of the usual 90 degrees. Arrange slices of beetroot on each plate to create a large circular shape, overlapping the slices as you go. Repeat with a smaller circle in the centre of the plate. Lightly brush the beetroot slices with 1 tablespoon of olive oil to prevent them from drying out. If you're preparing this a few hours ahead, stop at this stage and cover the plates with plastic film (there's no need to refrigerate them).

3 Place the shallot, garlic, thyme, ½ tablespoon of salt, pepper and soaked porcini in a bowl and add 4 tablespoons of the porcini liquid. Combine with a stick blender, then add the remaining 2 tablespoons of olive oil and continue to blend to form a thick, mayonnaise-like puree (you may need to add the remaining tablespoon of liquid). Season the porcini puree to taste, keeping in mind that mushrooms need lots of salt!

4 To serve, sprinkle the sliced beets with salt and pepper and spoon over the porcini puree. Season the reserved leaves with a tiny pinch of salt and pepper and arrange a scant amount on each plate to garnish.

POTATO AND CHEDDAR TORTELLINI

SERVES 4

9 CLOVES GARLIC, SKIN ON

150 ML MILK

80 G UNSALTED BUTTER,
CUT INTO KNOBS

SALT FLAKES AND CRACKED
BLACK PEPPER

800 G NICOLA OR DUTCH
CREAM POTATOES

100 ML POURING CREAM

GOOD PINCH OF FRESHLY
GRATED NUTMEG

GOOD PINCH OF CAYENNE PEPPER,
PLUS EXTRA TO GARNISH

LOTS OF FRESHLY GROUND
WHITE PEPPER

4 TABLESPOONS CHOPPED FLAT-LEAF
PARSLEY, PLUS SPRIGS TO GARNISH

30 ML EXTRA VIRGIN OLIVE OIL,
PLUS A LITTLE FOR DRIZZLING

¾ CUP (90 G) GRATED
TOP-QUALITY CHEDDAR
(PREFERABLY CLOTH-WRAPPED)

PASTA DOUGH

500 G STRONG PLAIN FLOUR
(SEE INGREDIENTS)

3 FREE-RANGE EGGS,
AT ROOM TEMPERATURE

9 FREE-RANGE EGG YOLKS,
AT ROOM TEMPERATURE

A mind-boggling array of spuds has hit our markets in recent years. As a rule of thumb, it's useful to remember that dry-fleshed, floury potatoes (also known as starchy potatoes), such as colibans and kennebecs, make good chips, crisp up nicely on cut surfaces when roasted and are best for a light and fluffy mash. Really waxy potatoes, such as bintjes and kipflers, have great moisture content and are generally the guys that hold their shape well when boiled. They feel a little more compact, are a little creamier on the palate and are good eaten cold. For this dish, you'll need something in the middle. Go for a slightly waxy variety, like nicola or Dutch cream, with enough creaminess to make the filling smooth but not so much that it becomes heavy. Along with the waxy potato, you need a really rich pasta dough (9 egg yolks!), or the dish will be too floury.

Once you have the potatoes sorted, you'll need to find the right cheddar. Luckily, you don't have to go to Somerset and pull a wheel from a cave (the traditional ageing home for good cheddars, as it provides a constant temperature). Some cheese-makers in Australia are sourcing excellent milk and following traditional methods to create top-quality cheddars. The cloth wrapping is generally a sign that the cheese-maker is putting their heart and soul into the process. It's a good indicator that the cheese will be sharp and crumbly, which is essential for the dish.

1 To make the pasta dough, place the flour in the bowl of an electric mixer fitted with a dough hook. Start on low speed and add the eggs and yolks, working into a dough. Mix on low speed until the dough is smooth and silken, about 6 minutes. Alternatively, place the flour in a bowl, make a well and add the eggs and yolks. Bring the flour into the egg mixture, then turn it out onto your benchtop and knead by hand for about 10 minutes until the dough has a good stretch and sheen. Place the dough in a lightly floured bowl and cover with plastic film. Leave it to rest for 1 hour at room temperature.

2 Preheat the oven to 180°C fan-forced (200°C conventional). Place the garlic and milk in a small saucepan and bring to a simmer. Cook over low heat for about 10 minutes until the garlic is tender. Drain, discarding the milk, and place the garlic on a baking tray. Add 40 g of butter and season with salt. Bake for 15 minutes or until the garlic smells nutty and the skins are golden. When cool enough to handle, squeeze 5 cloves from their skins and set aside. Reserve the remaining 4 cloves, with skins on, to garnish.

3 Place the spuds in a saucepan of cold salted water and bring to a gentle simmer. Cook for about 15 minutes (it doesn't matter if they're a little over-cooked), then drain well and return the potatoes to the dry saucepan over low heat for a couple of minutes to help loosen the skins and dry them out. When the potatoes are cool enough to handle, rub the skins off with a tea towel. The best way to make mash is to pass the still-warm potatoes and the roasted garlic through a mouli or ricer, but a potato masher will also do the job.

POTATO AND CHEDDAR TORTELLINI (CONT.)

4 Add the remaining butter and the cream, nutmeg, cayenne, white and black peppers, parsley, olive oil and cheddar, holding back a little of the cheddar to garnish. Fold all the ingredients together using a large spoon, being careful not to overwork the potato or the filling will become tough.

5 Divide the pasta dough into two or three pieces. Shape each one into a ball, dust lightly with flour and flatten slightly with the palm of your hand. Roll the dough until it is about 1 cm thick, so you can feed it through the widest setting on a pasta machine. Lightly flour the rollers on the pasta machine and roll the dough through each setting, gradually working down to the second-finest setting, and re-flouring as required if the dough starts to stick to the rollers. Stack the rolled pasta dough between layers of baking paper, cover with a tea towel sprayed lightly with water and leave to rest for 20 minutes.

6 Lightly flour the benchtop. Use an 8–12 cm pastry cutter (depending on how thin your pasta sheets are) to cut 24 discs from the dough, 6 tortellini per serve. Cover the discs with a tea towel sprayed lightly with water to prevent the dough from drying out.

7 Place a tablespoon of the potato filling in the centre of a pasta disc and brush around the edge with a little water. Fold over the disc to form a semi-circle and pinch the edges together to seal. Gently roll the edges outwards using a small rolling pin (see page 134). Grab the two ends and bring them together by stretching them away from the curve of the semi-circle to meet each other. Overlap them by a centimetre and pinch firmly to make a tortellini shape. Repeat with the remaining discs and filling, covering the finished tortellini with the moist tea towel as you work.

8 Bring a large saucepan of salted water to a rolling boil. Working in batches to avoid overcrowding the pan, cook the tortellini until they float to the surface, about 3 minutes. Remove them with a spider or slotted spoon and transfer them to a lightly oiled tray.

9 To serve, divide the tortellini among four plates. Sprinkle with the reserved cheddar and season with the extra black pepper and cayenne. Garnish each serving with a parsley sprig or two, a good splash of olive oil and a roasted garlic clove.

SPINACH PAKORAS

SERVES 6 AS A STARTER

1 LARGE BUNCH SPINACH,
WASHED AND DRAINED

3 CUPS (450 G) BESAN
(CHICKPEA) FLOUR
(SEE INGREDIENTS)

½ TEASPOON BAKING POWDER

3 TEASPOONS SALT FLAKES

3 TEASPOONS GROUND TURMERIC

1½ TEASPOONS CHILLI POWDER
(OPTIONAL)

3 TEASPOONS GROUND CORIANDER

1 ONION, FINELY DICED

1 LARGE FLOURY POTATO (SEE PAGE
117), PEELED AND GRATED

FLAVOUR-NEUTRAL OIL (SEE
INGREDIENTS), FOR DEEP-FRYING

APPLE, HONEY AND MINT RAITA
(SEE BASIC RECIPES) OR TOMATO
KUSUNDI (SEE PAGE 66), TO SERVE

This is one of my favourite snacks. It's a great fridge-emptier, as the spinach doesn't have to be in tip-top condition for the dish to still be good. In fact, you can use just about any vegetable for these pakoras. I like to add a little potato to soften the dense spinach flavour and I also use baking powder to lighten the texture, but if you prefer a heavier pakora, you can just omit it. If the raita is not your thing, the kusundi on page 66 also makes a good accompaniment.

1 Trim off the bottom half of the spinach stems and discard them. Roughly chop the remaining stems and the leaves. In a large mixing bowl, combine the spinach, flour, baking powder, salt, spices, onion and potato. Fold in 1 cup (250 ml) of room-temperature water and combine well to mix the spices evenly through the mixture. Leave the mixture to sit for 20–30 minutes at room temperature.

2 Working in batches if necessary, transfer the mixture to a food processor and pulse until the mixture begins to form a loose ball. You do not want to puree the ingredients, just chop and combine them. Grab a bit of the mixture in your hands and see if it will just hold together; if it doesn't, add another 50 ml of water. It should not be a batter, but rather a sticky mess of vegetables! If the mixture is still a little loose, let it sit for a while to allow the flour to absorb the water. This should happen within 10 minutes on a warm day, but it will take a little longer if it's cold.

3 Heat the oil in a small wok over medium–low heat until just shimmering (about 180°C). Grab golfball-sized amounts of the pakora mixture and flatten them into discs. Working in batches to avoid overcrowding the wok, carefully place the pakoras in the hot oil and fry them for about 4 minutes or until they're dark brown and cooked through. It's important not to let the oil get too hot or the batter will over-crisp on the outside while the centre remains raw and gooey. If the oil starts smoking, turn the heat right down before proceeding with the next batch. Remove the pakoras from the oil with a slotted spoon and leave them to drain on paper towel. Allow them to sit for about 2 minutes as the batter in the centre will continue to steam through in the residual heat.

4 Serve the pakoras warm with the Apple, honey and mint raita or Tomato kusundi for dipping.

POMEGRANATE, YELLOW CHARD AND WILD RICE SALAD

SERVES 4 AS A STARTER, LIGHT LUNCH OR SIDE SALAD

4 TABLESPOONS EXTRA VIRGIN OLIVE OIL

1 DECENT-SIZED BUNCH YELLOW CHARD, STEMS SLICED INTO 5 CM LENGTHS, LARGER LEAVES SLICED INTO 5 CM STRIPS

SALT FLAKES AND CRACKED BLACK PEPPER

4 POMEGRANATES

30 ML VERJUICE (SEE INGREDIENTS)

3 SPRIGS THYME, LEAVES PICKED AND FINELY CHOPPED, PLUS A FEW SPRIGS TO GARNISH

WILD RICE SALAD

½ CUP (90 G) WILD RICE

75 G UNSALTED BUTTER

1 ONION, FINELY DICED

4 CLOVES GARLIC, CRUSHED

½ CUP (100 G) BASMATI RICE

PINCH OF SAFFRON THREADS, SOAKED IN 1 TABLESPOON WATER FOR 1 HOUR

10 BLACK PEPPERCORNS

1 BAY LEAF

½ TEASPOON SALT FLAKES

Pomegranates are up there with figs for me: a little bit low-key on the outside but an absolute explosion on the inside. I never tire of their sweet aroma, bright crimson juice and little ruby jewels. The combination of soft dryness and sweet and sour flavours is unique. I hate losing any of the precious juice, so instead of chopping the pomegranates on a board, I hold them over a bowl, push my thumbs through the skin and proceed to dismember the fruit, picking the seeds from the white membranes and squeezing the juice as I go.

In this recipe, the little pop of the pomegranate seeds works spectacularly with the soft, chewy texture of the wild rice and the crunch of the nuts. A little basmati rice lightens up the dish, as the wild rice can be a bit too earthy. The trick here is to get the wild rice cooked through and the basmati tender at the same time; the method for this may seem a little convoluted but it does work. With a colour palette of pale yellow chard, deep red pomegranate and dusty brown rice, this dish screams autumn, but any chard or even silverbeet would do the job. I sometimes add a dollop of chevre to make it more of a meal.

1 For the wild rice salad, bring 3 cups (750 ml) of water to the boil in a small–medium saucepan. As it hits the boil, rain in the wild rice and stir once or twice. When the water returns to the boil, reduce the heat to very low. Cover with a lid and leave to simmer for 20 minutes while you prepare the basmati rice.

2 Preheat a small heavy-based sauteuse or frying pan over medium heat. Add the butter and allow it to melt, then add the onion and garlic and sweat them, stirring. When the onion is just soft and translucent, add the basmati rice and toast the grains by stirring them for a minute for two. Remove the pan from the heat. Allow the rice to cool for a couple of minutes, then add the saffron and its soaking water, along with the peppercorns and bay leaf. Place a lid on the pan to keep the rice warm.

3 When the wild rice has been simmering for about 20 minutes, pour the contents of the basmati pan into the wild rice pan. Stir to incorporate, then add the salt. Put the lid back on and simmer over low heat for a further 25 minutes or until the basmati rice is tender and the wild rice grains are starting to burst.

4 Meanwhile, preheat a heavy-based frying pan over medium heat. Add 1 tablespoon of olive oil to the pan, then add the chard and ½ teaspoon of salt and toss to wilt the chard (add a splash of water to expedite this, if you like). Remove the chard from the pan and set aside.

5 Lever out the pomegranate seeds into a bowl, gently crushing the fruit to release all the juice and discarding any pith. Add the remaining olive oil and ¼ teaspoon of salt to the bowl, along with the verjuice and chopped thyme.

6 Place the wild rice in a serving bowl and arrange the chard on top. Pour over the pomegranate dressing and season with black pepper. Serve garnished with a few small sprigs of thyme.

DAIKON, CARROT AND SALTY TURNIP OMELETTE

SERVES 4

1 CUP (150 G) RICE FLOUR

SALT FLAKES AND FRESHLY GROUND WHITE PEPPER

100 G DAIKON, PEELED AND COARSELY GRATED OR CUT INTO FINE MATCHSTICKS USING A MANDOLINE

100 G CARROTS, PEELED AND COARSELY GRATED OR CUT INTO FINE MATCHSTICKS USING A MANDOLINE

12 FREE-RANGE EGGS

3 TABLESPOONS LIGHT SOY SAUCE (SEE INGREDIENTS)

ABOUT 160 ML FLAVOUR-NEUTRAL OIL (SEE INGREDIENTS)

4 CLOVES GARLIC, CRUSHED

1½ TABLESPOONS CHOPPED SALTED PRESERVED TURNIP (SEE PAGE 89)

4 SPRING ONIONS, GREEN PARTS ONLY, CHOPPED

1 HANDFUL BEAN SPROUTS

BOTTLE OF KECAP MANIS (SEE INGREDIENTS), FOR THE TABLE

Some years ago, I worked next to the Adelaide Central Market, which has a dazzling array of Asian food stalls. Whenever I was fed up, I would bust out from work and buy this chai poh omelette, but then the place that served it took it off the menu, leaving me a little devastated. Over a few trips to Singapore, I ate one every time I had a spare minute and kept quizzing everyone about how it was made. After a bit of messing about, I finally made a version I was happy with. I have no idea how to do the dish 'properly' but as long as it tastes good, I really don't care! I drown it in kecap manis. It looks unruly but tastes great. For best results, make the rice flour cakes the day before and leave them to set in the fridge overnight.

1 Bring 2 cups (500 ml) of water to the boil in a saucepan, then remove it from the heat. Immediately shoot in the rice flour, a handful at a time, whisking with a stick blender to make a smooth paste. Chuck in ½ teaspoon of salt and a big pinch of pepper. Add the daikon and carrot and combine.

2 Line three or four side plates with lightly greased baking paper. Use a pastry card or spatula to smear over a 1–1.5 cm-thick layer of batter. Place the plates into a tiered bamboo steamer (you may need to work in batches), then set the steamer over a saucepan of gently simmering water and pop the lid on. Gently steam the rice flour cakes for 40 minutes. When they're done, they will turn a little opaque and shiny, and can be handled without breaking. Test by inserting a skewer – it should come out clean. Remove the plates from the steamer and cover the cakes with plastic film. Leave them in the fridge to set overnight.

3 The next day, cut or tear the rice flour cakes into matchbox-sized pieces. Lightly beat the eggs together with the soy sauce and add a pinch of salt and pepper. You will need to make one omelette at a time. Place a couple of tablespoons of oil in a medium (30 cm) wok over medium heat. Add a quarter of the cakes and fry until they're really coloured up, then flip them over with a spatula and fry the other side until well browned (they will stick a bit and may break up but don't worry). Add a quarter of the garlic and turnip and fry until aromatic, stirring as you go to prevent burning, then fold in a quarter of the spring onion and bean sprouts. Pour in a quarter of the egg mixture, swirling the pan just a little (the omelettes need to be thick). Fry the omelette until it's crispy on the bottom, then release it by poking a spatula underneath and shunting the wok around. Flip the omelette using a spatula – or toss it, if you're brave – and fry the other side for a few seconds to finish. If you find that the omelette starts to break up and is not so easy to flip, you can always flash the wok under a hot grill to set the egg instead. The compromise in crispiness is only negligible – just serve the omelette wok-ed side up. Repeat with the remaining ingredients to make four omelettes. (The cooked omelettes will keep well in a warm oven while you cook the rest.)

4 Serve immediately with lots of kecap manis drizzled over the top.

BLISTERED CAPSICUM SOUP WITH SMOKED PAPRIKA AND BUTTER BEANS

SERVES 4 AS A MAIN OR 8 AS A STARTER

200 G BUTTER BEANS, SOAKED
    OVERNIGHT IN COLD WATER

3 BAY LEAVES

4 LARGE RED CAPSICUMS (PEPPERS)

100 ML EXTRA VIRGIN OLIVE OIL,
    PLUS EXTRA TO SERVE

4 CLOVES GARLIC, CRUSHED

1 ONION, FINELY DICED

1 LARGE FLOURY POTATO
    (SEE PAGE 117), FINELY DICED

3 STALKS CELERY, FINELY DICED

SALT FLAKES AND CRACKED
    BLACK PEPPER

2 TABLESPOONS CHOPPED OREGANO

¼ TEASPOON SMOKED PAPRIKA,
    PLUS EXTRA TO SERVE

100 ML SOUR CREAM

JUICE OF ½ LEMON

CIABATTA, TO SERVE

1 BIG HANDFUL RIPPED BASIL LEAVES

I can't say I get overly enthusiastic when it comes to capsicums, but blackened capsicums are a different story. They look kind of wrong but they smell fantastic. The smokiness that permeates their flesh when they're cooked over an open flame is pushed even further by the paprika in this recipe. Of course you can cook the capsicums on a grill-plate, but I love making an absolute mess by placing them straight on top of the gas-burner trivets. I have this belief – I suspect scientifically unfounded – that they taste better this way and I'm sticking to it.

1 Drain the soaked beans, discarding the soaking water. Place them in a large saucepan, cover with cold water by 5–7 cm and add the bay leaves. Bring to a simmer and cook the beans for about 1 hour until tender to the bite (the cooking time will depend on their age); add more liquid as necessary. Take the pan off the heat and set it aside. Do not drain the beans.

2 Place the capsicums on your stove burner over medium–low heat and destroy them, turning them with tongs as they blacken. (If you do not have a gas stovetop, blacken the capsicums on a hot grill-plate or in a heavy-based frying pan.) Throw the cooked capsicums in a snug-fitting bowl and cover tightly with plastic film to help sweat the skin away from flesh.

3 Pry out the stalk-end of the capsicum, and most of the seeds and membrane should come out with it. Cut a single slit down the capsicum from top to bottom and gently scrape away the remaining seeds and membrane. Peel off the skin, but don't worry if a few pieces of blackened skin remain attached to the flesh – it's all flavour! Whatever you do, do not clean them under running water. Transfer the capsicum to a food processor and blend to a puree, adding just enough water from the beans to facilitate blending (a tablespoon should do it).

4 Heat the olive oil in a heavy-based sauteuse or frying pan over medium heat. Sweat the garlic and onion until the onion is soft and translucent, then add the potato, celery and 1 heaped teaspoon of salt. Turn up the heat to high and saute until the potato is a little caramelised. Add the oregano and paprika and cook for a minute longer.

5 Chuck this mixture into the pan of cooked beans, then stir through the capsicum puree. Return the pan to medium heat. Bring to a simmer to reheat the beans and emulsify the oil with the soup, then remove the pan from the heat and allow the soup to cool slightly.

6 Blob the sour cream into the middle of the soup (I rarely stir it through), then add the lemon juice and a good twist of pepper. Check the seasoning, adding salt to taste. To serve, I generally just throw the pan on the table with a loaf of good bread, a bottle of extra virgin olive oil, some ripped basil leaves and a little extra smoked paprika and let everyone do whatever they want.

POTATO POTSTICKERS
with CHILLI PEANUT SAUCE

SERVES 4

FLAVOUR-NEUTRAL OIL (SEE INGREDIENTS),
FOR BRUSHING AND FRYING

CHILLI PEANUT SAUCE (SEE BASIC
RECIPES), TO SERVE

DOUGH

3 CUPS (450 G) PLAIN FLOUR

PINCH OF SALT FLAKES

1¾ CUPS (430 ML) WATER,
AT ROOM TEMPERATURE

FILLING

4 FLOURY POTATOES (SEE PAGE 117),
PEELED AND HALVED

2 TABLESPOONS FLAVOUR-NEUTRAL OIL
(SEE INGREDIENTS)

1 TEASPOON CUMIN SEEDS

2 TABLESPOONS BROWN
MUSTARD SEEDS

1 ONION, VERY FINELY DICED

2 CLOVES GARLIC, CRUSHED

1 LONG GREEN CHILLI, FINELY CHOPPED,
SEEDS AND ALL

2 TEASPOONS GROUND TURMERIC

1 CARROT, VERY FINELY DICED

SALT FLAKES

2 TEASPOONS GARAM MASALA

200 G FIRM TOFU, CRUMBLED
INTO LITTLE PIECES

2 SPRING ONIONS, GREEN PARTS ONLY,
FINELY DICED

1 HANDFUL CHOPPED CORIANDER

I was once lucky enough to spend a morning learning how to make momos (Tibetan dumplings) from a group of visiting Buddhist monks. They were a cheeky bunch and laughed endlessly at my lack of dexterity while folding the dumplings. I learned something important that morning, and it wasn't the recipe (which I have long forgotten); it was the realisation that we often neglect the importance of ritual in our daily lives and especially in cooking. The monks make momos once a week, but they never seemed to tire of the process, splitting into little groups to care for the dough, the filling and the dipping sauce before coming together for the rolling, where a fair bit of banter was exchanged. I have fond memories of both the meal and the day itself.

I can't help feeling that in cooking (and in life, generally), we are always looking for something new and exciting. We often forget that there is a great deal of calm to be found by following a well-practised routine; this dish has become that to me. I love seeing the little rows of dumplings build up, and I am reminded how taste and memory are inextricably linked. Some of our best food memories are not so much about the food, but of the mood and company that made the meal exceptional.

This is my (very abstract) version of the soft little dumplings I made with the monks that day. I generally start with mashed potato as a base, spice it up and pop whatever is at hand in with it. I also like to fry the dumplings after steaming them to give them a nice crisp bottom (they're called potstickers because the dough just grabs the pan), which contrasts with the silky dough on top. If you're too busy to make the Chilli peanut sauce, just fold a little chilli sambal into a good-quality tomato sauce and you'll have a great dipping sauce in seconds.

⏐ To make the dough, place the flour in a bowl and make a well in the centre. Add the salt and water and gather the flour in, working it into a mass. Turn out the dough onto a floured benchtop and knead until it's smooth, silky and elastic, about 10–12 minutes. If the dough is still tacky after a couple of minutes of kneading, incorporate more flour by dusting the benchtop and just letting the dough grab it as you knead. Alternatively, if you have a good electric mixer with a dough hook, you can mix the ingredients at low–medium speed for about 6 minutes until the dough breaks away from the edge of the bowl and looks smooth and shiny. It should feel soft, like pizza dough. Place the dough in a lightly floured bowl and cover with plastic film. Leave it to rest for 1 hour at room temperature. (If your kitchen is hot, place the bowl in the fridge, as the dough can be very hard to work with if it's too warm.)

POTATO POTSTICKERS
WITH CHILLI PEANUT SAUCE (CONT.)

2 Meanwhile, for the filling, place the spuds in a large saucepan of cold salted water. Bring to a simmer over medium heat and cook the potatoes until they're tender, then drain well and return the potatoes to the dry saucepan over low heat for a couple of minutes to help dry them out. Pass through a mouli or ricer while still warm, or mash with a potato masher until smooth. Set the mash aside.

3 Preheat a heavy-based frying pan over medium heat. Add the oil and when it's slightly hazy, add the cumin and mustard seeds and stir for a second or two until they become highly aromatic (but not too long or they will burn and become bitter). Add the onion, garlic, chilli and turmeric and saute for a couple of minutes until the onion has softened. Add the carrot and salt to taste and cook for a further minute or two until the carrot is coated with the spices but still a little crunchy. Stir through the garam masala and tofu, then remove the pan from the heat. Fold the contents into the mash, combine well and leave to cool. Add the spring onion and coriander and set aside.

4 Lightly flour your benchtop (the less, the better). Roll the dough into a log about 3–4 cm in diameter. Pinch off little balls, each one slightly smaller than a ping pong ball, and roll them out into discs about 8–10 cm in diameter. Roll in all directions from the centre outwards to achieve evenness. Cover the discs with a tea towel as you work to prevent them drying out. You can stack the discs up if it's not too hot, but remember to flour between layers. You'll need about 32 dumplings to serve 4 – there is a little extra dough here to cover rejects!

5 Place a large bamboo steamer over a wok or saucepan half-filled with water and set at a gentle simmer.

6 Spoon about a tablespoon of the filling onto a disc and lightly wet the edges with a pastry brush or your finger. To create a half-moon shape, gather one side of the disc into pleats about 5 mm wide and fold it up to meet the unpleated side, pinching the edges to seal. Repeat with the remaining filling and discs.

7 Lightly brush the bamboo steamer with oil and, working in batches, steam the dumplings for about 10–12 minutes. When they're ready, the dough will shrink back and firm up.

8 Preheat a heavy-based frying pan with a tight-fitting lid over medium heat and add just enough oil to coat the base of the pan. When the oil is hot, place the dumplings into the pan, flat-side down (you may need to work in batches). Cover with the lid and shake the pan to get the dumplings sliding about in the oil; they will stick a bit, but try and get them all to move in the first 5 seconds of cooking to achieve an even layer of oil between the pan and the dumpling. Fry the dumplings until their bottoms are coloured and crispy.

9 Serve immediately with Chilli peanut sauce.

WARM CUCUMBER AND PARSLEY QUINOA TABBOULEH

SERVES 4 AS A SIDE SALAD OR SUBSTANTIAL STARTER

⅔ CUP (110 G) QUINOA SEEDS

SALT FLAKES AND CRACKED BLACK PEPPER

1 HANDFUL MINT LEAVES, TORN

1 HANDFUL FLAT-LEAF PARSLEY LEAVES, CHOPPED

1 HANDFUL CORIANDER LEAVES AND STEMS, CHOPPED

4 SPRING ONIONS, FINELY SLICED

4 LARGE TOMATOES, ROUGHLY DICED

2 LEBANESE (SMALL) CUCUMBERS, ROUGHLY DICED

JUICE OF 1 LEMON

4 TABLESPOONS EXTRA VIRGIN OLIVE OIL

A FEW COS LETTUCE LEAVES, TO SERVE

TAHINI SAUCE

3 TABLESPOONS HULLED TAHINI

1 TEASPOON SALT FLAKES

1½ TABLESPOONS WATER

JUICE OF 1 LEMON

FINELY GRATED ZEST OF ½ LEMON

½ TEASPOON GROUND CUMIN

I do like burghul tabbouleh, but this is a wheat-free alternative with the added benefit of complete protein, courtesy of the quinoa. The full set of amino acids that constitutes a complete protein is easily found in meat, fish and dairy but it's not so common in the plant world. Quinoa, however, is a one-stop shop. Don't get too bogged down about red, white or black variants of the grain as they're all pretty similar, although the subtler flavour of the white quinoa is probably best suited to this dish. It is, however, important to use seeds rather than flakes for this recipe as the latter will produce a sticky porridge, which is not the texture you're after.

The tail-end of the season's tomatoes and cucumbers lack a bit of flavour but this will not compromise the final result as the dish is drenched in a fair whack of lemon juice and extra virgin olive oil and a nice dollop of tahini sauce. If your tomatoes are particularly bland, however, you can emulate a summer tomato flavour by sprinkling a little salt, sugar and good red-wine vinegar onto the diced tomato and allowing it to sit for a few minutes.

1 Rinse the quinoa for a minute or so in a colander under cold running water, then drain. Place the quinoa, 1 teaspoon of salt and 1⅓ cups (330 ml) of water in a heavy-based saucepan over high heat and bring to a simmer. Stir, then cover the pan with a tight-fitting lid and turn down the heat to low. Cook the quinoa for 12–15 minutes or until the water has been absorbed and the quinoa is tender to the bite. (When a few of the seeds have popped open and split, it's a sure sign that the cooking time is sufficient.) Turn the quinoa out into a large bowl, fluff the grains with a fork and leave it, uncovered, for 10 minutes or so to cool slightly.

2 Meanwhile, to make the tahini sauce, whisk all the ingredients together in a small bowl. Set aside.

3 When the quinoa has cooled, fold in the mint, parsley, coriander, spring onion, tomato, cucumber, lemon juice and olive oil. Season with pepper.

4 Serve the tabbouleh on cos lettuce leaves with the tahini sauce on top.

GINGER AND MUSHROOM CONGEE

SERVES 4 FOR SUPPER

½ CUP (100 G) JASMINE RICE

2 TABLESPOONS FLAVOUR-NEUTRAL OIL (SEE INGREDIENTS), PLUS ½ TEASPOON FOR THE RICE

SALT FLAKES

4 CM PIECE YOUNG GINGER, SKIN ON, THINLY SLICED (ABOUT 2 HEAPED TABLESPOONS IN TOTAL)

2 TABLESPOONS SHAOHSING (SEE INGREDIENTS)

3 TABLESPOONS PICKLED MUSTARD GREENS, WASHED, DRAINED AND FINELY CHOPPED

3 RED SHALLOTS, HALVED AND FINELY SLICED LENGTHWAYS

1 LARGE HANDFUL CORIANDER LEAVES WITH 3–4 CM STEM

1 BIRD'S EYE CHILLI, CHOPPED, SEEDS AND ALL

¼ TEASPOON GROUND SICHUAN PEPPER

1 TEASPOON CRISPY SHALLOT CHIPS (SEE BASIC RECIPES)

2 TABLESPOONS CHINESE LIGHT SOY SAUCE (SEE INGREDIENTS)

STOCK

2 CUPS (500 ML) WATER

12 DRIED SHIITAKE MUSHROOMS

2 STAR ANISE

3 SPRING ONIONS, TIED IN A KNOT

2 CM PIECE GINGER, BASHED

2 CLOVES GARLIC, BASHED

This congee is ideal for autumnal nights. It's not just the comforting smell; one of ginger's volatile oils is a sedative and it also has analgesic properties, so if you have chilly bones this is the best supper dish. You'll find young ginger at the markets in late summer and early autumn. It has none of the fibre of the later, mid-year ginger, and it requires no peeling and very little cooking. Choose unwrinkled thumbs with pinky tips on the roots, and skin that slips off with a fingernail push – it should weep a little juice immediately or it's too old. Young ginger has a delicate, subtle flavour, which means you can add bucketloads to a dish without it stomping all over the accompanying flavours. In this, it brings a nice crunchy contrast to the velvety rice.

Any pickled Asian green or cabbage works here. I generally use mustard greens (available from Asian grocers) because they kick the subtle zing of the ginger and shallot up a notch. You'll need to start the rice a day ahead.

1 Place the rice in a colander and wash it several times by running cold water over the top while agitating the rice. Drain well. Place the rice, ½ teaspoon of oil, 2 teaspoons of salt and 1 litre of water in a large saucepan. Leave the rice to soak in the fridge overnight (there's no need to cover the pan).

2 Meanwhile, to make the stock, place all the ingredients in a small saucepan and bring to a gentle simmer. Cook for 1 hour (you may need to place a plate on top to keep the shiitakes immersed). Strain the stock, reserving the shiitakes and discarding the aromatics. Chuck the shiitakes in a container and store them in the fridge. You'll need 6 mushrooms for the congee; the rest will keep for up to a week.

3 The following day, add the stock to the rice and its soaking water. Add a pinch of salt and bring to a gentle simmer. Simmer with the lid on for 2 hours, stirring occasionally, until the rice is creamy and broken down to a smooth porridge consistency.

4 Remove and discard the stems of 6 shiitakes and finely slice the caps. Heat a small heavy-based frying pan over medium heat, then add the oil and sliced shiitakes. Fry for 2–3 minutes until the shiitakes are just colouring and crisping a little, then add the sliced ginger and fry for a further minute or so until the shiitakes are well browned. Deglaze the pan with the shaohsing, then remove the pan from the heat and set aside.

5 Add the mustard greens and half the shallots to the rice and cook for a few minutes over medium heat, stirring to combine and warm through.

6 Serve the congee in one big bowl or smaller individual bowls, sprinkled with the fried ginger and shiitakes and remaining raw shallots. Top with coriander, chilli, Sichuan pepper, Crispy shallot chips and soy sauce. Add salt to taste. Serve with a little extra soy on the side if you like.

BEETROOT RAVIOLI WITH ROAST GARLIC AND LEMON-ZESTED CHEVRE AND WALNUTS

SERVES 4 AS A MAIN

50 G UNSALTED BUTTER

1 TABLESPOON WALNUT OIL

2 HEAPED TABLESPOONS WALNUTS, TOASTED AND ROUGHLY CHOPPED

1 TABLESPOON EACH FINELY CHOPPED CHIVES AND LEMON THYME

FINELY GRATED ZEST OF ¼ LEMON

SALT FLAKES AND CRACKED BLACK PEPPER

1 HANDFUL FLAT-LEAF PARSLEY LEAVES

SHAVED PARMESAN, TO SERVE

PASTA DOUGH

120 G BEETROOT, PEELED AND ROUGHLY CHOPPED

250 G STRONG PLAIN FLOUR (SEE INGREDIENTS)

1 FREE-RANGE EGG

1 FREE-RANGE EGG YOLK

1 TABLESPOON EXTRA VIRGIN OLIVE OIL, PLUS EXTRA FOR COATING

FILLING

4 CLOVES GARLIC, SKIN ON

150 G CHEVRE

50 G RICOTTA

3 TABLESPOONS GRATED PARMESAN

2 TABLESPOONS ROUGHLY CHOPPED CHIVES

2 TABLESPOONS CHOPPED FLAT-LEAF PARSLEY

1 TABLESPOON LEMON THYME LEAVES

FINELY GRATED ZEST OF ¼ LEMON

½ TEASPOON SALT FLAKES

CRACKED BLACK PEPPER

The carpaccio on page 114 demands sweet young beets; here's one for any sad guys sitting in the back of the fridge. The cheese, however, does need to be top quality. Luckily, in Australia we're spoilt for world-class chevre. Cheese-makers live in a world of patience and gentle coaxing, waiting for curds to form, moulds and blooms to develop and aged cheeses to mature. There's something soothing about peeking into their coolrooms containing rows of little cheeses all lined up and growing into something special. It's like a nursery of infants – but silent. That's why I like these people and their craft so much. They provide a nice contrast to commercial kitchens (and their chefs), where it's noisy, hot and bothered, and everything needs to be ready 5 minutes ago.

I prefer a subtle chevre with a really good tang for this dish, but trust your palate and go with what you like. The ricotta boots up the texture inside but it could be omitted and then you will get a really squishy, oozy filling when you cut open the ravioli. Together, chevre, lemon zest, black pepper and herbs are a sublime and brilliant combination of flavours. The addition of beetroot and walnut makes the whole dish one of my all-time autumn favourites.

1 For the pasta dough, place the beetroot in a saucepan and add just enough cold water to nearly cover (it's really important to cook the beetroot using the minimum amount of water as you need a firm puree). Don't season the water; just plonk the lid on and bring to a simmer. Cook the beetroot until it's soft and slightly overdone. You might need to stir after 5 minutes to submerge any beetroot that is poking above the water.

2 Preheat the oven to 180°C fan-forced (200°C conventional).

3 Puree the beetroot and its cooking water using a stick blender or food processor. You should have a firmish pulp, like a banana puree. Place the flour in a bowl and make a well in the centre. Add the egg, yolk, olive oil and beetroot puree. Using a pastry cutter or your hands, bring the flour into the egg mixture and combine to make a dough. Turn out the dough onto a very lightly floured benchtop and knead for a couple of minutes until it's firm and smooth, a little shiny and elastic. Place it in a lightly floured bowl, cover with plastic film and leave it to rest in the fridge for at least 30 minutes.

4 Meanwhile, for the filling, wrap the garlic in foil and pop it in the oven for 30 minutes or until it's nice and mushy. When cool enough to handle, unwrap the foil and nip the sprouting end of the cloves with a sharp knife. Squeeze out the roasted garlic (the back of a knife is good for this). Place it, along with all the other filling ingredients, in a food processor and pulse until just combined. Be careful not to blend to a green puree; you want a few lumps from the ricotta for texture and visible herbs throughout. Season to taste (you may need a little extra salt, depending on the amount already in the chevre). Place the filling in the fridge if you're not using it immediately.

BEETROOT RAVIOLI WITH ROAST GARLIC AND LEMON-ZESTED CHEVRE AND WALNUTS (CONT.)

5 Divide the pasta dough into two or three pieces. Shape each one into a ball, dust it lightly with flour and flatten it slightly with the palm of your hand. Roll the dough until it is about 1 cm thick, so you can feed it through the widest setting on a pasta machine. Lightly flour the rollers on the pasta machine and roll the dough through each setting, gradually working down to the second-finest setting, and re-flouring as required if the dough starts to grab on the rollers. Stack the rolled pasta dough between layers of baking paper, cover with a tea towel sprayed lightly with water and leave to rest for about 20 minutes. (You can leave the dough to rest on a well-floured benchtop instead of baking paper, if you must, but you risk compromising the vibrant colour of your ravioli.) Very lightly dust the benchtop and use an 8–12 cm pastry cutter (depending on how thin your pasta sheets are) to cut about 24 discs from the dough. Cover the discs with a tea towel sprayed lightly with water to prevent the dough drying out.

6 Place about a heaped tablespoon of filling – depending on the size of your discs and how fat you like your ravioli – on half of the discs. Run a wet finger around the edges of each one and place the remaining discs on top, floured-side up as they will adhere better this way. Press down with your fingers to seal, then gently roll the edges of the ravioli outwards using a small rolling pin. (Be mindful that you have a double layer of dough on the sealed edge and this will be tough when cooked so you need to roll this edge back to the thickness of your original rolled dough. I roll the pin back towards the filling gently without pressure, press down and roll it towards the edge, then spin the dough around and repeat this until all the edges are even.) Cover the finished ravioli with the moist tea towel as you work.

7 Bring a large saucepan of salted water to a simmer. Shake off any excess flour from the ravioli and, working in small batches, plonk them into the pan and cook them until they rise to the surface. Lift the ravioli out with a spider or slotted spoon, draining off excess water, and place them on a large tray. Coat them lightly with a little olive oil, gently agitating the tray to ensure all of the ravioli are oiled, or they will stick together from the residual heat. Cover with a tea towel and set aside in a warm spot.

8 Melt the butter in a heavy-based frying pan over medium heat until it's fizzy and just starting to darken, then add the walnut oil and walnuts and stir for 1 minute. Remove the pan from the heat and allow it to cool slightly before adding the chives, lemon thyme, lemon zest, salt and pepper.

9 Divide the ravioli among plates and drizzle the walnut sauce over the top. Garnish with parsley and serve with shaved parmesan on the side.

MUSHROOM AND FONTINA CALZONES WITH PRESERVED LEMON

SERVES 4

POLENTA, FOR DUSTING

DOUGH

450 G STRONG PLAIN FLOUR
(SEE INGREDIENTS)

¾ CUP (180 ML) WARM WATER

1 FREE-RANGE EGG

FINELY GRATED ZEST AND JUICE OF
1 LEMON

½ CUP (40 G) GRATED PARMESAN

2 TABLESPOONS EXTRA VIRGIN
OLIVE OIL

FILLING

1 TABLESPOON EXTRA VIRGIN OLIVE OIL

100 G UNSALTED BUTTER

2 ONIONS, SLICED

4 CLOVES GARLIC, FINELY SLICED

2 LEEKS, WHITE PART ONLY, HALVED
LENGTHWAYS AND SLICED INTO
HALF-MOONS 3–4 MM THICK

800 G MIXED MUSHROOMS
(FIELD, BUTTON, PINE, SWISS
BROWN, WHATEVER), SLICED,
CHOPPED AND DICED

SALT FLAKES AND CRACKED
BLACK PEPPER

GOOD SPLASH OF DRY WHITE WINE
(ABOUT 3 TABLESPOONS)

1 PRESERVED LEMON, PITH AND FLESH
REMOVED, RIND FINELY CHOPPED

3 TABLESPOONS OREGANO
LEAVES, CHOPPED

4 TABLESPOONS CHOPPED
FLAT-LEAF PARSLEY

200 G FONTINA (OR ANY GOOD MELTING
CHEESE, LIKE GRUYERE), GRATED

4 FREE-RANGE EGGS

A few years back, I was lucky enough to spend a bit of time kicking around with Russell Jeavons, the legendary wood-oven pioneer. He was knocking up strudels one day while explaining the finer points of wood-oven building to me, and the resulting pastry was so crisp and light, I was inspired to make a savoury version.

This recipe makes four jumbo-sized pasties with a little dough left over, which comes in handy to patch up holes. The kneading is best done on a cool benchtop, otherwise the dough can become a little hard to handle. Using a pizza stone in the oven makes all the difference. It holds a soft, constant heat, which prevents your pizza base going soggy.

As for the filling, autumn brings an array of wild mushrooms to the market. My two favourites are vibrant orange pine mushrooms and slippery jacks. They're definitely worth seeking out for their bold flavours and textures that will add real punch to your little pasties, but Swiss browns and field mushrooms will also do the trick. When it comes to the chopping, it's good to have a mixture of textures and shapes, so get creative!

1 To make the dough, place the flour on your benchtop and make a well in the centre. Combine the water, egg, lemon zest and juice, parmesan and olive oil in a bowl and pour it into the well. Gather the flour in from the outside, fold it into the well and bring the ingredients together. They should come together nicely, but if this does not start to happen in the first minute of kneading, add a tablespoon of room-temperature water. Knead the dough until it's smooth, silky and elastic, about 6–8 minutes. Divide the dough into four pieces and shape each one into a seamless ball. Cover with a tea towel and leave the dough to rest at room temperature for 30 minutes.

2 Meanwhile, if you have a pizza stone, put it in the oven, and preheat the oven to 200°C fan-forced (220°C conventional). For the filling, preheat a large heavy-based frying pan with a lid over medium heat. Add the oil and butter, then add the onion, garlic and leek and saute until the onion is soft and translucent. Fold in the mushrooms, 1 heaped tablespoon of salt and lots of pepper and stir to coat with the butter. Pop the lid on for 5–6 minutes, shaking the pan or stirring occasionally. Remove the lid and deglaze with the wine, then turn the heat up until all the moisture has evaporated (otherwise the bottom of the calzone will go soggy). Add the preserved lemon, oregano and parsley. Remove the pan from the heat immediately and check the seasoning – mushrooms need salt to really shine.

3 Roll each dough ball into a round about 20 cm in diameter and 4 mm thick. Spread half of each round with mushroom mixture, then sprinkle with fontina and crack an egg on top. Fold over to make a semi-circle and twist the dough along the edge to seal. Sprinkle polenta onto the hot pizza stone and place the calzones, egg-side up, on top. Cook for 20–25 minutes or until golden brown on top and bottom. Lift a calzone up and give it a tap – a nice hollow sound indicates it's ready. Cool on a wire rack for 10 minutes, then serve.

GRILLED JAPANESE EGGPLANTS with WHITE MISO, SOBA NOODLES and BROTH

SERVES 4

6 JAPANESE EGGPLANTS

FINE SALT

3 TABLESPOONS FLAVOUR-NEUTRAL OIL
(SEE INGREDIENTS)

50 G WHITE MISO PASTE

1 TABLESPOON SUGAR

1 TABLESPOON SAKE

1 TABLESPOON MIRIN

1 FREE-RANGE EGG YOLK

1 TEASPOON JAPANESE SEVEN SPICE,
PLUS A LITTLE EXTRA

300 G SOBA NOODLES

1½ TABLESPOONS SESAME SEEDS

BROTH

1 LEEK, WHITE PART ROUGHLY CHOPPED

1 SMALL DAIKON, ROUGHLY CHOPPED

1 ONION, CHOPPED

2 CLOVES GARLIC, PEELED AND
LIGHTLY BRUISED

1 LITRE COLD WATER

4 CM PIECE KOMBU

2 TABLESPOONS WHITE MISO PASTE

1 TEASPOON FINE SALT

1 SHEET NORI

2 SPRING ONIONS, GREEN PARTS ONLY,
THINLY SLICED DIAGONALLY

Long, skinny Japanese eggplants have the best sweet flavour, and the skins become palatable with just the teeniest amount of cooking. They also generally have fewer seeds than the large, round eggplants. Salting the eggplant in this recipe is not to remove bitterness, but rather it helps to prevent the flesh sucking up all the oil during cooking. The oil remains on the surface, which enables quicker, more effective grilling with less oil.

Traditional Japanese broth (or dashi) is made from dried bonito shavings, and for a while I struggled to create a fish-free alternative that delivered the same sweetness and depth as the original. I was complaining about this in my kitchen one day when a Korean chef, Kaye Kang, explained that his mum always pops a daikon in her dashi, and this remedies both sweetness and body. Like most root veg, daikon (or Asian radish) becomes tougher the longer it's left in the ground, but it's worth knowing that there are different varieties that grow to different sizes, so larger doesn't always mean older. For this reason, don't judge a daikon by its size, but rather look for a smoother, whiter skin as an indicator of youth and tenderness.

Miso is a fermented, living food and boiling it will knock the probiotic good guys on the head with a hammer. If you want the maximum nutritional benefits, follow the recipe carefully by removing the stock from the heat before adding the miso. Japanese seven spice (or shichimi togarashi) is a seasoning blend that typically includes chilli peppers, sesame seeds, orange peel and nori; this, kombu and nori are available from Japanese supermarkets.

1 To make the broth, place the leek, daikon, onion and garlic in a heavy-based saucepan and pour in the water. Bring up to a simmer over medium heat, then turn the heat to low and simmer for 30 minutes. Add the kombu and simmer for a further 30 minutes. Strain, discarding the vegies and seaweed. Return the strained broth to the pan and set aside.

2 Meanwhile, cut the eggplants in half lengthways (if they're thicker than 3 cm, cut them into three slices or they will burn before the inside flesh is cooked). Sprinkle with ½–¾ teaspoon of fine salt. Leave the eggplant slices on a tray or plate for 30 minutes at room temperature or until a little liquid has pooled around them.

3 Preheat a grill-plate or oven grill to medium. Rinse the salted eggplants in cold water, then drain and pat dry with a tea towel or paper towel. Brush both sides with a little oil. Grill for 2–3 minutes on each side or until the flesh is slightly soft and just cooked through. Remove the eggplants and preheat the oven grill to high. Place the eggplants on a baking tray, flesh-side up. Combine the miso, sugar, sake, mirin and egg yolk in a bowl. Spread the miso topping over the eggplants and lightly sprinkle with Japanese seven spice.

GRILLED JAPANESE EGGPLANTS with WHITE MISO, SOBA NOODLES and BROTH (CONT.)

4 Place the miso eggplants under the hot oven grill and grill them for about 2 minutes or until the miso topping bubbles and slightly blackens in places. Transfer the eggplants to the bottom of the oven to keep warm, along with four small heatproof soup bowls (the residual heat from the grill should do the trick).

5 For the noodles, bring 1.5 litres of cold water and ½ teaspoon of fine salt to a simmer over medium heat.

6 Place the broth over medium heat to warm. When it's hot, but before any tiny bubbles appear in the water, remove the pan from the heat and add the miso paste and salt. Whisk or stir to combine, then adjust the seasoning if necessary. Place a lid on top to keep the broth warm. Toast the nori by waving it over a flame for a second using tongs, then rip it into roughly 3 cm pieces. Toast the sesame seeds in a heavy-based frying pan over low heat for a few minutes, stirring occasionally, until they turn a shade darker and become aromatic.

7 When the noodle water is boiling, add the noodles. This will immediately take the water off the boil, so turn the heat up to full. When the water returns to the boil, pour 1 cup (250 ml) of cold water into the pan; this inhibits the starches in the soba, giving a better final texture. When the water returns to the boil, cook the noodles for 3–4 minutes or until they're tender to the bite, then drain and run under cold water for a minute. Place the soba noodles on a large serving plate or a bamboo mat.

8 To serve, divide the broth among the warmed bowls and garnish with toasted nori and spring onion greens. Arrange the warm eggplant on a serving plate and sprinkle with toasted sesame seeds. Place it in the middle of the table along with the soba noodles. Encourage everyone to plonk the noodles and eggplant into their soup. (Alternatively you can put the noodles in individual shallow bowls, pour over the soup and float the eggplant slices on top.) Serve with extra Japanese seven spice on the side.

MUSHROOM DAL

SERVES 6

140 ML GHEE (SEE INGREDIENTS)

2 TEASPOONS BROWN MUSTARD SEEDS

2 TEASPOONS CUMIN SEEDS

1 SPRIG CURRY LEAVES, STRIPPED

2 ONIONS, DICED

3 TOMATOES, ROUGHLY CHOPPED
(SEEDS AND SKINS OKAY)

1 CUP (200 G) CHANA DAL
(SEE INGREDIENTS)

300 G BUTTON MUSHROOMS,
THICKLY SLICED

2 TABLESPOONS SALT FLAKES,
OR TO TASTE

1 TABLESPOON TAMARIND
CONCENTRATE OR LEMON JUICE

3 CM PIECE GINGER, PEELED AND
CUT INTO THIN MATCHSTICKS

½ BUNCH CORIANDER, LEAVES PICKED
AND CHOPPED

1 LONG GREEN CHILLI, FINELY DICED,
SEEDS AND ALL

CHAPATTIS (SEE BASIC RECIPES),
TO SERVE

SPICE MIX

1 TABLESPOON CORIANDER SEEDS

1½ TEASPOONS CHILLI POWDER

½ TEASPOON FENUGREEK SEEDS

1 TEASPOON CUMIN SEEDS

1 TEASPOON GROUND TURMERIC

PINCH OF ASAFOETIDA

2 TABLESPOONS DESICCATED COCONUT

1 TABLESPOON HULLED AND SPLIT
URAD DAL (SEE INGREDIENTS)

A hearty autumn meal, this dal works brilliantly with mushrooms because they bring a contrasting texture to the soft lentils, but you can add any vegies you like. This is a staple dinner in my house, so I usually make up a decent batch of the spice mix, which means it's one less job next time round (it stores well in an airtight container for a few months). The urad dal in the spice mix act as a thickener and give the dal body. In fact, as the mix is fried in ghee and added near completion, the method is really not that dissimilar to using a roux to thicken a soup or sauce in French cookery. The asafoetida brings a pungent garlicky onion flavour to the dish. (It also tends to help with the less desirable side effects of eating legumes . . .) If you can't find it, add a couple of garlic cloves to the onion; it will impart a similar flavour profile if it's left slightly under-sauteed.

While the dal is cooking, you might want to knock up some very quick Chapattis (see Basic recipes) as an accompaniment. If you can't be bothered, simply serve the dal with rice or pappadams.

1 To make the spice mix, place all of the ingredients in a heavy-based frying pan and toast them over low heat for 30 seconds–1 minute until aromatic. Leave the spice mix to cool, then run it through a spice grinder or pound it using a mortar and pestle. The lentils need to be very finely ground to a fine flour, or the spice mix will not thicken the dish properly in its final stage. Set the spice mix aside.

2 Preheat a large saucepan over medium heat. Add 3 tablespoons of ghee and the mustard seeds and cumin seeds, and let them pop for a few seconds while stirring. Fold in the curry leaves and onion and saute for about 3 minutes until the onion softens. Add the tomato and continue to cook, stirring, for about 5 minutes until it breaks down. Add the chana dal and cover with 4 litres of tepid water (it will look like there is too much liquid, but it will be absorbed). Simmer over medium heat for about 1 hour until the chana dal is tender. Add the mushrooms and salt and simmer for 15 minutes.

3 Warm the remaining ghee in a small frying pan over low heat and add the spice mix (you should have about 140 g). Saute for about 1 minute, stirring constantly, until the spice mix is well coated in ghee and drying out. Fold this into the dal and stir to combine, then add the tamarind or lemon juice and simmer for 2–3 minutes or until the dal becomes thick and creamy.

4 Divide the dal among bowls and garnish with ginger, coriander and chilli. Serve with Chapattis.

GREEN BEANS, MUSTARD SEED AND COCONUT WITH LEMON BASMATI RICE

SERVES 4

500 G GREEN BEANS, TAILED

1 HANDFUL CORIANDER LEAVES
  AND STEMS, CHOPPED

1 LONG RED CHILLI, SEEDED AND
  CHOPPED (OR SEEDS IN IF YOU
  LIKE IT HOT)

30 G DESICCATED COCONUT

1 TEASPOON SALT FLAKES

4 TABLESPOONS GHEE
  (SEE INGREDIENTS)

1 SPRIG CURRY LEAVES,
  LEAVES STRIPPED

2 TABLESPOONS POPPY SEEDS

1½ TABLESPOONS BROWN
  MUSTARD SEEDS

1 TABLESPOON CUMIN SEEDS

TOMATO KUSUNDI, TO SERVE
  (OPTIONAL, SEE PAGE 66)

LEMON BASMATI RICE

100 ML GHEE (SEE INGREDIENTS)

2 ONIONS, FINELY DICED

1 STAR ANISE

8 GREEN CARDAMOM PODS, SMACKED

2 CINNAMON STICKS

10 CLOVES

1 TABLESPOON BLACK PEPPERCORNS

2 CUPS (400 G) BASMATI RICE
  (UNWASHED)

1 LITRE BOILING WATER

½ TEASPOON SALT FLAKES

BIG PINCH OF SAFFRON THREADS

2 BAY LEAVES

1 CUP (150 G) SHELLED PISTACHIOS
  OR 1 CUP (80 G) ALMOND FLAKES

100 G CURRANTS

FINELY GRATED ZEST OF 2 LEMONS

I don't remember getting excited about green beans until I ate this dish. The combination of the coconut and the aromatics is just perfect. It's important to neither undercook the spices (or the dish will just taste flat) nor expose them to excess heat (as they will become bitter). Keep in mind that the addition of the beans will cause the temperature of the wok to drop quickly and thus prevent the spices from burning, so make sure you have them to hand.

I learnt my first rice pilaf at trade school and I remember the lecturer drilling the class not, under any circumstances, to lift the lid while the rice was cooking. To this day, I still don't know if this would really upset the process because as much as I long to peek into the pan, there is the little voice of a large Spanish TAFE chef terrifying me and I just can't lift the lid.

I do, however, have a very handy fix if you lift the lid at the end of cooking to discover your rice is not quite done (it can vary wildly in its absorption ratio). Simply dig a teaspoon ever so gently into the rice: if it's still a little crunchy and undercooked, rain a little boiling water on top and replace the lid. The trick is not to disturb the grain arrangement. If you stir or fluff the rice, then discover it's undercooked, you're stuffed!

1 For the rice, place a heavy-based saucepan with a tight-fitting lid over low–medium heat. Add the ghee and fry the onion until it's soft and translucent. Add the star anise, cardamom, cinnamon, cloves and peppercorns and stir for 30 seconds or so, then add the rice, continuing to stir until the rice is coated with ghee and is glossy. Carefully add the boiling water (it will sizzle quite hard), then add the salt. Reduce the temperature to the lowest setting until there is no more movement on the surface of the water. Add the saffron in patches around the pan and pop the bay leaves in. Cover with a tight-fitting lid and cook the rice gently for 15–20 minutes. (Oh, and no peeking!)

2 Meanwhile, blanch the green beans in boiling salted water for a couple of minutes until just tender. Refresh them in iced or running water, then drain them well and set aside.

3 When the rice is cooked and all the liquid has been absorbed, carefully turn out the rice into a large mixing bowl. Fold in the nuts, currants and lemon zest and mix gently. (If you do this in the pan, you will break the rice grains.) Discard the cinnamon and cover the bowl with foil to keep the pilaf warm.

4 Combine the coriander, chilli, coconut and salt in a medium-sized bowl and set aside. Heat a heavy-based frying pan over low heat. Add the ghee, then the curry leaves (be careful as the ghee will splatter) and allow them to darken a shade and become aromatic. Add the poppy seeds, mustard seeds and cumin seeds, and as soon as they become aromatic (this will only take a few seconds), add the blanched beans. Stir, shaking the pan to warm the beans through slightly and to coat them with the ghee and spices. Tip the beans into the coconut mixture and combine.

5 Serve the beans and pilaf with a small bowl of Tomato kusundi, if you like.

CORN AND TOFU TOM KAH

SERVES 4 AS A STARTER

- 8–10 DRIED SHIITAKE MUSHROOMS
- 2 BIG CORN COBS, KERNELS STRIPPED AND COBS RESERVED
- 4 STALKS LEMONGRASS, BRUISED
- 3 CM PIECE GALANGAL, FINELY SLICED
- 1 BUNCH CORIANDER, ROOTS AND STEMS SCRAPED AND CHOPPED, LEAVES RESERVED
- 2 RED SHALLOTS, HALVED AND FINELY SLICED
- 1 × 440 ML TIN COCONUT CREAM
- 1 TEASPOON GRATED COCONUT PALM SUGAR (SEE PAGE 52)
- 2 KAFFIR LIME LEAVES
- 375 G FIRM TOFU, CUT INTO 4 CM × 3 CM × 2 CM CUBES
- JUICE OF 2 LIMES
- 2 TABLESPOONS THAI LIGHT SOY SAUCE (SEE INGREDIENTS)
- SALT FLAKES AND FRESHLY GROUND WHITE PEPPER
- 1 LONG GREEN CHILLI, CHOPPED, SEEDS AND ALL

This is another 'old' corn dish, perfect for autumn when the last of the corn reaches the markets. There is so much flavour in the cobs, but more often than not they end up in the bin. In this recipe I use them to infuse a corn flavour into a stock so nothing is wasted.

I cook soup all year round; it's not just for winter, as far as I'm concerned. Buying ready-made soup might save us time but it costs us in many other ways. In fact, I reckon the world would be a better place if people just made soup and gave it away to random strangers. To me, making soup for someone is a way of saying, 'Don't worry, everything will be all right.' My philosophy is this: When someone is upset, make soup! If someone is sick, make soup! When you've argued with someone and you're too stubborn to admit you were wrong, make soup! Even if you're making soup at home for one, it's an important gesture that says you're truly caring for yourself. This is why I like soup so much.

1 Place the shiitakes and 1 litre of hot water in a large saucepan and leave to soak for 30 minutes or so.

2 Cut the stripped corn cobs into 6 cm lengths and add them to the saucepan containing the soaked shiitakes, along with the lemongrass, galangal and coriander roots and stems. Place the pan over low heat and simmer for 30 minutes. Strain the stock through a muslin-lined sieve into a clean saucepan, reserving the shiitakes and discarding the corn cobs, lemongrass, galangal and coriander.

3 Remove the shiitake stems and thinly slice the caps. Return the sliced shiitakes to the strained stock, along with the corn kernels, shallot, coconut cream, palm sugar and kaffir lime leaves. Bring to a simmer over medium heat, then reduce the heat to low and simmer for 15 minutes. Pulse a stick blender through the mixture to break down the corn a little, but retain some texture. Add the tofu and allow it to warm through for a minute or two. Remove the pan from the heat.

4 Season the soup with lime juice, soy sauce and about 1 teaspoon of salt. To serve, divide the soup among bowls and add the coriander leaves, white pepper and chilli.

LEEK AND POTATO TART WITH FETA

SERVES 6

COS LEAVES DRESSED WITH EXTRA
   VIRGIN OLIVE OIL AND LEMON JUICE,
   TO SERVE

SHORT PASTRY

280 G STRONG PLAIN FLOUR
   (SEE INGREDIENTS)

½ TEASPOON FINE SALT

180 G CHILLED UNSALTED BUTTER,
   DICED INTO 1 CM CUBES AND
   THEN ALLOWED TO COME UP
   TO ROOM TEMPERATURE

4 TABLESPOONS CHILLED SODA WATER

FILLING

20 G UNSALTED BUTTER

30 ML EXTRA VIRGIN OLIVE OIL

1 LARGE LEEK, WHITE PART ONLY,
   ROUGHLY SLICED

3 WAXY POTATOES (SEE PAGE 117),
   THINLY SLICED

2 SPRIGS THYME, LEAVES PICKED

1 BAY LEAF

SALT FLAKES AND CRACKED
   BLACK PEPPER

200 ML DOUBLE (RICH) CREAM

30 G PARMESAN, GRATED

3 FREE-RANGE EGGS

200 G FETA, CUBED

Leek and potato is one of those classic combinations. Add a good feta and you have a little magic. If you like the crumbly, slightly grainy texture of sheep's milk feta, feel free to use it, but for this tart I prefer creamy cow's feta with its softer texture and richer flavour. There are some great Australian artisan cheese-makers creating fantastic feta-style cheeses, but you can always use Danish feta, the most widely available cow's feta – you should have no trouble finding it in your local supermarket.

Now, I am the world's worst pastry chef. If it involves scales, I quickly lose interest. However, when I cook tart shells I do take great care with the method and technique. This pastry needs to be dangerously short and crisp to offer a contrasting texture to the smooth creamy filling, and the only way to achieve this shortness is to inhibit the swelly, stretchy gluten in the flour. Gluten loves water, heat and motion – deprive it of these and you have a short pastry. In this method, rubbing the butter into the flour before adding the water buffers the hydration rate; using cold water and your fingertips keeps the dough cool; and the complete lack of kneading minimises both heat and motion. Remember these tips and you will perfect short pastry.

The tart will come out of an ordinary baking tin easily when cooled, but a tart tin with a removable base is a worthwhile investment, especially if you wish to serve the tart hot. To expedite the cooking, pull the eggs, cream and cheese out of the fridge about 1½ hours before preparing. This will also give you a smoother-textured filling. The tart shell should still be a little warm when the filling is poured in, as this prevents the pastry becoming soggy.

1 To make the pastry, sift the flour into a large bowl, then add the salt and mix through. Rub in the butter cubes using your fingertips. When the butter is combined, add the soda water and bring the dough together with the absolute minimum of mixing, using your fingertips to prevent the heat from your hands affecting the dough. The dough should be a little crumbly still and definitely not one cohesive mass. A few visible lumps of butter here and there are not a major issue and will actually make the pastry flakier and nicer. Very roughly gather the dough into a ball.

2 Lightly sprinkle your benchtop with flour and roll the dough out from the centre in all directions to make a round about 34 cm in diameter. Grease a 23 cm tart tin and pop the pastry in – there should be plenty overhanging to allow for shrinkage during baking. Leave in the fridge for 40 minutes.

3 Preheat the oven to 190°C fan-forced (210°C conventional). Line the pastry with baking paper and add at least 1 cup (200 g) of pastry weights or dried beans. Blind bake the pastry for 15 minutes or until it's firm to the touch. Remove the weights or beans and paper and return the pastry to the oven for a couple more minutes to crisp and colour. Remove from the oven and leave the pastry in the tin. Reduce the oven temperature to 180°C fan-forced (200°C conventional).

4 Meanwhile, for the filling, melt the butter and oil in a heavy-based frying pan with a lid over medium heat. Add the leek and saute for a few minutes until softened, then add the potato, thyme, bay leaf and 2 tablespoons of cold water. Season with ½ teaspoon of salt, if necessary (I often omit this if the feta is heavily brined), and a good few twists of black pepper. Reduce the heat to low and pop a lid on the pan. Cook the potato slices for about 10 minutes, turning them a few times, until they're just tender. (They will cook a tiny bit more in the baking of the tarts, but they do need to be virtually ready to eat at this stage.) Remove the bay leaf and set the pan aside.

5 Mix the cream, parmesan and eggs together in a bowl and season with salt and pepper. Spoon the leek and potato mixture into the pastry shell, then pour over the egg mix and drop cubes of feta over the top. Bake for 25–30 minutes until the filling is just set. To check, insert a skewer: a little goo is okay as the tart will continue to set when it's removed from the oven; however, the mixture should definitely not wobble when you shake the tin. The tart top should also have patches that are coloured up nicely.

6 Serve the tart hot or cold with dressed cos leaves.

FIELD MUSHROOM FREEKEH 'RISOTTO'

SERVES 4

⅓ CUP (ABOUT 15 G) DRIED
WILD MUSHROOM MIX,
PACKED A LITTLE TIGHTLY

60 G UNSALTED BUTTER

4 GOLDEN SHALLOTS, FINELY DICED

4 CLOVES GARLIC, CRUSHED

1 TABLESPOON THYME LEAVES, CHOPPED

1 TABLESPOON OREGANO
LEAVES, CHOPPED

4 LARGE FIELD MUSHROOMS,
CHOPPED INTO 2 CM WEDGES

EXTRA VIRGIN OLIVE OIL, FOR FRYING
(IF NEEDED)

1 CUP (165 G) CRACKED FREEKEH

3 TABLESPOONS VERJUICE
(SEE INGREDIENTS)

1 BAY LEAF

SALT FLAKES AND CRACKED
BLACK PEPPER

⅓ CUP (25 G) GRATED PARMESAN

½ CUP (125 G) MASCARPONE

1 HANDFUL FLAT-LEAF PARSLEY LEAVES

Freekeh is young green wheat, which is harvested early and then roasted. It imparts a smoky, earthy flavour that's ideal for autumn and winter cooking. In this dish, it harmonises brilliantly with the straw overtones of a good field mushroom and robust aromatic herbs such as thyme and oregano. I prefer to use cracked freekeh grains as they're a little lighter on the palate than the whole grains, which can feel a little bit like hard work halfway through a dish. The cracked grains also take less time to cook.

Experiment with the array of wild harvest mushrooms that come into the markets in autumn, or swap the mascarpone for blue cheese if you want a bolder colder-weather meal. Just remember that this needs a fairly rich cheese, otherwise the freekeh can be a little dry and mealy.

A sauteuse is really the ideal vessel for this dish. If you use a saucepan to cook the garlic and mushrooms, you can end up steaming rather than frying and the resulting flavour is compromised. If you do not have a sauteuse, I recommend you cook the shallot, garlic, mushrooms and herbs in a frying pan and then transfer them to a saucepan before adding the freekeh.

1 Soak the dried wild mushrooms in 3 cups (750 ml) of warm water for 30 minutes or so at room temperature. Drain the mushrooms, reserving the soaking liquid. Squeeze them dry, then roughly chop. Strain the soaking liquid through a fine sieve to remove any grit.

2 Place a heavy-based medium–large sauteuse over medium heat. When warm, add the butter and allow it brown slightly (just past the stage when it fizzes and bubbles). Add the shallot and saute until it's soft and translucent, then add the garlic and continue to saute until the garlic becomes highly aromatic and a little coloured. Add the thyme and oregano and stir them for a minute or so, then add the chopped field mushroom and the wild mushrooms. Saute for 5 minutes or so until the field mushroom softens slightly and the wild mushrooms colour a little. (You may need to add a little oil if the pan becomes dry during cooking. This will depend on the quality and age of the mushrooms: very fresh mushrooms will absorb little butter but older ones will soak it up like hungry little sponges!)

3 Add the freekeh and continue to saute over medium heat for about 5 minutes, stirring frequently to prevent burning and to coat and toast the grains. Deglaze the pan with the verjuice, then add the bay leaf, reserved mushroom liquid and 1 heaped teaspoon of salt and reduce the heat to low. Cook for about 20 minutes, stirring periodically, until the freekeh is tender to the bite. You may need to top up the water during cooking; this will depend on the quality and age of the freekeh.

4 When the 'risotto' has the consistency of wet porridge, remove the pan from the heat and check the seasoning, adding more salt if required. Fold in the parmesan and mascarpone – I rarely stir them in, preferring to see them streak through the mixture – and season with pepper. Divide the 'risotto' among bowls, then scatter over the parsley and season with extra pepper.

TWICE-COOKED CHEESE SOUFFLE WITH PICKLED CHERRIES AND ALMOND PASTE

SERVES 6 AS A STARTER

½ CUP (80 G) ALMONDS

65 ML EXTRA VIRGIN OLIVE OIL

1 TEASPOON SALT FLAKES

½ CUP (75 G) PICKLED CHERRIES
(SEE BASIC RECIPES) AND A SPLASH
OF THE PICKLING VINEGAR

1 HANDFUL ROCKET LEAVES

SOUFFLES

45 G UNSALTED BUTTER, PLUS EXTRA,
MELTED, FOR BRUSHING MOULDS

100 G GRATED ROMANO OR PARMESAN,
PLUS EXTRA, FINELY GRATED,
FOR LINING MOULDS

45 G PLAIN FLOUR

260 ML MILK, AT ROOM TEMPERATURE

1 TEASPOON CHOPPED THYME

3 TABLESPOONS CHOPPED
FLAT-LEAF PARSLEY

1 TEASPOON DIJON MUSTARD (OPTIONAL)

2 FREE-RANGE EGG YOLKS,
AT ROOM TEMPERATURE

SALT FLAKES AND CRACKED
BLACK PEPPER

3 FREE-RANGE EGG WHITES,
AT ROOM TEMPERATURE

6 TABLESPOONS DOUBLE (RICH) CREAM

Why a twice-cooked souffle? Well, they're idiot-proof. They also allow you to do all the scary work in advance and then act all nonchalant as you whip perfect souffles out of the oven for your guests. This recipe yields some spare mixture that could do a couple of extra souffles if you like (although this does depend on the volume you achieve with your egg whites). I've included this as a bit of an insurance policy, just in case one or two souffles either do not rise or over-rise due to an uneven oven (this is rare, but it can happen). You can buy all sorts of fancy silicone moulds to bake souffles in, but I am quite happy to use my beaten-up moulds that cost about a dollar each. Whatever moulds you use, just make sure they're flexible enough for the souffles to easily pop out after the first bake. For finishing the dish you need double (rich) cream, which has a fat content of around 48 per cent. Do not confuse this with thickened cream, which has less fat and contains thickening agents (see Ingredients).

This recipe includes Pickled cherries (see Basic recipes), which you will need to crack on to in late summer. They're not absolutely essential, but the combination of cheese, almonds and cherries is a stunner.

1 For the souffles, brush six ½ cup (125 ml) flexible souffle moulds with a little melted butter. Line them with the extra finely grated cheese. Preheat the oven to 180°C fan-forced (200°C conventional). Prepare a water bath by filling a 5 cm-deep roasting tin with hot water to a depth of 3 cm. The tin will need to be a minimum of 20 cm square to avoid overcrowding the souffle moulds. Preheat the water bath in the oven for a good 20 minutes to ensure it's up to temperature.

2 Melt the butter in a medium saucepan over medium heat until it's foaming. Add the flour and cook it, stirring constantly, for 2–3 minutes until a thick paste forms and the flour smells slightly nutty. Working slowly to avoid lumps, gradually whisk in the milk and bring the mixture to a simmer. Remove the pan from the heat and add the cheese, thyme, parsley and mustard, if using. Allow the mixture to cool for 5 minutes so that the egg yolks will not scramble when added. Stir in the egg yolks, one at a time, with a wooden spoon, adding the second yolk only when the first has been incorporated. Season with ½ teaspoon of salt and black pepper, then transfer the mixture to a large bowl and set aside.

3 Place the egg whites in a really clean bowl (any oil residue will stuff up the aeration) or in an electric mixer with a whisk attachment and whisk until they form stiff peaks. They should hold their shape if you scoop some out with the whisk and hold it horizontally. If the peaks drop after a few seconds, they need a little more whisking. Be careful not to over-whisk, though, or the souffle will be grainy. A sign of over-whisking is when the water separates out from the foamed egg whites in the bowl – if this happens, start again!

TWICE-COOKED CHEESE SOUFFLE WITH PICKLED CHERRIES AND ALMOND PASTE (CONT.)

4 Gently fold a third of the whisked egg whites into the yolk mixture and mix through with a pastry card or with your hands. Do not whisk! You're trying not to knock out the bubbles trapped in the egg whites. A cut-and-fold action with a pastry card works well. When the egg whites have been incorporated, add another third and repeat the folding through. Finally, add the last third of the whites and incorporate. The mixture doesn't need to be absolutely combined, as there is a trade-off between mixing it through perfectly and losing the bubbles; a few egg-white streaks through the mix is fine.

5 Gently spoon the mixture into the moulds until they're two-thirds full (about 4 tablespoons per mould) to allow for expansion. Remove the preheated water bath from the oven and place the souffles carefully into it, spacing them well to allow airflow between them. Return the water bath to the oven and bake the souffles for about 15 minutes or until they're just a little firm to the touch and are well-puffed. Remove the water bath from the oven and take out the souffles. Allow them to cool slowly at room temperature. They will drop – a little over half of the rise gained will be lost – but do not be alarmed, as the second cooking will fix this.

6 While the souffles are cooling, spread the almonds on a baking tray and roast them in the oven for 10 minutes. Allow them to cool slightly, then place them in a food processor with the olive oil and salt and blend to a pesto-like consistency. If the almonds are old, the paste will be a little thick, so you may need to add a little more oil. Set aside.

7 When the souffles are cool, release them from their moulds by gently running a wet paring or small butter knife around the inside edge of each mould. Invert onto a greased tray and squeeze the mould gently to create an air gap – the souffle should slide out. If it doesn't release, give it a little tap on the base. Make sure the souffles are well-spaced on the tray. (If you're not using them within the hour, carefully cover them with plastic film and place them in the fridge, where they can be kept for a couple of days. Just bring them up to room temperature before the second cooking.)

8 Preheat the oven grill to high. Spoon a tablespoon of cream over the top of each souffle to moisten it. (You can also sprinkle them with a little extra cheese if you like.) Place them under the grill with about 5 cm clearance from the souffle tops to the element and grill for 3–5 minutes or until they're well-puffed and golden on top.

9 Arrange the Pickled cherries and rocket leaves around each plate. Using a spatula, gently lift up the souffles and slide them onto the centre of each plate. Drizzle the almond paste on and around the souffles. Serve immediately.

FRIED JASMINE RICE with SOYBEAN SPROUTS

SERVES 4

2½ CUPS (500 G) JASMINE RICE

4 FREE-RANGE EGGS

4 TABLESPOONS LIGHT SOY SAUCE (SEE INGREDIENTS)

4 DROPS OF SESAME OIL

SALT FLAKES AND FRESHLY GROUND WHITE PEPPER

6 CORIANDER ROOTS AND STEMS SCRAPED AND FINELY CHOPPED, LEAVES RESERVED

2 TABLESPOONS PEANUT OIL

4 CLOVES GARLIC, CRUSHED

2 CM PIECE GINGER, GRATED

3 SPRING ONIONS, WHITE PARTS FINELY CHOPPED, GREEN PARTS SLICED DIAGONALLY

1 CARROT, PEELED AND CUT INTO 1 CM DICE

1 CUP (120 G) FROZEN PEAS

1 BUNCH CHINESE BROCCOLI (GAI LAN), LEAVES SHREDDED INTO 1 CM STRIPS, STEMS SLICED DIAGONALLY INTO 2 CM LENGTHS

1 CUP (80 G) SOYBEAN SPROUTS (SEE PAGE 55) OR BEAN SPROUTS IF UNAVAILABLE

2 TABLESPOONS VEGETARIAN OYSTER SAUCE (SEE INGREDIENTS)

½ TEASPOON SUGAR

1 LONG RED CHILLI, FINELY SLICED, SEEDS AND ALL

Contrary to popular belief, long-grain rice does not contain less starch than short-grain rice: it's just a different type. Short-grain rice is high in amylopectin, which busts out of the grain during cooking and makes the rice sticky and creamy (see my notes on making risotto on page 38). Long-grain rice, on the other hand, is usually high in amylose, which doesn't become gluey, so the grains remain separate. Jasmine rice, however, is the exception to the rule. It contains a significant amount of amylopectin (the short-grain starch), and this can turn your fluffy fried rice into a sticky mess. But do not fear! Armed with this knowledge, you can employ a few tactics to inhibit the starch and achieve a slightly creamy texture without clumping. All you need to do is wash the rice well, steam it without excess water and, most importantly, refrigerate it to cool completely, preferably overnight (or spread it out and chuck it in the freezer if you're in a rush). If you follow these steps and still don't end up with nice soft grains that cling ever so slightly, it may be because you're using new-crop rice, which contains more available starch. I suggest you buy rice from an Asian supermarket, as it is often labelled with this info.

1 Wash the rice a few times in cold water until the water becomes less milky. Drain well, then place in a rice cooker or a small heavy-based saucepan and add 3½ cups (875 ml) of water. If you're using a pan, cover with the lid, bring to a rapid simmer over high heat, then immediately reduce the heat to the lowest setting. Steam for 15 minutes or until the water is absorbed and the rice is tender. Gently empty the rice out onto a tray about 20 cm square. Allow to cool to room temperature, then immediately place in the fridge.

2 The next day, break the eggs into a bowl. Using a fork, gently mix them with 1 tablespoon of soy sauce, sesame oil, pepper and coriander roots and stems. Break the yolks but don't scramble the mixture. Preheat a small heavy-based frying pan over low heat. Add 1 teaspoon of peanut oil and coat the pan with a thin layer of the egg mixture. Cook the omelette through (it will only take a minute), then transfer it to a plate. Repeat with the remaining mixture, stacking the omelettes up as you go; the oil from the pan will prevent them sticking together. (You shouldn't need to add more oil to the pan, but feel free to add a few drops if the omelettes begin to stick.) Roll up the omelettes into cigars and slice them into 5 mm-wide 'noodles'. Set aside.

3 Preheat a wok over high heat. Add the remaining peanut oil and the garlic, ginger and white spring onion. Stir-fry for 30 seconds until the garlic is soft. Add the carrot, peas, cold rice, ½ teaspoon of salt and broccoli stems, and fry while gently lifting and folding the mix. Continue to fry for 4–5 minutes or until the rice is coated and the vegies are just tender. Add the broccoli leaves, soybean sprouts, remaining soy sauce, oyster sauce and sugar and stir through, then remove the wok from the heat.

4 To serve, divide the fried rice among bowls and top with chilli, green spring onion and coriander leaves.

CAVOLO NERO WITH GREEN OLIVES, FENNEL AND RUBY GRAPEFRUIT

SERVES 4 AS A STARTER OR SIDE SALAD

2 SMALL OR 1 LARGE BULB FENNEL

FINELY GRATED ZEST AND JUICE
OF 1 LEMON

3 RUBY GRAPEFRUIT, AT ROOM
TEMPERATURE, PEELED AND
PITH REMOVED

1 BUNCH CAVOLO NERO

120 ML EXTRA VIRGIN OLIVE OIL

SALT FLAKES AND CRACKED
BLACK PEPPER

20 GREEN OLIVES

2 TABLESPOONS AGED SWEET RED
VINEGAR (SEE INGREDIENTS)
OR BALSAMIC VINEGAR

½ BUNCH DILL, LEAVES PICKED

Cavolo nero is just a fancy name for black kale or cabbage. I love the flavour, which is milder than your regular stinky cabbage, and the fact that the leaf retains its structure when cooked. The little lumps give an interesting, almost otherworldly, look on the plate. I'm also a big fan of the texture of icy cold, thinly shaved fennel but I find the chill can sometimes close down the flavour. Warming the fennel in this recipe enables the top notes to sing without compromising the raw crunch. I understand if you can't be stuffed with this bit, but may I suggest as a compromise that you serve the fennel at room temperature rather than straight from the fridge? If it's a really cold day, slice the fennel slightly thicker and give it a lightning-quick sear on a barbecue grill-plate for smokiness. Add a few waxy spuds to push the whole dish into a more wintry domain. A handful of diced feta is another nice addition.

1 Bring a saucepan of water to a gentle simmer. Remove and discard the tough outer layers from the fennel, if necessary, then pick off a dozen or so fronds and set aside. Cut off the fennel stems and very finely shave the bulb using a mandoline (if the fennel is old, you may have to quarter the bulb and remove the core before shaving it). Coat the shaved fennel in half of the lemon juice to prevent it discolouring, then place in a heatproof bowl and set it over the saucepan of simmering water. Turn off the heat and just let the fennel sit while you prepare the rest of the dish.

2 Using a small sharp knife, prize out the segments from 2 of the grapefruit, holding them over a bowl to collect any juices. Set the segments aside. Squeeze all the juice from the grapefruit flesh remaining after the segments have been removed and add this to the bowl, then add the juice from the third grapefruit. Strain the juice into a small saucepan and place it over medium heat. Reduce for about 3–5 minutes or until syrupy; you should end up with about 2 tablespoons. Remove the pan from the heat and pop the segments into the warm syrup. Let them macerate until you're ready to put the dish together. They'll become extra-juicy and taste like super-grapefruits!

3 Trim the cavolo nero by removing the bottom of the stems. If the leaves are small, use the whole leaf; if they're large, cut them across their width into two or three slices. Preheat a heavy-based frying pan over medium–high heat. Add 1 tablespoon of olive oil and about 1 teaspoon of salt, then add the olives and blister the skins a little. Fold in the cavolo nero and saute rapidly until the leaves blister slightly in places, then add the remaining lemon juice and allow the leaves to wilt a bit. They will turn a slightly darker shade of green when ready – less than a minute. Season with lots of black pepper.

4 To serve, divide the warmed shaved fennel, cavolo nero and olives among four plates. Drizzle with the remaining olive oil and the vinegar, then add the grapefruit syrup and segments. Season, then add the lemon zest. Finally, garnish with dill and a few fennel fronds.

PEA AND POTATO SAMOSAS
WITH TAMARILLO AND CHILLI CHUTNEY

MAKES 12–16

2½ CUPS (425 G) PLAIN FLOUR

½ TEASPOON FINE SALT

100 ML GHEE (SEE INGREDIENTS), JUST WARMED (NOT TOO HOT)

FLAVOUR-NEUTRAL OIL (SEE INGREDIENTS), FOR DEEP-FRYING

TAMARILLO AND CHILLI CHUTNEY (SEE BASIC RECIPES), TO SERVE

FILLING

500 G LARGE FLOURY POTATOES (SEE PAGE 117)

½ TEASPOON FINE SALT

4 TABLESPOONS PEANUT OIL

1 ONION, CUT INTO 1 CM DICE

2 CLOVES GARLIC, CRUSHED

1 TEASPOON FINELY CHOPPED GINGER

1 TABLESPOON CUMIN SEEDS

1 TABLESPOON GROUND CORIANDER

1 LONG GREEN CHILLI, CHOPPED, SEEDS AND ALL

300 G FRESH PEAS, SHELLED OR ½ CUP (60 G) FROZEN PEAS

1 TABLESPOON CHAAT MASALA (SEE PAGE 37)

1 TABLESPOON AMCHOOR (DRIED MANGO POWDER; SEE PAGE 32)

1 TABLESPOON LEMON JUICE

½ TEASPOON SALT FLAKES

1 BUNCH CORIANDER, LEAVES PICKED AND ROUGHLY CHOPPED

The hardest thing about making samosas is getting the shaping down pat. My favourite shape is a cone. You can always just make little pasty shapes and crimp the edges, but the ratio of filling to dough is reduced and I reckon the subsequent flavour is compromised. If you attempt the cones, the first few batches will probably look like a three-year-old's art project. I have allowed for a bit of extra dough in the recipe, so you can just pull the filling out of your rejects until you get the method sorted out. See, I am being nice to you!

Be aware that the dough will become hard to handle if it gets too warm (depending on the room temperature and your hands – some people's are way hotter than others), so you may want to periodically pop the dough in the fridge for a minute. If it becomes too cold, however, it has no pliability, so it's a matter of finding a balance.

1 Sift the flour into the bowl of an electric mixer fitted with a dough hook and add the salt. Pour in the ghee, then mix on the lowest speed for about a minute until the ghee is combined. (You may have to pause to scrape down the sides of the mixer bowl.) Continue to mix on the lowest speed and slowly add ¾ cup (180 ml) of room-temperature water. When the water has been absorbed, increase the speed to medium for 3–4 minutes until a smooth dough forms. Alternatively, if you're making the dough by hand, rub the ghee into the flour and salt with your fingertips until well combined, then add 3 tablespoons of water and bring the ingredients together until the water is absorbed. Repeat twice more until the water is all absorbed. Turn it out onto your benchtop and knead for 8 minutes to make a smooth dough. Wrap the dough in plastic film and leave it to rest in the fridge for 1 hour.

2 Meanwhile, for the filling, place the potatoes in a saucepan, cover them with cold water and add the fine salt. Bring to a simmer and cook until the potatoes are tender, then drain and allow to cool slightly. Rub off the skins using a tea towel (it doesn't matter if a little skin remains in the final mix). Place the potatoes in a bowl and use a spatula to lightly smash them into chunks, ideally 2 cm cubes with a few smaller crumbly bits. You need some texture to the filling, so do not mash the potato.

3 Preheat a heavy-based sauteuse or frying pan over medium heat and add the peanut oil. Saute the onion until soft and translucent, then add the garlic and ginger and continue to fry until the ginger is a little softened, a minute or two. Stir in the cumin seeds, ground coriander and chilli and fry for about 30 seconds. Add the potato and peas and cook until the peas are tender. Add the chaat masala and amchoor, then stir to coat the potato and peas with the spices and cook for a further minute. Remove the pan from the heat and allow the mixture to cool for a couple of minutes. Splash in the lemon juice and add the salt flakes and chopped coriander.

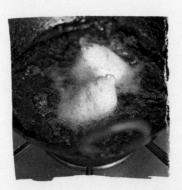

PEA AND POTATO SAMOSAS WITH TAMARILLO AND CHILLI CHUTNEY (CONT.)

4 Remove the dough from the fridge and roll it out to a thickness of about 3 mm. Cut the dough into 12–16 triangles with a 15 cm bottom edge and 22 cm sides. Brush the edges (about 1 cm wide) of each triangle with water. With the bottom edge facing you, fold the bottom right corner across to meet the left edge. Fold the top corner towards you and wrap around to make a cone. Pinch the seams together to seal. Holding the cone in your hand, fill it with about 1–1½ heaped tablespoons of the filling. Fold the base over and pinch the edges together to seal – easy! Place the samosa base-side down on a tray lined with a tea towel. Gently re-form the shape to achieve a perfect cone. Repeat with the remaining dough and filling.

5 Pour the oil into large saucepan or wok until it's about 8 cm deep. Heat it over low–medium heat to about 160°C (not quite shimmering). Deep-fry the samosas a few at a time to avoid overcrowding. They may need to be turned using a slotted spoon or tongs during cooking to avoid hot spots on the bottom, but don't be perturbed by little blisters forming on the dough.

6 The samosas will take about 5–6 minutes to cook as the dough is quite thick. If the dough colours past golden brown but is not cooked through, the temperature of your oil is too hot. If this is the case, you can pop the samosas in the oven at 180°C fan-forced (200°C conventional) for about 5 minutes to finish them off or simply remove them from the wok, turn the temperature down and re-fry them when the oil is cooler.

7 Serve the samosas with Tamarillo and chilli chutney.

PUMPKIN TEMPURA WITH HONEY SESAME DIPPING SAUCE

SERVES 4 AS A LIGHT MEAL OR STARTER

2 CUPS (400 G) SHORT-GRAIN
    WHITE RICE

TEMPURA

100 G SIFTED PLAIN FLOUR

10 G CORNFLOUR

4 TABLESPOONS COLD WATER

1 HANDFUL ICE CUBES

1 FREE-RANGE EGG

1 KG PUMPKIN, PEELED, SEEDED AND
    SLICED INTO 5 CM × 2 CM × 3 MM
    THICK PIECES

2 CUPS (500 ML) NON-GM,
    COLD-PRESSED CANOLA OIL
    (SEE INGREDIENTS)

HONEY SESAME DIPPING SAUCE

2 TEASPOONS HONEY

2 TEASPOONS TOASTED SESAME SEEDS

JUICE OF 1 LIME

½ TEASPOON SESAME OIL

1 TABLESPOON JAPANESE LIGHT SOY
    SAUCE (SEE INGREDIENTS)

1 TEASPOON GRATED GINGER

2 SPRING ONIONS, GREEN PARTS ONLY,
    FINELY CHOPPED

To me, pumpkin with honey, soy and sesame is just one of those perfect flavour combinations. However, you can also use any leftover vegies you have lurking in the fridge for this – mushrooms, cauliflower, carrot, sweet potato and green beans all work well. Frying tempura requires immaculately clean oil so it's essential to have a skimmer handy to prevent impurities spoiling the last few batches. Oil in a small wok will eventually reach a very high temperature but this can plummet in seconds with the addition of just a handful of ingredients – which will lead to soggy, oily batter. Without the luxury of a commercial deep-fryer, you will need to adjust the heat as you go to keep a constant temperature. For this reason, a deep-frying thermometer is a must-have for this recipe.

1 Whisk all the dipping-sauce ingredients together. Set aside.

2 Cover the rice with cold water and run your fingers through the grains until the water becomes cloudy. Discard the water and repeat a couple of times, then drain. Place the rice in a rice cooker with 3 cups (750 ml) of water and cook for 15 minutes or until the rice is tender and the water has been absorbed. Alternatively, place the rice and water in a saucepan with a tight-fitting lid. Bring to a simmer over high heat, then immediately turn down the heat to very low. Leave to cook undisturbed for 15–18 minutes or until tender.

3 For the tempura, combine the flour and cornflour in a large bowl and make a large well in the centre. Place the water, ice and egg in a jug and stir with chopsticks until the yolk breaks and combines with the water (but do not over-mix). Pour into the well in the flour but do not combine. The mixture will start to suck the flour in and create a light batter in the centre of the bowl; leave for a few minutes to thicken. Dust both sides of the pumpkin pieces with the flour at the edge of the bowl. Leave it there until you're ready to fry.

4 Carefully heat the oil in a small wok or saucepan over low–medium heat to 190°C. Working in batches of five or six pieces, use chopsticks to drag the pumpkin slowly through the batter. Hold for a few seconds over the bowl and allow excess batter to drip away. Don't worry if the coating is a bit random for the first few pieces and contains the occasional pocket of flour. The mixture will thicken and become more consistent as more flour is incorporated. (You might need to add a smidge of water later on if the batter becomes too thick.) Use chopsticks to gently lower the coated pumpkin into the hot oil. Once crisp, about a minute or two, remove the tempura and drain on paper towel. The coating should still be quite pale; if it's past golden, the oil is too hot. The pumpkin may be a little underdone in the centre, but the residual heat will cook it through. Coat and fry the remaining pumpkin, skimming the oil between batches. The oil temperature must remain at 190°C: you may have to adjust it depending on how quickly you're working and how many tempura you're frying at once.

5 Serve the pumpkin tempura with the honey sesame dipping sauce and bowls of steamed rice.

RAPINI with PENNE and CHICKPEAS

SERVES 6

½ CUP (100 G) DRIED KABULI
 CHICKPEAS (SEE INGREDIENTS),
 SOAKED OVERNIGHT IN COLD WATER

500 G PENNE

4 TABLESPOONS EXTRA VIRGIN
 OLIVE OIL

½ CUP (40 G) FLAKED ALMONDS

6 CLOVES GARLIC, CRUSHED OR
 1 TEASPOON GRANULATED GARLIC

SALT FLAKES AND CRACKED
 BLACK PEPPER

JUICE OF 1 LEMON

2 BUNCHES RAPINI, STEMS ROLL-CUT
 (SEE PAGE 83) INTO 4 CM LENGTHS,
 LEAVES RIPPED OR SLICED

½ CUP (40 G) SHAVED PARMESAN

1 HANDFUL FLAT-LEAF PARSLEY LEAVES

Rapini, also known as broccoli rabe, is a leafy green vegetable with flowering heads that resemble broccoli florets. It hits the farmers' markets and better fruit vendors in the cooler months. The seeds are also becoming more readily available, and it's fairly easy to grow. (I am the worst brassica grower in the Southern Hemisphere, but even I have had success with rapini.) At a pinch, you can use Chinese broccoli (gai lan) in this dish, but you should look for a slightly older bunch with darker green leaves and a good amount of flowering heads, because the young stuff lacks the required bitterness.

The flaked almonds really bring out the subtle nutty undertones of the rapini, as does frying the garlic beyond a sweat to golden brown. You will need to stand over the pan, ready to arrest the cooking with a splash of lemon juice or white wine when you're doing this, as the difference between nuttiness and burnt is about 10 seconds. This is actually one dish where I would consider using granulated garlic: you will lose that wonderful fresh garlic aroma, but the granules will deliver the desired flavour and texture without burning.

1 Drain the chickpeas, discarding the soaking water. Place them in a saucepan and cover with cold water. (The less water you use, the quicker the chickpeas will cook, so cover them by just a few centimetres and top up the water during cooking if necessary.) Bring to a simmer over medium heat and cook for about 1 hour until tender to the bite. Drain and set aside.

2 Cook the penne in a large saucepan of boiling salted water until al dente. Drain, then toss the pasta in about 2 teaspoons of olive oil and spread it out on a large tray or plate to prevent clumping.

3 Meanwhile, preheat the oven to 180°C fan-forced (200°C conventional). Toast the flaked almonds, shaking the tray halfway through cooking, for 5–10 minutes or until they're aromatic and slightly browned. Set aside.

4 Preheat a heavy-based sauteuse or frying pan over medium heat and add 30 ml of olive oil, the garlic and a good pinch of salt (this will speed up the caramelisation of the garlic). Fry the garlic, stirring constantly, until it's golden brown, then immediately add half of the lemon juice to the pan. Add the chickpeas and rapini stems and saute for a couple of minutes until the chickpeas are warmed through and the stems are just tender. Fold in the rapini leaves, then add the penne and stir to warm through. Season well with salt and pepper, then add the remaining lemon juice and olive oil and stir to coat all ingredients.

5 Transfer the rapini, penne and chickpeas to a large serving bowl. Toss through the parmesan, toasted flaked almonds and parsley. Serve immediately.

CORN TAMALES WITH LIME, CORIANDER AND RED ONION SALSA

SERVES 4 (MAKES 12 PARCELS)

3 CORN COBS, HUSKS STRIPPED
AND RESERVED

100 G GRATED CHEDDAR OR
CRUMBLED FETA

1 CUP (180 G) MASA LISTA

SALT FLAKES AND CRACKED
BLACK PEPPER

2 TABLESPOONS VEGETABLE OIL

1 RED ONION, DICED

500 G CHERRY TOMATOES, QUARTERED

1 BUNCH CORIANDER, LEAVES
AND STEMS CHOPPED

JUICE OF 2 LIMES

FINELY GRATED ZEST OF 1 LIME

1 LONG GREEN CHILLI, SEEDED
AND FINELY CHOPPED

SMALL PINCH OF SWEET PAPRIKA

3 TABLESPOONS EXTRA VIRGIN
OLIVE OIL

Tamales are a traditional Latin American dish, used by the ancient Aztec and Maya peoples to feed armies and travellers. They are made from masa lista (maize flour with limewater added), which is rehydrated and cooked with vegies and seasoning, then wrapped in a corn husk parcel. I was curious to learn how to make them and convinced a local restaurateur, Caesar Aguillar, to teach me a few tricks. He invited me to his home for a cooking lesson, followed by an unexpected invite to dinner and a glimpse of how El Salvadoreans share their table. It was an amazing experience, and it reminded me just how lucky we are in Australia to have food and people from just about every corner of the world to enrich our lives and kitchens.

The last of the season's corn, still around in early autumn, is ideal here. Look for big cobs with plenty of husk intact. When corn is plentiful, I set aside a few husks to dry every time I use a cob, then chuck them in a 50°C fan-forced (70°C conventional) oven for a few hours and store the dried husks in an airtight container until I get a tamale craving. This way I can still make tamales when corn is long gone and just season the masa with different vegies. Alternatively, you can buy pre-dried husks from Mexican grocers, where you'll also find masa lista.

1 Strip the corn kernels from 2 of the cobs by snapping them in half and running your knife down the cob. Lightly crush the kernels with a rolling pin or potato masher, then mix together with the cheese, masa lista and 3 cups (750 ml) of water; the mixture should be like stiff mashed potato. Season with a big pinch of salt and pepper. Place it in a small heavy-based saucepan over very low heat and cook for 10 minutes, stirring constantly, to create a soft dough. It should be fairly dry but not crumbly.

2 Lightly oil a fresh corn husk with the vegetable oil. (If you're using dried husks, rehydrate them first in warm water and pat dry before oiling.) Spread a heaped tablespoon of the masa mixture over the thick end of the husk, and wrap it up into a matchbox-sized parcel. Place another oiled husk perpendicular to the first one and wrap it up again to seal the sides. Tie the parcel with a fine strip of husk. Repeat with the remaining mixture and husks to make 12 tamales.

3 Place a large tiered steamer over a large saucepan of simmering water. Place the tamales in the steamer, then cover and steam for 20–25 minutes. Remove the steamer from the pan. Allow the tamales to sit for 5–10 minutes to finish steaming and to cool a fraction.

4 Meanwhile, blacken the remaining corn cob on a dry char-grill plate or pan over high heat. Turn the cob regularly, as it will go from blackened to completely burnt very quickly. You just need to achieve a smoky flavour and create a few black contact spots on the kernels. Leave the corn cob to cool slightly, then strip the kernels with a knife. Place them in a bowl along with the remaining ingredients and a pinch of salt. Combine to make a salsa.

5 Arrange three tamales on each plate with the salsa alongside.

WALNUT AND HONEY SYRUP CAKE

SERVES 12

380 G WALNUTS, TO MAKE 3 CUPS
(360 G) GROUND WALNUTS

9 FREE-RANGE EGGS

200 G GRANULATED SUGAR

30 ML BRANDY

2 CUPS (140 G) BREADCRUMBS,
FROM 2 SMALL DAY-OLD BAGUETTES

80 G CHOPPED TOASTED WALNUTS

SYRUP

400 G GRANULATED SUGAR

2 CINNAMON STICKS

JUICE OF 1 LEMON

200 ML HONEY

I have made a habit of surrounding myself with people who have the culinary skills that I lack. Not only do I find this inspiring, but it's also pretty damn useful seeing as I have two left hands when it comes to baking and pastry work! I am really not a cake person, so when I find a recipe that requires very little skill to achieve a spectacular result, I am pretty happy. This one comes from my assistant on *The Cook and The Chef*, Steph the Chef. Even if she weren't one of the loveliest people around (which she is), I would tolerate her as a friend just to rob her of her excellent pastry skills!

I like this cake because, despite being outrageously sweet, it's not just a pile of fluff and sugar. It has great texture and body from the walnuts and breadcrumbs. A lot of packaged walnut meal is fairly unimpressive and the oils can turn rancid quite quickly. I prefer to lightly roast whole walnuts, then rub off the skins and coarsely grind the nuts. Likewise, homemade breadcrumbs will taste so much better than the bought stuff, which always reminds me of sand. A couple of half-sized day-old baguettes will do the job. I rarely trim the crusts, and I prefer a slightly coarse grind to give the cake some decent texture.

1 Preheat the oven to 180°C fan-forced (200°C conventional). To make the ground walnuts, roast the 380 g of walnuts for 10–12 minutes, giving them an occasional stir. Leave to cool, then use a tea towel to rub off the skins. Pulse the walnuts in a food processor until they're breadcrumb-sized. Increase the oven temperature to 200°C fan-forced (220°C conventional).

2 To make the syrup, place the sugar and 3 cups (750 ml) of water in a heavy-based saucepan over medium heat and heat until the sugar dissolves. Add the cinnamon and lemon juice, then turn up the heat and boil for 15 minutes. Remove from the heat, fold in the honey and allow the syrup to cool at room temperature. Discard the cinnamon and set the syrup aside.

3 Using an electric mixer fitted with a whisk attachment, beat the eggs on high speed until they're thick and pale. Turn off the mixer and add the sugar and brandy, then mix at a lower speed to incorporate. Use a wooden spoon or spatula to fold in the walnut meal and breadcrumbs and combine well. (Alternatively, put a paddle on the mixer and run for a minute or two at low speed.)

4 Grease a 20 cm square cake tin and line it with baking paper. Pour the cake mixture into the prepared tin (it should be about 8 cm deep). Bake for 30–40 minutes or until a skewer inserted into the centre comes out clean. Remove the cake from the oven but leave it in the tin.

5 Placing the cake tin over a baking tray to catch any drips, gradually pour the cooled syrup all over the hot cake. You may not need all of the syrup, but allow the cake to take in as much as it will absorb. Sprinkle the top of the cake with the chopped toasted walnuts. Allow the syrup to soak in and set for an hour or so before slicing and serving the cake.

WINTER

In winter,
I like to hunker down,
make some mess and
steam up the kitchen windows.

It's a time to experiment with the bold flavours and unusual textures the season has to offer. The markets are filled with enormous pumpkins and knobbly celeriac. Brussels sprouts tower like architectural masterpieces, and morning beads of frost rest on cabbage leaves and cauliflower clusters. Asian greens are at their peak, and the cold earth has turned root vegies into explosive bundles of flavour. Cumquats hang over fences, just ripe for stealing...

In winter, fire becomes your best friend, so drag out the cast-iron casseroles and ramp up the heat. Chuck parsnips, cauliflower or pumpkin in the roasting tin, braise some fennel or artichoke, or knock up a warming vegie curry. Preserve some limes or lemons while they're cheap and plentiful. Make the most of grains and legumes and pair them with your favourite winter vegies for a hearty meal.

COFFEE AND COCOA CEREAL WITH WATTLESEED AND VANILLA

MAKES 8–10 SERVINGS

360 G ROLLED OATS (OR ROLLED RICE FLAKES, FOR A GLUTEN-FREE VERSION)

150 ML HONEY

1 TABLESPOON GROUND ROASTED WATTLESEED

2 TABLESPOONS GRATED COCONUT PALM SUGAR (SEE PAGE 52)

3 TABLESPOONS COCOA POWDER

2 VANILLA BEANS, SEEDS SCRAPED

240 ML (8 SHOTS) ESPRESSO COFFEE

200 ML ORANGE JUICE

3 TABLESPOONS SWEET ALMOND OIL

3 TABLESPOONS EXTRA VIRGIN OLIVE OIL

1 CUP (160 G) CHOPPED ALMONDS

1 CUP (50 G) FLAKED COCONUT

½ CUP (85 G) MUSCATELS

½ CUP (95 G) CHOPPED DRIED FIGS (I LIKE THE TURKISH-STYLE WILD FIGS)

½ CUP (75 G) DRIED CRANBERRIES

John Downes is a pioneer of the 'real bread' movement in Australia. He was playing about with old grains and artisan baking back in the 1970s, when the only bread most of us were eating was the sliced white kind. John is passionate about all types of real foods and one summer morning, during a walk along Port Willunga Beach, he spilled a few secrets about his baked cereals – another one of his passions.

Now I am not a morning guy, and I struggle with breakfast. I have heard rumours about people who spring out of bed and eat breakfast. Apparently it gets even scarier: these people *talk* in the morning. I suspect they're lunatics; I know for a fact that they're not chefs! But after chatting with John, I was inspired to have a shot at making my own cereal with all of the things that I might consider getting out of bed for – bitter chocolate, dried figs, honey, almonds and, most importantly, coffee!

The honey you choose for this recipe needs to be one that can stand up and punch with the other bold flavours. Really light honey just won't cut it, so go for a blue gum or bush mallee or any other thick and robust variety that can fight it out with the coffee and chocolate. The wattleseed is here because, when it's combined with coffee, it creates an intense roast coffee flavour, and the mere smell of it is enough to wake me up. Probably one of the most accessible native foods in terms of both availability and flavour, wattleseed is the one spice I buy pre-ground because it's so hard it tends to blow up even the best spice grinders. If you are messing around with wattleseed in other recipes, it's worth noting that the flavour can be a little underwhelming and flat if there is no accompanying fat in the dish; it tends to carry so much better in cream or, in the case of this recipe, oil. See Ingredients for more about native spices.

1 Preheat the oven to 80°C fan-forced (100°C conventional). Combine all of the ingredients except for the almonds, coconut, muscatels, figs and cranberries in a bowl. Mix until the oats are coated and slightly moist. If the mixture is too wet, add a few more oats; if it's too dry, add a touch of water. Spread the mixture out on a large baking tray and top with the almonds and coconut. Bake the cereal mixture for a couple of hours until it crisps up, stirring a few times during baking.

2 Remove the cereal from the oven and while it's still slightly warm, toss through the muscatels, figs and cranberries.

3 Store the cereal in an airtight jar in a cool, dark cupboard for up to 6 months. Serve with soy or cow's milk.

CARROT, FARRO, CORIANDER, MINT and ORANGE SOUP

SERVES 4

3 TABLESPOONS CRACKED FARRO, SOAKED OVERNIGHT IN COLD WATER

SALT FLAKES AND CRACKED BLACK PEPPER

100 ML EXTRA VIRGIN OLIVE OIL, PLUS A SPLASH FOR DRIZZLING

1 ONION, DICED

4 CLOVES GARLIC, CRUSHED

1 TABLESPOON GROUND CORIANDER

1 TEASPOON GROUND CUMIN

1 CINNAMON STICK

1 KG CARROTS, DICED

4 TABLESPOONS DRY WHITE WINE OR SPARKLING WHITE WINE

FINELY GRATED ZEST AND JUICE OF 1 ORANGE

1 HANDFUL EACH MINT AND CORIANDER LEAVES, CHOPPED

½ CUP (140 G) GREEK-STYLE YOGHURT

Carrot soup runs the risk of becoming one-dimensional if the sweetness of the carrots is allowed to dominate. This recipe acknowledges the sweetness, but it's rescued by the cumin and coriander, which nudge the flavours more to a savoury spectrum, and the yoghurt and orange zest, which deliver tang. The farro brings an earthy dimension to the dish and almost turns it into a complete meal.

I don't get too fussy about the quality of the carrots for this. I believe very strongly in buying the best ingredients I can, but in this case I would rather spend the money on a great extra virgin olive oil to finish the dish.

Farro usually requires quite a bit of soaking. You can get away without it in this recipe, if you're in a hurry, but make sure you rinse the farro a few times under cold running water, then up the water content by ½ cup (125 ml) and add 15–20 minutes to the cooking time.

Oh, and a note about using wine in cooking: if you wouldn't drink it, don't cook with it. You will notice undesirable flavours in your dish if you skimp on the wine. In this case, you are after something dry; I often use sparkling white if I don't have a suitable dry white wine on hand.

1 Drain the farro, discarding the soaking water. Place it in a heavy-based saucepan with ¾ cup (180 ml) of cold water and 1 teaspoon of salt and bring to a gentle simmer. Cook the farro for 20 minutes until it's tender to the bite, then drain and set aside.

2 Meanwhile, heat the olive oil in a large heavy-based saucepan over medium heat and sweat the onion until it's soft and translucent. Add the garlic, coriander, cumin and cinnamon and saute for 5 minutes, then add the carrots and 3 teaspoons of salt and saute for a further 5–8 minutes until the carrot is coated with the spices and slightly coloured. Deglaze the pan with the wine. Add 800 ml of water and simmer over low heat for about 10 minutes until the carrot is tender.

3 Remove the pan from the heat and discard the cinnamon. Carefully blend the diced carrots to a smooth consistency using a stick blender. Stir in the orange juice, then check the seasoning, adding more salt to taste.

4 Fold the orange zest and chopped herbs through the yoghurt and add a pinch of salt. Place a large spoonful of farro into four warmed soup bowls and ladle the carrot and orange soup over the top. Garnish with a dollop of the herb yoghurt. Finish with an extra splash of olive oil and a good twist of black pepper.

ARTICHOKE AND LEMON TAGINE WITH HARISSA

SERVES 4

100 G DRIED KABULI CHICKPEAS (SEE INGREDIENTS), SOAKED OVERNIGHT IN COLD WATER

SALT FLAKES AND CRACKED BLACK PEPPER

300 G MOGRABIAH

100 ML EXTRA VIRGIN OLIVE OIL

JUICE OF 2 LEMONS

6 ARTICHOKES

2 ONIONS, CHOPPED

2 CLOVES GARLIC, CHOPPED

2 TEASPOONS GROUND CORIANDER

1 TEASPOON GROUND CUMIN

2 CINNAMON STICKS

1 PRESERVED LEMON, PITH AND FLESH REMOVED, FINELY SLICED

2 BAY LEAVES

PINCH OF SAFFRON THREADS

1 HANDFUL CORIANDER LEAVES AND STEMS, ROUGHLY CHOPPED

1 HANDFUL FLAT-LEAF PARSLEY LEAVES, ROUGHLY CHOPPED

100 G ROASTED ALMONDS, CHOPPED

HARISSA (SEE BASIC RECIPES), TO SERVE

Globe artichokes are a 'love them or hate them' type of veg. I think most people are put off by the perception that they're hard to prepare, but this is simply not true and they're worth every minute of their short preparation time. (Maggie Beer taught me a great trick: boil the artichokes for a few minutes, and the paring back of the outer leaves becomes easier.) To prepare artichokes, cut off the top third of the leaves, trimming the older outer leaves back until you see a paler green or almost yellow patch on the base of the leaves. Scoop out the hairy choke from the centre of the artichoke, then nip the stem about 5 cm from the lowest leaves. I sometimes run a peeler down the stems if they look a little woody (as you would with the base of old asparagus). Then just plonk the artichokes into some water with a squeeze of lemon juice to prevent them discolouring, which happens very rapidly. When you are selecting artichokes, avoid those that look a bit dull or have splayed leaves as this means they have been sitting around for a while. Instead, go for those with a fairly tight formation. Give a leaf a little tug: it should resist and want to spring back.

You can add any root vegies to this dish (pumpkin, swedes, carrots, whatever) but I like this just with chickpeas and preserved lemon, and tons of harissa thrown all over the top. Whenever lemons are cheap, I buy and preserve them. Don't fall for the trap of adding water. For every lemon, I use a heaped tablespoon of fine salt, the juice of half a lemon and a dash of good extra virgin olive oil, and the resulting flavour is really intense and rounded. Mograbiah is a jumbo couscous. You can buy it from good delis.

1 Drain the chickpeas, discarding the soaking water. Place them in a saucepan and cover with cold water. (The less water you use, the quicker the chickpeas will cook, so cover them by just a few centimetres and top up the water during cooking if necessary.) Bring to a simmer over medium heat and cook for about 1 hour until tender to the bite. Drain and set aside.

2 Place 2 litres of water in a saucepan over high heat and add ½ teaspoon of salt. When the water boils, add the mograbiah and cook it for about 20–25 minutes or until tender to the bite. Drain, then place the mograbiah in a large bowl and splash it with a tablespoon of olive oil to prevent clumping. Cover with plastic film to keep the mograbiah warm.

3 Meanwhile, bring a very large saucepan of salted water to a simmer over high heat. Fill a large bowl with about 2 cups (500 ml) of water and add the lemon juice. Prepare the artichokes as per the above instructions, placing them in the lemon water as you go and rotating them periodically so that all surfaces are exposed to the liquid.

ARTICHOKE AND LEMON TAGINE WITH HARISSA (CONT.)

4 Add the prepared artichokes to the simmering water and simmer them for 10 minutes. (You may need to place a plate on top to sink the chokes and ensure even cooking.) The artichokes will still be a little firm but they will finish cooking in the next stage of recipe. Drain and place on a chopping board. When the artichokes are cool enough to handle, slice them in half straight down the middle of the stem and through the head.

5 Place a heavy-based casserole or lidded frying pan (or tagine, if you have one) over medium heat. Add the remaining olive oil and saute the onion and garlic until soft. Add the ground coriander, cumin and cinnamon and saute for a minute to coat the onion and garlic with the spices, then add the artichokes and chickpeas, preserved lemon, bay leaves and saffron. Top up with 3 cups (750 ml) of water and season with a teaspoon of salt and a few twists of black pepper. Place a lid on top, reduce the heat to low and simmer for 20 minutes to heat the artichokes and chickpeas and to meld all the flavours together. You should be left with about 200–250 ml of sauce.

6 Divide the mograbiah among bowls and place the artichokes and chickpeas on top. Sprinkle with herbs and almonds, spoon over the harissa, and serve.

SWEET POTATO, PEANUT AND MANDARIN CURRY

SERVES 4

700 G SWEET POTATOES, CHOPPED INTO 4 CM PIECES, SKIN ON

50 ML KECAP MANIS (SEE INGREDIENTS)

3 TABLESPOONS PEANUT OIL

½ CUP (75 G) UNSALTED PEANUTS

500 G IMPERIAL MANDARINS, PEELED

1 × 400 ML TIN COCONUT MILK (OR MAKE YOUR OWN, SEE PAGE 26)

2 PIECES DRIED MANDARIN PEEL

4 KAFFIR LIME LEAVES

2 TABLESPOONS GRATED COCONUT PALM SUGAR (SEE PAGE 52)

30 ML TAMARIND CONCENTRATE

1 TABLESPOON THAI LIGHT SOY SAUCE (SEE INGREDIENTS)

SALT FLAKES

½ BUNCH CORIANDER, LEAVES PICKED

STEAMED JASMINE RICE, TO SERVE

ROASTED ONION PASTE

8 LARGE DRIED RED CHILLIES, SEEDED

1 LARGE ONION, ROUGHLY CHOPPED

4 CLOVES GARLIC, PEELED

3 CM PIECE GINGER, CHOPPED

3 CM PIECE GALANGAL, CHOPPED

4 STALKS LEMONGRASS, WHITE PARTS ONLY, CHOPPED

1 LOOSE HANDFUL CORIANDER LEAVES, STEMS AND SCRAPED ROOTS

2 TABLESPOONS PEANUT OIL

ROASTED SPICE MIX

2 CM PIECE CASSIA BARK

5 OR 6 GREEN CARDAMOM PODS

¼ BLADE MACE

1 TABLESPOON CORIANDER SEEDS

2 TEASPOONS CUMIN SEEDS

4 OR 5 CLOVES

4 OR 5 WHITE PEPPERCORNS

Massaman curry is a great example of what happens when cooking cultures collide. It is thought to have emerged when Indian traders arrived in Southern Thailand, and it features key ingredients from each cuisine. The cardamom, cinnamon, mace, cumin and coriander give the curry that familiar Indian note, but it crosses into Thai cooking with the inclusion of galangal, lemongrass and a rich coconut sauce.

Sweet potato is packed full of vitamin A and has joined the ranks of the so-called superfoods with the claim it protects against carcinogens. It's always piled high in our markets from late autumn through winter. The crunchy peanuts give a great contrast to the soft textures of the dish and they also boost the protein content. Imperials are my favourite mandarin, and they have a perfect sweet–sour balance for this dish; the juice really makes the curry sing of citrus. Cassia is the brasher (and cheaper) cousin of cinnamon. The latter is a delicate quill of several thin layers, while cassia is a thicker bark, robust enough to take the heat required in the spice roasting.

1 Preheat the oven to 190°C fan-forced (210°C conventional). Place the sweet potato in a bowl and coat it with the kecap manis and 1 tablespoon of oil. Transfer to a baking tray and roast the sweet potato for 10–15 minutes, turning occasionally, or until it's dark brown. It does not need to be cooked; you are just aiming for a caramelised surface. Set the sweet potato aside.

2 To make the roasted onion paste, first soak the dried chillies in warm water for 10 minutes. Combine all the paste ingredients in a mixing bowl, lightly tossing through the oil to coat. Transfer the ingredients to a baking tray and roast in the oven for 20–25 minutes, stirring occasionally, or until caramelised and aromatic. Remove from the oven and leave to cool slightly, then transfer to a food processor and blend to a fine paste. Set aside.

3 Dry-roast all of the spice mix ingredients in the oven for 10–15 minutes or until highly fragrant. Leave to cool slightly, then grind using a spice grinder or mortar and pestle and set aside. Roast the peanuts in the oven, stirring occasionally, for 10–12 minutes or until they're golden and crunchy, then set them aside. Juice 2 of the mandarins. Segment the remaining mandarins and set the juice and segments aside.

4 Heat a heavy-based saucepan or sauteuse over medium heat. Add the remaining oil, then the roasted onion paste and spice mix. Saute for 10 minutes, stirring continuously. You may need to add a splash of water if the paste starts to stick to the base of the pan. Add the coconut milk, dried mandarin peel, kaffir lime leaves and ½ cup (125 ml) of water, then turn the heat to low and simmer for 10 minutes. Add the sweet potato and cook for 6–10 minutes or until soft. Remove the pan from the heat and add the mandarin juice and segments, palm sugar, tamarind, soy sauce and salt to taste. Stir to combine, then check the seasoning.

5 Garnish the curry with peanuts and coriander. Serve with jasmine rice.

ONION BHAJIS with APPLE, HONEY and MINT RAITA

SERVES 6 AS A STARTER

1 CUP (150 G) BESAN (CHICKPEA) FLOUR (SEE INGREDIENTS)

300 G NATURAL YOGHURT

2 TEASPOONS GARAM MASALA

2 TEASPOONS GROUND CUMIN, ROASTED

1 TEASPOON GROUND TURMERIC

1 TEASPOON AJWAIN SEEDS

REALLY BIG PINCH OF CHILLI POWDER

1 TEASPOON SALT FLAKES

4 ONIONS, SLICED INTO 1 CM THICK RINGS WITH CENTRES PUSHED OUT

2 TABLESPOONS LEMON JUICE

2 LONG GREEN CHILLIES, CHOPPED, SEEDS AND ALL

1 BUNCH CORIANDER, LEAVES PICKED AND CHOPPED

ABOUT 1 LITRE FLAVOUR-NEUTRAL OIL (SEE INGREDIENTS)

APPLE, HONEY AND MINT RAITA (SEE BASIC RECIPES), TO SERVE

MINT SPRIGS, TO GARNISH

I had no idea how good an onion could taste until I ate my first bhaji. This is another great snack recipe that I picked up from my time working in Indian restaurants. I love the concept of hawker food: little bits and pieces that you can grab on the street and just scoff down as you are going about your business. I am reminded of food writer Michael Pollan's admonition, 'It's not food if it arrived through the window of your car.' His words are aimed at all types of 'fast food', but to me it seems particularly relevant when it comes to the way we snack. With street food, you can actually see how the food is being prepared, have a chat with the cook and maybe learn a trick or two by watching them in action. It's one thing that I would like to see more of in Australia. Ajwain seeds are a popular Indian spice, closely related to caraway and cumin. You can buy them from Indian grocers.

1 Place the flour in a large bowl. Add ⅔ cup (160 ml) of room-temperature water and the yoghurt, and stir to form a smooth batter. Add the spices and salt. Cover with plastic film and leave the batter in a warm spot for 2 hours.

2 Add the onion rings to the batter along with the lemon juice, green chilli and chopped coriander. Stir gently to mix through and coat the onion.

3 Heat the oil in a wok or heavy-based saucepan over medium heat until just shimmering (about 180°C). Working in batches (about five at a time), pull the coated onion rings out of the batter, shaking them gently to remove excess batter. Carefully slip the onion rings into the hot oil and fry, turning occasionally with a slotted spoon or tongs, until the batter is deep brown and the onion has cooked through, about 5 minutes. Remove the bhajis with a slotted spoon and leave them to drain on paper towel. Repeat with the remaining onion rings.

4 Serve the onion bhajis immediately with Apple, honey and mint raita alongside for dipping. Garnish with mint sprigs, if you like.

ROASTED BRUSSELS SPROUTS WITH RED ONION JAM AND TOASTED BREADCRUMBS

SERVES 4 AS A SIDE

500 G BRUSSELS SPROUTS, BASES TRIMMED

75 G UNSALTED BUTTER

2 SMALL RED ONIONS, SLICED

2 TABLESPOONS AGED SWEET RED VINEGAR (SEE INGREDIENTS) OR BALSAMIC VINEGAR

2 TEASPOONS BROWN SUGAR

40 G PLAIN FLOUR

2 CUPS (500 ML) COLD MILK

70 G GRATED CHEDDAR, PLUS A HANDFUL EXTRA FOR SPRINKLING

2 FREE-RANGE EGG YOLKS

SALT FLAKES AND CRACKED BLACK PEPPER

PINCH OF FRESHLY GRATED NUTMEG

⅔ CUP (50 G) COARSE BREADCRUMBS, FROM DAY-OLD WHITE BREAD

CELERIAC, POTATO AND LENTIL SHEPHERD'S PIE (SEE PAGE 206), PARSNIPS WITH ORANGE ZEST, SHAVED FENNEL AND CAPERBERRIES (SEE PAGE 192) OR PUY LENTILS, TO SERVE

I was one of those weird kids who actually liked Brussels sprouts, and they remain a favourite. I can eat a whole bowl of them just steamed and tossed in a little good extra virgin olive oil and salt. The common complaint is that Brussels sprouts smell, but this will only happen if you overcook them. In this recipe, they're only briefly steamed before being roasted, and this ensures they remain on the crisp side of tender. When choosing sprouts, go for compact heads with tightly clinging outer leaves.

Good chefs are very aware of how the taste of a final dish can depend on the smallest margins in preparation. When you are beginning the roux for the sauce (cooking the flour in the butter), be very careful not to overcook the flour. If you take it to a dark brown colour, it will dominate the whole dish and bury the fresh sprout flavour, so make sure you go easy at this stage.

1 Using a small sharp knife, cut a cross on the bottom of each sprout. Boil or steam the sprouts for 6 minutes until they're just tender, then drain. Transfer the sprouts to a shallow roasting tin.

2 Melt 20 g of butter in a heavy-based saucepan over low heat and add the onion. Stir to coat, then add the vinegar and sugar and cook for 20 minutes, stirring occasionally, until the onion is soft and caramelised. Set the onion jam aside.

3 Preheat the oven to 200°C fan-forced (220°C conventional). Melt the remaining butter in a small heavy-based saucepan over low heat. Add the flour and stir for a few minutes to cook, but not colour, the flour. Slowly add the milk, stirring continuously to prevent lumps. Turn up the heat to medium and cook, stirring, for about 5 minutes to cook out the flour, then remove the pan from the heat. Stir in the 70 g of cheddar. When the mixture has cooled a little, add the egg yolks one at a time, stirring to incorporate the first before adding the next, then season with salt, pepper and nutmeg.

4 Pour the cheese mixture over the Brussels sprouts. Add a layer of onion jam, then top with the breadcrumbs. Sprinkle over the extra cheddar and season with more pepper.

5 Roast in the oven for 10–15 minutes or until the topping is golden. Serve with Celeriac, potato and lentil shepherd's pie, Parsnips with orange zest, shaved fennel and caperberries, or just a bowl of puy lentils.

RADICCHIO WITH CUMQUAT AGRODOLCE AND BAKED SEMOLINA

SERVES 4

1 SMALL RADICCHIO

75 ML EXTRA VIRGIN OLIVE OIL

SALT FLAKES AND CRACKED
    BLACK PEPPER

60 G UNSALTED BUTTER

1 LARGE RED ONION,
    SLICED LENGTHWAYS

1 HEAPED TABLESPOON BROWN SUGAR

3 SPRIGS ROSEMARY

24 CUMQUATS, HALVED

100 ML AGED SWEET RED VINEGAR
    (SEE INGREDIENTS) OR
    BALSAMIC VINEGAR

75 ML WHITE-WINE VINEGAR

BAKED SEMOLINA

2 CUPS (500 ML) MILK

50 G UNSALTED BUTTER

¾ CUP (110 G) COARSE SEMOLINA

2 FREE-RANGE EGG YOLKS

SALT FLAKES AND CRACKED
    BLACK PEPPER

BIG PINCH OF FRESHLY GRATED NUTMEG

½ CUP (40 G) GRATED PARMESAN

You will find variants of agrodolce (sweet and sour) flavours in just about every cuisine, from Italian to Chinese. It's an irresistible combination but it can be a little pedestrian if the sweetness is derived from sugar alone and the sourness from cheap vinegar. The key to success with this recipe is to achieve the sweetness mainly from the onions and use the sugar just to drive that process. Red onions are best because they rapidly caramelise and produce the desired sweetness. It doesn't mean the dish won't work with brown onions, but they will have to work a little harder (and longer).

Your mouth can get bored if the textures of a dish don't provide a few surprises, and I think it's fair to say this is a common oversight in a lot of vegetarian cooking – after all, there are no bones to chew or crispy pieces of seared meat to crunch. Here, the coarse semolina brings an interesting texture contrast to the silky onions and cooked cumquats, and baking it with cheese on top provides another dimension to the texture of the robust grains.

1 For the baked semolina, preheat the oven to 180°C fan-forced (200°C conventional). Heat the milk in a heavy-based saucepan over medium heat. When the milk is hot but not yet simmering, add half the butter and stir until it melts. Take the pan off the heat and add the semolina in a slow, steady stream, whisking quickly and continuously. Place over low heat and stir the semolina for 5–10 minutes until it thickens and comes away from the sides of the pan. Remove the pan from the heat. Add the egg yolks one at a time, stirring to incorporate the first before adding the next. Season with 1 teaspoon of salt, pepper and nutmeg. Add half of the parmesan and combine.

2 Transfer the semolina to a small greased bread or cake tin, 18 cm square or thereabouts (ideally the semolina should be 2–3 cm deep). Sprinkle with the remaining parmesan and dot with the remaining butter. Bake the semolina in the oven for about 15–20 minutes or until the top is golden brown and the mixture has puffed up slightly. Remove the semolina from the oven and when it has cooled a little, spoon it out onto plates.

3 While the semolina is baking, preheat a char-grill pan or heavy-based frying pan over medium–high heat. Quarter the radicchio lengthways, with the wedges held together by the heart. Brush with a little olive oil and season with salt and pepper. When the pan is extremely hot, add the radicchio quarters. Turn them over after a minute or so when the leaves just start to darken and wilt. Add more oil if the radicchio begins to dry out, but remember that the aim is to grill rather than fry the leaves.

4 Heat the butter and remaining oil in a heavy-based frying pan over medium heat. Saute the onion for 3–5 minutes until soft and caramelised, then add the sugar, rosemary and cumquats. Saute for a few minutes until the cumquats start to soften, then add the vinegars and 3 teaspoons of salt. Ramp up the heat and reduce until the sauce is syrupy and slightly sticky.

5 To serve, place a wedge of grilled radicchio and some baked semolina on each plate, then spoon out the cumquats and pour the sauce over the top.

CABBAGE COLCANNON

SERVES 4

600 G FLOURY POTATOES
(SEE PAGE 117), PEELED

⅓ SAVOY CABBAGE, FINELY SHREDDED

60 G UNSALTED BUTTER

1 TABLESPOON EXTRA VIRGIN OLIVE OIL

4 TABLESPOONS MILK

2 SPRING ONIONS, WHITE AND GREEN
PARTS FINELY SLICED

1 HANDFUL FLAT-LEAF PARSLEY LEAVES,
CHOPPED

SALT FLAKES AND FRESHLY GROUND
WHITE PEPPER

Like Brussels sprouts, cabbage has an undeserved reputation for being stinky. A malodorous dish will only happen if you overcook the cabbage, so stick to the brief steaming time with this recipe. My criteria for a fine cabbage are a tight, heavy head, squeaky leaves that don't fall away from the main body too much, and a good weight. The dish works simply because the slight bitterness in the cabbage is balanced with the hint of sweetness a starchy spud has when cooked. I always seem to be going on about balance in my cooking, because I really do believe that good cooks either have an intuitive feel for how to balance dishes or they have learnt it through repetition and trial and error.

The colcannon will keep for a few days and I love to fry leftovers in olive oil with a few peas (or any other vegies) thrown in for a quick supper. The over-caramelised bits of fried mashed potato take me straight back to being a kid with a plate of bubble and squeak and a bottle of tomato sauce in front of me, and I can't help smiling as I eat.

1 Place the potatoes in a large saucepan and cover them with cold water and a pinch of salt. Bring to the boil, then simmer for 20–30 minutes (depending on size) or until tender but not falling apart. Drain off the water and leave the potatoes to steam-dry in the pan.

2 Steam the cabbage for 2–3 minutes until it's tender but still crisp. Warm the butter, olive oil and milk in a saucepan over medium heat until the butter has melted. Set aside.

3 While the potatoes are still warm, pass them through a mouli or ricer, or mash them with a potato masher until smooth. Stir through the steamed cabbage and the spring onion, then add the warm milk mixture and stir until combined. Finally, stir through the parsley and season with salt and white pepper. Serve immediately. This is also great served with the Radicchio with cumquat agrodolce (see page 182) in place of the baked semolina.

JACKFRUIT BIRYANI

SERVES 4 AS PART OF A SHARED MEAL

1 CUP (200 G) BASMATI RICE

SALT FLAKES

JUICE OF 1 SMALL LEMON

400 G GREEN JACKFRUIT

30 ML FLAVOUR-NEUTRAL OIL
(SEE INGREDIENTS),
PLUS EXTRA TO OIL KNIFE

130 G ATTA FLOUR (SEE INGREDIENTS)

3 TABLESPOONS GHEE
(SEE INGREDIENTS)

2 GREEN CARDAMOM PODS, BRUISED

2 CLOVES

1 CINNAMON STICK

2 BAY LEAVES

1 SMALL ONION, FINELY CHOPPED

3 CM PIECE GINGER, PEELED AND
FINELY GRATED

2 CLOVES GARLIC, CRUSHED

2 TEASPOONS GROUND CORIANDER

1 HEAPED TABLESPOON NATURAL
YOGHURT

1 TABLESPOON POURING CREAM

PINCH OF GROUND MACE

1 LONG GREEN CHILLI, CHOPPED
AND SEEDED

PINCH OF SAFFRON THREADS,
CRUSHED WITH A PESTLE OR
BACK OF A SPOON AND SOAKED
IN 1 TABLESPOON WARM WATER

½ SMALL BUNCH CORIANDER, LEAVES
AND STEMS ROUGHLY CHOPPED

BITTER MELON BALTI (SEE PAGE 201),
MUSHROOM DAL (SEE PAGE 141)
AND CHICKPEA AND KIPFLER POTATO
CURRY (SEE PAGE 203), TO SERVE
(OPTIONAL)

Jackfruit is available throughout the dry season in the north of Australia (roughly April to October). I use young green jackfruit in this recipe. Often referred to as 'cooking' jackfruit, it's less sticky than the ripe fruit and has an appealing meaty texture. Choose one that has just the slightest give and a few brown tinges, as this indicates the fruit is just about to ripen. Use a well-oiled knife as the sap is incredibly sticky. (And make sure you wash the knife before the sap dries.) To prepare the jackfruit, peel it and cut it open, then chuck away the white stringy bits called the rags. Pry out the solid little cloves of fruit, then cut them open and pop out their seeds. I love the seeds, but some people find them bitter, so have a little taste after you boil them. You can always proceed using just the flesh if the seeds are not to your liking.

1 Wash the rice well, then place it in a saucepan with enough water to cover. Soak for 30 minutes, then drain. Bring 3 cups (750 ml) of water to the boil in a small saucepan. Add the rice and 1½ teaspoons of salt and bring back to the boil. Add the lemon juice and cook at a rolling boil, stirring occasionally, for 8 minutes or until the rice is almost cooked and most of the water has evaporated (the rice should be just tender, but not quite ready to eat). Drain and set aside.

2 Using an oiled knife, peel and quarter the jackfruit, then prise out the fruit segments. Pop the seeds out, reserving the fruit and seeds separately. Discard the skin and the white stringy bits. Heat the oil in a large heavy-based frying pan and add the jackfruit and a pinch of salt. Fry over medium heat for 3–5 minutes until it colours a little, then set aside. Boil the seeds in a small saucepan of water for 10 minutes until tender, then drain and set aside.

3 Blend the flour with a pinch of salt and 100 ml of lukewarm water and squish together for a minute or so. Place the dough on a floured benchtop and roll into a round the same diameter as the dish you'll be using to bake the rice. Set aside.

4 Preheat the oven to 200°C fan-forced (220°C conventional). Heat the ghee in a large heavy-based saucepan, then add the cardamom, cloves, cinnamon and bay leaves and stir over medium heat until fragrant. Add the onion, ginger, garlic and ground coriander and fry for about 3–4 minutes until the onion just softens. Stir in the yoghurt, and heat for a minute or so, then add 75 ml of water and bring to the boil. Reduce the heat to low and simmer for a few minutes. Discard the cardamom, cinnamon and bay leaves, then add the jackfruit and its frying oil and the seeds. Simmer for 2–3 minutes, then remove from the heat and stir through the cream, mace and chilli.

5 Spoon a third of the jackfruit mixture into a 1.5–2 litre casserole dish and cover with a third of the rice. Repeat this twice more, finishing with a layer of rice and gently patting it down with a spoon. Dot with the saffron paste, then place the dough on top to form a lid, pressing it around the outside edge of the casserole to seal. Bake for 12–15 minutes or until steam starts to escape through the seal. To serve, break through the dough using a fork and sprinkle with coriander (you can eat or discard the dough).

BABY PURPLE CARROTS AND BEETS WITH HERBED SPATZLE

SERVES 4

400 G BABY PURPLE CARROTS
(OR REGULAR BABY CARROTS,
IF UNAVAILABLE), TRIMMED

400 G BABY BEETS, TRIMMED

FINE SALT

2 TABLESPOONS EXTRA VIRGIN
OLIVE OIL

¼ BUNCH FLAT-LEAF PARSLEY,
LEAVES PICKED AND CHOPPED

¼ BUNCH THYME, LEAVES PICKED
AND CHOPPED

¼ BUNCH MARJORAM, LEAVES PICKED
AND CHOPPED

CRACKED BLACK PEPPER

4 TABLESPOONS VERJUICE
(SEE INGREDIENTS)

40 G UNSALTED BUTTER

HERBED SPATZLE

500–700 G PLAIN FLOUR

4 FREE-RANGE EGGS

3 TABLESPOONS POURING CREAM

SALT FLAKES AND CRACKED
BLACK PEPPER

TOUCH OF FRESHLY GRATED NUTMEG

1 SMALL BUNCH FLAT-LEAF PARSLEY,
LEAVES PICKED AND CHOPPED

40 G UNSALTED BUTTER

SPLASH OF EXTRA VIRGIN OLIVE OIL

1 CLOVE GARLIC, VERY FINELY SLICED

You need to find some really fresh baby beets and carrots for this recipe because there is no peeling involved. I always take into account the textures of the final dish and I reckon you need a few fibrous bits from the skins to keep this interesting. The spatzle has a great chewy texture but the plain flour makes it a little too refined for my taste, so I find the unpeeled vegies help create an earthier meal. The recipe calls for baby purple carrots, but regular baby carrots are fine as long as they're really crisp and firm. If your carrots are a little sad and floppy, nip the leaves off, submerge them in water overnight in the fridge and they should crisp up.

Making spatzle is a messy process but flicking the little dough squiggles into the water is a lot of fun. I guarantee a fair few will not make it to the table because the cooked spatzle are so moreish you can't help popping a few into your mouth along the way. They're delicious just simmered in water, but once sauteed until golden and crispy in places, they're sensational.

1 To make the herbed spatzle, mix the flour, eggs, cream and 240 ml of room-temperature water in a bowl. Add 2 teaspoons of salt and the pepper, nutmeg and parsley. Cover the bowl with plastic film and leave the mixture to rest for 1 hour at room temperature to form a stiff batter. (You may need to add a touch more water, but keep in mind you need a firm batter with the consistency of creamed honey.)

2 Bring a large saucepan of salted water to the boil. Pour about 4 tablespoons of the spatzle mixture onto a dry wooden chopping board. Using a wet spatula or pastry card, and keeping as close as possible to the boiling water, cut the batter to form strips measuring about 6 mm × 4 cm, flicking them into the pan as you do so. Cook the spatzle for 3–4 minutes or until they float. Remove them using a spider or slotted spoon and drain well, then place on a lightly greased baking tray. Repeat with the remaining spatzle mixture.

3 To prepare the carrots and beets, place them in a large saucepan of cold water with 1 teaspoon of salt. Bring to a simmer and cook until the carrots and beets are just tender (this will probably take around 5 minutes, but will depend on the size of your vegies). Drain them well and set them aside.

4 To fry the spatzle, heat the butter and olive oil in a large heavy-based saucepan over medium heat until nut-brown. Add the garlic and a pinch of salt and toss in the spatzle. Fry the spatzle, tossing or stirring, for 3 minutes or until they're golden and a little crispy in places.

5 Throw the carrots and beets into a separate large frying pan with the olive oil, herbs and black pepper, and saute for 3–5 minutes or until they're well coloured and blistering slightly. Deglaze the pan with the verjuice, then remove the vegies from the pan. Remove the pan from the heat and add the butter to the pan juices. Whisk to make a slightly thick sauce.

6 Serve the beets and carrots with the sauce poured over the top and the fried spatzle alongside.

FENNEL CONFIT

SERVES 4

4–6 BULBS BABY FENNEL, TRIMMED LEAVING 1 CM STEM INTACT, FRONDS RESERVED

ABOUT 200 ML EXTRA VIRGIN OLIVE OIL, PLUS EXTRA FOR DRIZZLING

2 TABLESPOONS ROUGHLY GROUND CORIANDER SEEDS

1 TABLESPOON ROUGHLY GROUND FENNEL SEEDS

SALT FLAKES AND CRACKED BLACK PEPPER

16 GREEN OLIVES

3 RUBY OR YELLOW GRAPEFRUIT, PEELED AND SEGMENTED, JUICE SQUEEZED FROM MEMBRANE AND RESERVED

2 HANDFULS ROCKET OR BABY CHARD

SPLASH OF LEMON JUICE

Sweet baby fennel, the first of the year's grapefruit and extra virgin olive oil is a great combination. New-season olive oils hit the markets around late autumn and early winter. They often have a nice grassy flavour and some pepperiness to them before they mellow with time. You may notice a difference in butteriness between blends, and you might need to add more lemon or vinegar to dressings when using some oils – although how you balance your dishes will always depend on your own palate, of course. When you buy fennel, look at the condition of the stalks. Dry, shrivelled stems are a telltale sign that the bulb has been sitting around for a while. Good baby fennel should have tender outer layers, which don't need to be removed before cooking. Also look out for fat, round bulbs, as they have superior flavour to flat, skinny ones.

I am not particularly loyal to any variety of green olive. In South Australia, we have fantastic examples of both the French variety verdale and the Spanish manzanilla. I tend to taste what the current season offers and my choice is mainly based on how well cured the fruit is. I just can't tolerate a badly cured olive. For this dish, it's especially important to avoid green olives with any sign of mushiness, as they will lose all structure during cooking.

1 Preheat the oven to 200°C fan-forced (220° conventional). Slice each fennel bulb in half lengthways. Choose a shallow cast-iron baking dish that will hold the fennel halves snugly and place them in, cut-side up. Pour enough olive oil into the baking dish so that the fennel is partly submerged with about 1 cm left exposed. Sprinkle the coriander and fennel seeds and a good pinch of salt and pepper over the exposed fennel, then finish with just a smidge more olive oil to moisten the surface. It's fine if a few spices spill into the oil, but try to get a good spice crust on the fennel.

2 Braise the fennel in the oven for 20 minutes, then scatter in the olives. Return to the oven and cook for 20 minutes or until the fennel is tender and has a nice golden crust. (If you find the outside starts to burn before the inside becomes tender, reduce the oven temperature by 20°C or so and cook for a while longer.) The olives should be slightly wrinkled and just beginning to bubble. Set the dish aside to cool for 10 minutes or so, then tip off about 4 tablespoons of oil.

3 To serve, arrange the grapefruit, reserved juice, salad leaves and fennel fronds on top of the cooled fennel and olives, and season well. Taste, and add a splash of lemon juice to sharpen the dish if you feel it's too oily. Leave to stand for a minute or two to allow the ingredients to warm through with the residual heat before serving. Alternatively, to serve the grapefruit salad separately, throw the grapefruit, juice, salad and fennel fronds into a bowl and season well. Give them a toss, then add a splash of lemon if you like. Serve the salad beside the fennel confit and let everyone dig in.

COCONUT AND MACADAMIA LAKSA

SERVES 2

30 ML PEANUT OIL

600 ML COCONUT CREAM

2 BOK CHOY, QUARTERED LENGTHWAYS

½ BUNCH CHINESE BROCCOLI (GAI LAN)

JUICE OF 1 LIME (ABOUT 30 ML)

4 TABLESPOONS THAI LIGHT SOY SAUCE
(SEE INGREDIENTS)

SALT FLAKES

200 G FRESH HOKKIEN NOODLES

80 G FRIED TOFU PUFFS, SLICED

3 SMALL RED CHILLIES, SLICED,
SEEDS AND ALL

80 G BEAN SPROUTS

½ SMALL BUNCH CORIANDER, LEAVES
PICKED WITH 3–4 CM STEM

½ BUNCH VIETNAMESE MINT,
LEAVES PICKED

2 TEASPOONS CRISPY SHALLOT CHIPS
(SEE BASIC RECIPES)

2 KAFFIR LIME LEAVES, FINELY SLICED

LAKSA PASTE

2 LARGE DRIED RED CHILLIES, SEEDED

50 ML PEANUT OIL

2 TEASPOONS VEGETARIAN BELACAN
(SEE INGREDIENTS)

2 ONIONS, CHOPPED

2 CLOVES GARLIC, PEELED

FINELY GRATED ZEST OF 1 KAFFIR LIME

2 STALKS LEMONGRASS, WHITE PARTS
ONLY, FINELY SLICED

1 TABLESPOON PEELED AND ROUGHLY
CHOPPED GALANGAL

1 TEASPOON FRESH CHOPPED TURMERIC,
OR ½ TEASPOON GROUND TURMERIC

30 G MACADAMIAS

1 TABLESPOON CORIANDER SEEDS,
ROASTED AND GROUND

3 CORIANDER ROOTS, SCRAPED
AND TRIMMED

There are so many arguments about what makes a laksa authentic, and which kind of noodle is the 'correct' one to use . . . yawn. You could spend a lifetime sampling laksa from every hawker stall in Malaysia and Singapore to find the answers, but I reckon if you have a recipe that you like, then you are a winner. This particular recipe is completely inauthentic and has been tweaked countless times over a number of years. It came about because so many customers would ask if they could have a vegetarian or vegan laksa and this was always problematic: the laksa contained either dried prawns in the paste (in the case of coconut curry laksa) or fish stock (in sour tamarind-based laksa). So I created this recipe using vegetarian belacan (see Ingredients) to produce the extreme savoury flavour (umami) that you would normally get from shrimp belacan.

I also use macadamia nuts instead of the more 'authentic' candlenuts, because I strongly believe in a common-sense approach to cooking and I tend to look at what an ingredient actually does in a traditional recipe before I have a foot-stamping hissy fit and demand that it must be used. Both candlenuts and macadamias are waxy and their role in this recipe is to fatten the palate and thicken the broth. As one nut is imported and one grows really well in Australia, it's a pretty easy choice for me.

I always use a ratio of one part coconut cream to two parts water for laksa; otherwise I find the dish is magnificent for one mouthful but then becomes just way too rich to finish.

1 To make the laksa paste, first soak the dried chillies in warm water for 10 minutes. Place all of the laksa paste ingredients in a blender and blend to a smooth paste. You should have roughly 6 tablespoons of paste.

2 Heat 30 ml of peanut oil in a heavy-based saucepan over medium heat and fry the laksa paste until fragrant. Add the coconut cream and simmer for 10 minutes, then add 1.2 litres of water and simmer for a further 5 minutes. Add the bok choy and Chinese broccoli and simmer for 1 minute. Remove the pan from the heat and add the lime juice and soy sauce, and season with salt to taste.

3 Place the noodles in a large bowl and cover them with boiling water. Allow the noodles to soften for a minute or so, then drain. Immediately divide the noodles among serving bowls, along with the tofu. Pour the soup over the noodles, making sure every bowl gets some bok choy and Chinese broccoli.

4 Garnish each laksa with chilli, bean sprouts, coriander, Vietnamese mint, Crispy shallot chips and kaffir lime leaves. Serve immediately.

PARSNIPS WITH ORANGE ZEST, SHAVED FENNEL AND CAPERBERRIES

SERVES 4

500 G YOUNG PARSNIPS, TRIMMED, PEELED AND HALVED LENGTHWAYS

50 G UNSALTED BUTTER

100 ML EXTRA VIRGIN OLIVE OIL

2 TEASPOONS CHOPPED ROSEMARY

JUICE OF 1 ORANGE

THICK STRIPS OF ZEST OF ½ ORANGE

2 SMALL BULBS FENNEL, TRIMMED

THIN STRIPS OF ZEST AND JUICE OF 1 LEMON

16 CAPERBERRIES, HALVED LENGTHWAYS

CRACKED BLACK PEPPER

I have brazenly stolen this idea from Maggie Beer. She cooked up some parsnips in orange juice one day and I was sold on the first mouthful! The parsnips need to be really young and fresh for this recipe or you will need to double both the blanching and roasting times. The most important thing is to try not to roast the parsnips for longer than 10 minutes once the orange juice hits them in the final part of the recipe, or the citrus flavour will start to disappear.

The razor-thin fennel releases a waft of anise as it meets the warm parsnips, and its flavour pairs well with the hint of bitterness from the citrus zest. And a word about the caperberries, which bring the whole dish together: if you don't like capers, it doesn't mean you won't like caperberries. They're a completely different ball-game. The caper is the bud of the plant, which will eventually become a flower if left to its own devices, while the caperberry is the fruit. It contains less of the mustardy overtone of the buds, and there are none of the salty flavours that come from packing the buds in salt. Caperberries also have a great texture, which works brilliantly in this dish.

1 Preheat the oven to 200°C fan-forced (220°C conventional).

2 Blanch the parsnips in boiling salted water for 3–4 minutes, then drain.

3 In a small heavy-based saucepan over medium heat, melt the butter until it's frothy and nut-brown, then add 3 tablespoons of olive oil. Pour this into a stainless-steel bowl, add the parsnips and toss to coat. Transfer the parsnips to a baking tray, cut-side down, and scatter over the rosemary. Bake the parsnips for about 15 minutes or until they're golden brown.

4 Remove the parsnips from the oven and turn up the heat to 220°C fan-forced (240°C conventional). Deglaze the tray with the orange juice, then toss in the strips of orange zest. Return the parsnips to the oven for about 10 minutes or until most of the juice has evaporated or stuck to the parsnips.

5 Meanwhile, using a mandoline or a very sharp knife, carefully shave the fennel into slices 1–2 mm thick. Place the shaved fennel in a bowl of water with the lemon juice added to prevent discolouration.

6 To serve, drain the fennel well and arrange it on a serving plate. Arrange the parsnips on top and scatter them with thin strips of lemon zest and the caperberries. Season with black pepper and drizzle over the remaining oil.

SAGE AND GARLIC PUMPKIN WITH BRAISED RED RICE

SERVES 4

150 ML EXTRA VIRGIN OLIVE OIL, PLUS EXTRA FOR DRIZZLING

2 ONIONS, DICED

4 CLOVES GARLIC, CRUSHED

2 CUPS (400 G) ITALIAN RED RICE

SALT FLAKES AND CRACKED BLACK PEPPER

3 TABLESPOONS DRY WHITE WINE

80 G UNSALTED BUTTER

100 G PARMESAN, GRATED

1 KG JAP PUMPKIN, CUT INTO WEDGES

1 HEAD OF GARLIC, CLOVES SEPARATED

1 TABLESPOON DRIED GREEK OREGANO

½ SMALL BUNCH SAGE, LEAVES PICKED

I love the amazing sweetness and weight of jap pumpkins, but most of all I love the way they look. Stripy, dotty and gnarly, they have a stunning prehistoric ugliness to them. These big fellas sweeten for a long period of time after they're picked, so I like to leave one sitting on the kitchen table for a while to ramp up the sugars. That way, I can also spend time pondering the numerous ways of preparing this versatile vegie before I eventually get around to cooking it. In this dish, the roasted pumpkin marries perfectly with the Italian red rice, which is so full of flavour there's no need to use a stock; water will work just fine. The pumpkin's deep green skin and vibrant orange flesh and the red juices of the rice paint a lovely winter palette on the plate.

This is a skin-on dish, with the garlic, rice and pumpkin all presented in their winter jumpers. I can never understand our obsession with peeling, skinning and refining all of our food. The textures of these skins add body and contrast and give you something to get stuck into.

1 Fill a large saucepan with 2 litres of water and bring to the boil. Reduce the heat and keep the water at a steady simmer.

2 Heat 50 ml of olive oil in a large heavy-based saucepan over medium heat and saute the onion and garlic until the onion is soft and translucent. Reduce the heat to low, add the rice and toast it, stirring constantly, for 3 minutes. Increase the heat to high and wait for just a few seconds, then add 1 teaspoon of salt and a good twist of black pepper and deglaze the pan with the wine. Once the wine has evaporated (this should take a few seconds and a couple of stirs), turn down the heat to low. Add the simmering water to the pan one ladleful at a time, stirring occasionally and adding another ladleful as the liquid in the pan evaporates. Continue in this way until the rice is cooked, about 50 minutes. (It's ready when the husks burst slightly and the mixture becomes creamy; the rice will not be as sticky as it is in a regular risotto.) Fold in the butter and check the seasoning, adding more salt to taste. The rice should be slightly wet, and definitely not dry and claggy. Stir through the parmesan.

3 While the rice is cooking, preheat the oven to 200°C fan-forced (220°C conventional). Place the pumpkin wedges and garlic cloves on a baking tray and coat with the remaining 100 ml of olive oil, oregano, sage, 2 teaspoons of salt and a grinding of pepper. Roast for 30 minutes or until the garlic is crispy on the outside and mushy on the inside and the pumpkin is blistered and soft but still holding its shape.

4 Divide the braised red rice among shallow bowls and arrange the roast pumpkin slices and garlic on top. Drizzle over a little more oil and serve.

PRESERVED LIME PILAF

SERVES 4 AS PART OF A SHARED MEAL

CHICKPEA AND KIPFLER POTATO CURRY
(SEE PAGE 203) OR CAULIFLOWER
ROASTED WITH PANCH PHORAN AND
FRESH TURMERIC (SEE PAGE 198),
TO SERVE (OPTIONAL)

PRESERVED LIMES

750 G LIMES (ABOUT 15 LIMES),
WASHED, DRIED AND HALVED

¼ CUP (55 G) FINE SALT

3 TABLESPOONS CHILLI POWDER

125 G LONG GREEN CHILLIES

1 LITRE MILD MUSTARD OIL

½ CUP (40 G) FENUGREEK SEEDS

1½ TABLESPOONS GROUND TURMERIC

1½ TABLESPOONS ANISE SEEDS

7–10 STAR ANISE, POUNDED GENTLY
UNTIL BROKEN

2 TABLESPOONS NIGELLA SEEDS
(OPTIONAL)

The idea for this pilaf recipe came about one day when I was just about to start cooking an Indian lemon rice dish. Then I spotted a jar of preserved limes on my shelf and thought, 'Why not?' The highly aromatic preserved lime recipe was taught to me by my assistant, who picked it up during a sabbatical in Northern India. It's nothing like the fiery Indian pickle you may be familiar with. The limes are preserved in oil and partially fermented in a warm spot for a week. Buy the limes when they hit rock-bottom prices and make a batch to keep and use as an accompaniment to your Indian meals. It has become a favourite of mine, and most people are amazed that you can actually eat the whole lime chunks, unlike preserved lemons where you discard the pith and flesh. I sometimes add a little of the preserving oil, spices and lime to yoghurt to make a quick, zingy raita.

1 For the preserved limes, place the limes in a large bowl and sprinkle over a third (about 2 tablespoons) of the salt and half of the chilli powder. Mix well, packing the salt into the lime flesh. Cover the bowl with plastic film and leave the limes to marinate at room temperature for 24 hours.

2 The next day, drain off all the liquid in the bowl. Re-cover the bowl with plastic film and leave the limes to marinate for another 24 hours. Wash the chillies and dry them well. Carefully cut them almost in half, leaving them held together at the stalk. Place the chillies in a separate bowl and sprinkle with another third of the salt. Mix well, packing the salt into the chillies. Cover the bowl with plastic film and leave the chillies to marinate overnight.

3 The next day, gently squeeze out all the water released by the limes and chillies, taking care not to squeeze the juice from the limes.

4 Heat the mustard oil in a heavy-based saucepan until it's smoking. Remove the pan from the heat and leave the oil to cool to 80°C. In a large bowl, mix together the remaining salt and chilli powder and the fenugreek seeds, turmeric, anise seeds, star anise and nigella seeds, if using. Add the marinated limes and chillies and just enough hot oil to bind the spices. Mix everything together with your hands, preferably wearing gloves as this is really hot and spicy!

5 Place the limes, chillies and spices in a large sterilised jar (see page 223). Pour in the remaining oil to cover by about 3 cm, then cover the jar with muslin or seal with a lid. Keep the jar in a sunny or warmish spot for a week, stirring the contents or tipping the jar upside-down at least once a day to ensure that everything is completely coated in the oil. The preserved limes will be ready to eat after a week. Once opened, they will keep in the fridge for up to a year.

PILAF

120 ML GHEE (SEE INGREDIENTS)

2 ONIONS, CHOPPED

1 STAR ANISE

8 GREEN CARDAMOM PODS, BRUISED

2 CINNAMON STICKS, SNAPPED IN HALF

10 CLOVES

16 BLACK PEPPERCORNS

2 BAY LEAVES

2 CUPS (400 G) BASMATI RICE

1 LITRE BOILING WATER

BIG PINCH OF SAFFRON THREADS

1 CUP (150 G) SHELLED PISTACHIOS OR
   1 CUP (160 G) CHOPPED ALMONDS

100 G CURRANTS

2 PRESERVED LIMES,
   ROUGHLY CHOPPED (SEE OPPOSITE)

6 To make the pilaf, heat the ghee in a heavy-based saucepan over medium heat. Fry the onion until it's soft and translucent, then add the star anise, cardamom, cinnamon, cloves, peppercorns and bay leaves. Stir a little, then add the rice and continue to stir until the rice is coated with ghee and is glossy. Carefully add the boiling water (this will sizzle quite hard), then reduce the temperature until there is no more movement on the surface. Dot the saffron in patches over the top. Cover the pan with a tight-fitting lid and cook the rice gently for 15–20 minutes or until the liquid has been absorbed and the rice is tender to the bite. Carefully fold the nuts, currants and preserved lime through the rice.

7 Serve the pilaf with extra preserved lime on the side. This is also good with the Chickpea and kipfler potato curry or Cauliflower roasted with panch phoran and fresh turmeric.

CAULIFLOWER ROASTED WITH PANCH PHORAN AND FRESH TURMERIC

SERVES 4

1 CAULIFLOWER, TRIMMED

120 ML GHEE (SEE INGREDIENTS)

1 TABLESPOON FRESHLY GRATED TURMERIC OR 1 TEASPOON GROUND TURMERIC

4 TABLESPOONS PANCH PHORAN

1 TABLESPOON SALT FLAKES

1 LONG GREEN CHILLI, SLICED, SEEDS AND ALL

1 SMALL BUNCH CORIANDER, LEAVES PICKED

JUICE OF 1 LEMON

PRESERVED LIME PILAF (SEE PAGE 196) OR JACKFRUIT BIRYANI (SEE PAGE 185), TO SERVE (OPTIONAL)

Whenever I visualise cauliflower, I always think of my vegie patch on a frosty winter morning after overnight rain with the cauliflowers nestling in their leaves like they're tucked up in blankets, and a drop or two of rainwater gleaming on their flowery tops. I was never a kid who hated vegies, but I did think that boiled cauliflower smelt a bit like old socks (and overcooking it pushed that smell to somewhere nearer rotten eggs). I've since learnt that the trick is to leave the cauliflower a little undercooked or to roast it. As a young chef, I was a little reluctant to do the latter because I thought it made the florets look a bit sad and wilted, but my appreciation for messy-looking things has grown with the years (old dogs, dented cars, beaten pots and pans . . .) and I now think roast cauliflower looks rather compelling.

Panch phoran is my choice of spice for this. It's essentially a blend of fennel, fenugreek and cumin seeds and sometimes wild celery or mustard seeds, but absolutely always nigella seeds. I always think it smells slightly medicinal. I especially love the combination of the fennel seeds with the cauliflower. This, along with the slight bitterness of the fenugreek and the way the turmeric stains the cauliflower a vibrant yellow, makes the dish another favourite of mine.

1 Preheat the oven to 200°C fan-forced (220°C conventional). Cut the cauliflower into quarters. Working from the stem end up, cut each quarter into florets about 4 cm wide at the top with a trailing stem. The stem is the best bit so do not trim it all off.

2 Heat the ghee in a small frying pan over medium heat. Add the turmeric and panch phoran and fry until a few seeds crackle ever so slightly. Do not allow the panch phoran to get too hot as the fenugreek will become very bitter. Add the salt to the pan and stir to combine. Transfer the spice mix to a large bowl.

3 Add the cauliflower to the bowl and toss to coat with the spice mix, adding a little more ghee if the cauliflower is not properly coated, and pressing the seeds onto the florets. Transfer the cauliflower to a roasting tin.

4 Roast the cauliflower for about 25 minutes or until it's tender; a few burnt tips are nothing to worry about. When you are ready to serve, toss the roast cauliflower with the chilli, coriander and lemon juice. This works really well served with Preserved lime pilaf or Jackfruit biryani.

BITTER MELON BALTI

SERVES 4

1 KG BITTER MELON, PEELED, HALVED LENGTHWAYS AND SEEDED, THEN SLICED INTO 2 CM HALF-MOONS

1 TABLESPOON COARSE-GRAINED SALT

100 ML GHEE (SEE INGREDIENTS)

PRESERVED LIMES (SEE PAGE 196), TO SERVE (OPTIONAL)

BALTI SAUCE

3 TABLESPOONS GHEE

2 CLOVES GARLIC, CRUSHED

2 CM PIECE GINGER, CHOPPED

5 ONIONS, CHOPPED

6 TOMATOES, CHOPPED

1 TEASPOON GROUND CUMIN

1 TEASPOON GARAM MASALA

1 TEASPOON KASHMIRI CHILLI POWDER

1½ TEASPOONS FENUGREEK LEAF

2 TEASPOONS GROUND CORIANDER

2 TEASPOONS GROUND TURMERIC

¼ TEASPOON GROUND BLACK PEPPER

2 BAY LEAVES

4 GREEN CARDAMOM PODS, SMASHED

1 SMALL BUNCH CORIANDER, LEAVES PICKED AND CHOPPED

CHIPS

4 FLOURY POTATOES (KENNEBECS ARE BEST), PEELED AND CUT INTO FINGERS

SALT FLAKES

FLAVOUR-NEUTRAL OIL (SEE INGREDIENTS), FOR DEEP-FRYING

Baltis are one of those amazing mix-ups of cultural and culinary influences. They're said to have originated in the English city of Birmingham, when Pakistani immigrants adapted their traditional curries (cooked in a deep cast-iron wok called a balti) to local tastes. This is a great example of how cuisines evolve with people's migratory paths. Food is part of culture, and neither is a static concept – I reckon if a dish tastes good, you should just enjoy eating it and stop banging on about 'authenticity' . . .

This is my favourite way to eat bitter melon. It stands up well to all the spices in the balti and has an almost cooling effect on the palate. However, Western palates tend not to enjoy bitterness, so this dish is not for everyone. I had to include it, though, because I always see people pick up bitter melon at the market, then swiftly put it back down with a puzzled look on their face. You prepare it in a similar way to eggplant, using salt to draw out its bitter liquid. (Coarse-grained salt, like kosher salt, is best as it does this without dissolving and is therefore easier to remove after it has done its job.) You'll then need to blanch the melon briefly to further remove bitterness before cooking it. The melon will still be a little bitter – that's the point – but in a refreshingly different way. So the next time you are intrigued by this other-worldly looking vegetable, you'll know how to prepare it.

In the UK, it's not unusual to find baltis served with chips. They're an ideal accompaniment, so I rarely serve this curry with rice. There is a science to cooking the perfect chip. In this recipe, the simmering cooks the potato and makes the centre fluffy and light, the low-temperature fry crisps the delicate skin, and the high-temperature frying creates the golden, crackling-like coating. Kashmiri chilli powder is a stunning red spice with an almost sweet taste. It's available from Indian grocers.

1 To make the chips, place the potatoes in a large saucepan and cover with cold water and a pinch of salt. Bring to the boil, then simmer gently over medium–low heat for 10–12 minutes until really soft and almost breaking up. Do not allow the water to boil rapidly or the chips will break apart completely. You want them to be soft but still intact. Drain the chips on paper towel, then spread them out on a tray and leave them in the fridge for 1 hour until completely cool. This will help to 'set' the chips in preparation for frying.

2 Place the chilled chips and the oil in a large heavy-based saucepan over low–medium heat and bring the temperature up to 100°C. Fry the chips for a further 10 minutes until the skins are really crisp but have absolutely no colour; the outside of the chips should feel like tracing paper to the touch. Drain the chips on paper towel and return them to the fridge for 30 minutes.

BITTER MELON BALTI (CONT.)

3 Meanwhile, lay the bitter melon on a tray, sprinkle it with the salt and leave it for 30 minutes.

4 To make the balti sauce, heat the 3 tablespoons of ghee in a large saucepan over medium heat and add the garlic, ginger and onion. Sweat until the onion is soft and translucent. Add 1 cup (250 ml) of water and bring to a simmer, then add all the remaining ingredients except the coriander leaves and simmer for 30 minutes until the tomatoes are really mushy. Remove from the heat and discard the bay leaves and cardamom pods. Add the coriander, then transfer the balti mixture to a blender and puree to a sauce. This is now ready to be made into whatever flavour balti you want to make. (If you don't fancy this bitter melon balti, try my favourite combinations of sweetcorn and wilted spinach or mushroom and potato.)

5 Wash the bitter melon under running water to remove the excess salt and the droplets of bitter liquid that it has drawn out, then blanch it for 3 minutes in plenty of boiling water. Drain, then pat dry with paper towel. Heat the ghee in a frying pan over medium heat and add the bitter melon. Saute for 5 minutes until the melon is caramelised, then add the balti sauce to warm through.

6 Reheat the oil to 180°C and fry the chips for 5 minutes until crisp and golden. Drain on paper towel and season with salt to taste.

7 Serve the balti in bowls with chips on the side. This is also really good with a side of Preserved limes.

CHICKPEA AND KIPFLER POTATO CURRY

SERVES 6

200 G DRIED KABULI CHICKPEAS (SEE INGREDIENTS), SOAKED OVERNIGHT IN COLD WATER

2 CLOVES GARLIC, PEELED

2.5 CM PIECE GINGER, ROUGHLY CHOPPED, PLUS EXTRA SLICED, TO GARNISH (OPTIONAL)

100 ML GHEE (SEE INGREDIENTS)

1 ONION, DICED

1 × 400 G TIN DICED TOMATOES

2 TEASPOONS SALT FLAKES

2 BAY LEAVES

2 LARGE KIPFLER POTATOES, CUT INTO 2.5 CM PIECES

1 CINNAMON STICK

100 G GREEN BEANS, CUT INTO 2 CM LENGTHS

JUICE OF 1 SMALL LEMON

½ TEASPOON GARAM MASALA

CHOPPED CORIANDER LEAVES, TO GARNISH

CHAPATTIS (SEE BASIC RECIPES), TO SERVE

SPICE MIX

2 TEASPOONS GROUND TURMERIC

½ TEASPOON CHILLI POWDER

½ TEASPOON GARAM MASALA

1 TEASPOON GROUND CORIANDER

1 TEASPOON GROUND CUMIN

1 TEASPOON AMCHOOR (DRIED MANGO POWDER; SEE PAGE 32)

¼ TEASPOON GRATED NUTMEG

PINCH OF GROUND FENUGREEK

A few years ago, I had the pleasure of a visit from gardening guru Peter Cundall. That morning I was absolutely terrified, running around making sure that my vegie garden was 'acceptable' for a visit from horticultural royalty. Peter is an amazing guy. Among many other achievements, he is a dedicated environmentalist and studied organic gardening in the 1970s – well before the organic movement had become mainstream. He arrived at my place with a dizzying array of spuds under his arms and, with his machine-gun banter (and sharp sense of humour), he began a lesson on all things potato.

This dish is an example of how a little knowledge can really change your cooking. I had always used a starchy potato in this simply because that was the way I was taught, but after Peter's visit, I decided to try this curry using a waxy spud. While the kipfler doesn't absorb the flavours in the sauce as much as a starchy variety, it definitely delivers a fuller mouth-feel and is less dry. As an added bonus, it also holds its shape well.

1 Drain the chickpeas, discarding the soaking water. Place them in a saucepan and cover with cold water. (The less water you use, the quicker the chickpeas will cook, so cover them by just a few centimetres and top up the water during cooking if necessary.) Bring to a simmer over medium heat and cook the chickpeas for about 1 hour until tender to the bite. Drain, reserving 200 ml of the cooking water, then set the water and chickpeas aside.

2 Place the garlic and chopped ginger in a blender and puree to a paste, then set aside. Combine all of the ingredients for the spice mix and set aside.

3 Heat the ghee in a large frying pan with a lid over medium heat. Fry the onion until it browns, then add the ginger and garlic paste and the spice mix. Fry for a couple of minutes until the raw ginger and garlic smell disappears, then add the tomatoes, reduce the heat slightly and simmer for 15 minutes. Add the salt, bay leaves, potato and cooked chickpeas and stir to coat. Add the reserved chickpea cooking water and the cinnamon, then cover and cook for 15–20 minutes or until the potato is just tender. Add the green beans and cook for a further 5 minutes or until they're just tender, then add lemon juice to taste and the garam masala.

4 Garnish the curry with chopped coriander and ginger, if you like. Serve with Chapattis.

PAPPARDELLE WITH DILL, CAPERS AND LEEK SOUBISE

SERVES 4

6 LEEKS, WHITE PARTS ONLY, CUT INTO MATCHSTICKS

60 G UNSALTED BUTTER

4 TABLESPOONS DRY WHITE WINE

SALT FLAKES AND CRACKED BLACK PEPPER

600 ML POURING CREAM

2 TABLESPOONS EXTRA VIRGIN OLIVE OIL

3 CLOVES GARLIC, FINELY SLICED

3 TABLESPOONS SALTED CAPERS, RUBBED IN A CLEAN TEA TOWEL TO REMOVE EXCESS SALT

6 SPRIGS OREGANO, LEAVES PICKED AND FINELY CHOPPED

½ CUP (40 G) SHAVED PARMESAN

FINELY GRATED ZEST OF 1 LEMON

12 SPRIGS DILL, ROUGHLY RIPPED INTO 4 CM LENGTHS

PASTA DOUGH

200 G STRONG PLAIN FLOUR (SEE INGREDIENTS)

1 FREE-RANGE EGG

1 FREE-RANGE EGG YOLK

ABOUT 3 TABLESPOONS WATER, AT ROOM TEMPERATURE

Strictly speaking, a soubise is made with onion, but I like to use leek whites. As they braise slowly in the cream, their sweetness intensifies and the cream reduces and thickens, giving a lush, rich sauce. Get a good Australian caper for this and you will be amazed what a difference the flavour makes to the dish. Don't wash them; rather just rub the salt off gently with a tea towel and the residual saltiness will balance wonderfully with the sweetness in the sauce. Dill is a delicate herb, so make sure it only hits the top of the dish just before serving. As a rule of thumb, robust and woody herbs go into your cooking early and delicate, soft herbs, like coriander, chervil, tarragon and dill, are last-minute jobs.

1 To make the pasta dough, mix together the flour, egg and yolk in a food processor by pulsing a few times to combine, then gradually add enough water to make a stiff dough (you may need up to 3 tablespoons). Alternatively, place the flour in a bowl, make a well and add the egg and yolk. Bring the flour into the egg mixture and gradually combine until you have a dough. Turn it out onto a lightly floured benchtop and knead the dough for 10 minutes until smooth and silky. Place the dough in a lightly floured bowl and cover with plastic film. Leave to rest for 1 hour at room temperature.

2 Meanwhile, in a heavy-based saucepan over low heat, saute the leek in the butter for a few minutes. Stir in the wine and 2 teaspoons of salt, then pour in the cream. Cook over the lowest heat for 1 hour until the cream is thickened and sweetened by the leeks, stirring periodically so as not to burn the cream. Remove the pan from the heat and cover with a lid to keep warm.

3 Divide the pasta dough into two or three pieces. Shape each one into a ball, dust lightly with flour and flatten slightly with the palm of your hand. Roll the dough until it is about 1 cm thick, so you can feed it through the widest setting on a pasta machine. Lightly flour the rollers on the pasta machine and roll the dough through each setting, gradually working down to the second-finest setting, and re-flouring as required if the dough starts to grab on the rollers. Stack the rolled dough between sheets of baking paper, cover with a tea towel sprayed lightly with water and leave to rest for 20 minutes. Lightly flour the dough, fold it in half like a book and cut into 2 cm-wide strips.

4 Cook the pasta in a large saucepan of lightly salted boiling water for 2 minutes or until just tender to the bite, then drain well. Place the pasta in a large bowl and pour over the warm leek soubise, then toss to coat well. Check the seasoning.

5 Heat the olive oil in a heavy-based shallow pan over medium heat. Saute the garlic and capers for about 2 minutes or until the garlic is really well coloured and the capers are starting to burst. Throw in the oregano and stir once, then remove the pan from the heat. Divide the pasta among warmed plates and spoon over the garlic, capers and oregano. Top with the parmesan and lemon zest, and garnish with dill. Season with black pepper and serve.

CELERIAC, POTATO AND LENTIL SHEPHERD'S PIE

SERVES 4

150 G UNHULLED RED LENTILS (SEE INGREDIENTS), SOAKED OVERNIGHT IN COLD WATER

3 TABLESPOONS EXTRA VIRGIN OLIVE OIL

1 ONION, DICED

2 CLOVES GARLIC, CRUSHED

2 STALKS CELERY (INCLUDING THE HEART), DICED

1 CARROT, DICED

1 TEASPOON CARAWAY SEEDS

1 SPRIG ROSEMARY

2 BAY LEAVES

4 SPRIGS THYME

100 G BUTTON OR FIELD MUSHROOMS, DICED

25 ML RED-WINE VINEGAR

1 TABLESPOON TOMATO PASTE

10 G DRIED WILD MUSHROOM MIX, GROUND TO A FINE POWDER

200 G TINNED DICED TOMATOES

SALT FLAKES AND CRACKED BLACK PEPPER

2 TEASPOONS FINELY GRATED LEMON ZEST

75 G GREEN BEANS, CUT INTO 1 CM LENGTHS

1 LOOSE HANDFUL FLAT-LEAF PARSLEY LEAVES, CHOPPED

GOOD TOMATO KETCHUP, TO SERVE

CELERIAC AND POTATO MASH

375 G CELERIAC, PEELED AND CUT INTO 3 CM CHUNKS

375 G FLOURY POTATOES (SEE PAGE 117), PEELED AND CUT INTO 3 CM CHUNKS

100 G UNSALTED BUTTER, CUBED

150 ML MILK

½ CUP (40 G) GRATED PARMESAN

¼ TEASPOON GROUND MACE

SALT FLAKES AND FRESHLY GROUND WHITE PEPPER

Shepherd's pie will never be that sexy because it always brings to mind farmers in gumboots who speak with thick accents, but this sheep-free version is a perfect winter dinner. You can knock the pies up beforehand and just pop them in the oven to brown the mash – which is especially good if you don't wear gumboots and return home cold, hungry and with wet feet. The real deal-breaker with this dish is using top-quality lentils and spiking them with an outrageous amount of dried wild mushroom mix, for it is this that makes the earthy tones of the lentils become almost 'meaty'.

You also need a really fluffy mash for the topping. A floury white-fleshed potato will have the necessary starch content to achieve the brown topping during baking. No waxy potatoes here – not only will they not brown, but they will make a mash that is far too heavy when paired with the lentils. The celeriac adds another dimension of flavour and prevents the mash becoming too gluey. A ricer or mouli is a worthwhile investment if you are a mash perfectionist. You can use an old-fashioned masher but the results won't be as smooth. Grab a bottle of good tomato ketchup and you have a fantastic meal.

1 Drain the lentils, discarding the soaking water. Place them in a saucepan and cover with cold water by about 5 cm. Bring to the boil over high heat, then reduce the heat to low–medium and simmer for 1 hour until just tender to the bite. (Top up the water if the lentils become too dry, but keep the liquid level low as you will lose flavour to the cooking water.) Drain and set aside.

2 Heat the olive oil in a large frying pan over medium heat and saute the onion and garlic until the onion is soft and translucent. Add the celery, carrot, caraway seeds, rosemary, bay leaves and thyme and saute for 5 minutes, then add the fresh mushrooms and saute for a further 5 minutes. Turn the heat up to full and deglaze the pan with the vinegar. Add the tomato paste, ground dried mushrooms and tomatoes and saute for 3 minutes, then add 2 teaspoons of salt, pepper and lemon zest. Add the green beans and cooked lentils with their cooking liquid and enough extra water to cover the lentils by about 4 cm. Simmer for 10 minutes or until the green beans are tender. Check the seasoning and remove the rosemary, bay leaves and thyme. Stir in the chopped parsley. Pour the lentil mix into four large souffle ramekins or one big baking dish.

3 Preheat the oven to 220°C fan-forced (240°C conventional). To make the mash, place the celeriac and potato in a saucepan with plenty of cold salted water and bring to a rapid boil. Reduce the heat and simmer for 10–15 minutes or until the vegies are tender. Drain, then return to the pan and place over very low heat for 5–10 minutes, stirring periodically to help evaporate any water. For best results, pass the celeriac and potato through a mouli or ricer, then gradually fold in the butter and milk, mashing to combine. Stir in the parmesan, mace, 2 teaspoons of salt and white pepper. Top the lentil mix with the mash and bake for 15 minutes or so until the topping is golden brown. Serve with tomato ketchup.

EGYPTIAN BEANS WITH LEMON AND CORIANDER SALAD

SERVES 4

320 G EGYPTIAN BROWN (FUL) BEANS, SOAKED OVERNIGHT IN COLD WATER

4 FREE-RANGE EGGS, HARD-BOILED

LEMON WEDGES, TO SERVE

LEMON PASTE

6 CLOVES GARLIC, PEELED

½ CUP (125 ML) EXTRA VIRGIN OLIVE OIL

1 TABLESPOON GROUND CUMIN

JUICE OF 3 LEMONS

3 TEASPOONS SALT FLAKES

1 TEASPOON CRACKED BLACK PEPPER

CORIANDER SALAD

1 BUNCH CORIANDER, LEAVES PICKED WITH 3–4 CM STEM

1 LARGE RED ONION, SLICED

1 CLOVE GARLIC, CHOPPED

3 TOMATOES, CHOPPED

30 ML EXTRA VIRGIN OLIVE OIL

JUICE OF ½ LEMON

SALT FLAKES AND CRACKED BLACK PEPPER

This Egyptian dish, known as ful medames, is usually eaten for breakfast, but it's also good served with a little flatbread for supper. Traditionally, the beans are left to soak in the morning, the eggs are added to the beans in the evening and the pot is buried in coals overnight. The beans and eggs are flavoured with lemon and herbs and served as a hearty breakfast the following morning. (In my version, I just add hard-boiled eggs to the salad.) The Egyptians describe this fortifying dish as a 'stone in the stomach'. It's especially welcome during Ramadan. If you can't find Egyptian brown beans, you can substitute broad (fava) beans instead, though they're lighter and larger than ful beans. This is really nice served with green tea spiked with sugar and tons of mint.

1 Drain the beans, discarding the soaking water. Place them in a saucepan and cover with a few centimetres of cold water. Simmer the beans over low heat for about 3 hours, until they're tender and mushy.

2 For the lemon paste, grind the garlic, olive oil and cumin to a paste using a mortar and pestle. Add the lemon juice, salt and pepper. Set aside.

3 Make a salad with the coriander, onion, garlic and tomato. Dress with a little olive oil and lemon juice and season with a large pinch of salt and pepper.

4 To serve, stir three-quarters of the lemon paste into the beans. Cut the hard-boiled eggs in half lengthways and arrange them on a platter with the coriander salad and lemon wedges. Serve the beans with a small bowl of the remaining lemon paste for those who like it zingy.

RED AND GOLDEN BEETS WITH GRUYERE POLENTA AND LENTILS

SERVES 4

2 BUNCHES RED BABY BEETROOT

2 BUNCHES GOLDEN BABY BEETROOT

SALT FLAKES AND CRACKED
 BLACK PEPPER

4 TABLESPOONS EXTRA VIRGIN
 OLIVE OIL

1 HANDFUL ROUGHLY CHOPPED
 FLAT-LEAF PARSLEY

ZEST OF ⅓ LEMON

LENTILS

3 TABLESPOONS EXTRA VIRGIN OLIVE OIL

1 ONION, DICED

2 CLOVES GARLIC, CRUSHED

¾ CUP (150 G) UNHULLED RED LENTILS
 (SEE INGREDIENTS)

1 SPRIG THYME

1 BAY LEAF

3 TEASPOONS SALT FLAKES

30 ML DRY WHITE WINE

GRUYERE POLENTA

1 CUP (250 ML) MILK

¾ CUP (125 G) COARSE POLENTA

SALT FLAKES AND CRACKED
 BLACK PEPPER

30 G UNSALTED BUTTER, CUBED

50 G GRUYERE, GRATED

There are a couple of things to look for when buying beetroots. Their leaves will give you a pretty good indication of how fresh they are, so ignore beets with wilted leaves and choose those with lively, crisp-looking leaves instead. The golden beets in this recipe add a little pepperiness (almost a radish-like flavour) and they combine really well with the sweetness of baby red beets. However, don't feel that you can't cook the dish if golden beets are not available; you'll just need to ramp up the pepper.

Way too much flavour ends up in the cooking water if the beets are peeled before you add them to the pan. If you must remove the skin (although there is absolutely no reason to if you are cooking baby beets), slip it off after cooking. In this recipe, you want to simmer the beets for about 10 minutes – somewhere between a blanch and a par-cook – before you finish them off in a hot oven. This method ensures the beets remain tender and juicy. Wilted and tossed with olive oil and lemon juice, the beetroot leaves go really well the Fennel confit on page 188. The stems are also delicious. Cut them into 5 cm lengths and saute them in olive oil until just softened.

l For the lentils, place a large saucepan over medium heat and add the olive oil. Saute the onion until soft and translucent, then add the garlic and when soft, remove the pan from the heat and leave to cool (you want a cold start for your lentils). Add the lentils, thyme and bay leaf to the pan and cover with water by about 5 cm. Return the pan to medium heat and bring to a steady simmer. Cook the lentils for 1 hour until they're just tender but holding their shape, adding a touch more water if the lentils become too dry. Stir in the salt and wine, then discard the thyme and bay leaf. The lentils should be slightly wet and nestled in the pan with about a third of their volume of water when finished; adjust the water as necessary.

2 Meanwhile, preheat the oven to 200°C fan-forced (220°C conventional). Cut the beetroot stalks about 1.5 cm above the beet. Give the beets a scrub with a vegie brush and place them in a large saucepan of cold water with 1 teaspoon of salt. Bring to a simmer over medium heat and cook for about 10 minutes or until they're half-softened. Drain, then coat the beets in 50 ml of olive oil and season them with another teaspoon of salt and the pepper. Transfer them to a baking tray and roast in the oven for 20 minutes or until they look a little wrinkly and are just tender.

3 To make the gruyere polenta, place the milk and 520 ml of water in a large saucepan and bring to an almost-simmer over low heat. Just before tiny bubbles appear, slowly rain in the polenta, stirring constantly. Add 1 teaspoon of salt, and pepper to taste. Turn the heat down to the lowest-possible setting and cook for 25 minutes, stirring all the time to prevent sticking, until the polenta is soft. Fold in the butter and gruyere.

4 To serve, divide the polenta among plates and top with the lentils and beets. Sprinkle with parsley and lemon zest, splash with the remaining olive oil and season with black pepper.

BAKED THREE-CHEESE PASTA WITH PARSLEY

SERVES 4

500 G SPAGHETTI

130 G PARMESAN, GRATED

3 TABLESPOONS EXTRA VIRGIN OLIVE OIL, PLUS EXTRA FOR DRIZZLING

30 G UNSALTED BUTTER

40 G PLAIN FLOUR

350 ML MILK

SALT FLAKES AND CRACKED BLACK PEPPER

¼ TEASPOON GRATED NUTMEG, PLUS A LITTLE EXTRA, TO SERVE

5 FREE-RANGE EGGS, SEPARATED, AT ROOM TEMPERATURE

80 G EMMENTAL, GRATED

½ BUNCH FLAT-LEAF PARSLEY, LEAVES PICKED AND CHOPPED, PLUS A LITTLE EXTRA FOR SERVING

100 G BOCCONCINI, CUT INTO 4 MM-THICK SLICES

Starring sweet, nutty emmental, sharp, salty parmesan and rich, creamy bocconcini, this three-cheese pasta is full of bold flavours. The dish also looks absolutely stunning, with the pasta set into a perfect mound of interlocking strands. A souffle base brings lightness to an otherwise heavy dish and, when baked, the airy inside contrasts nicely with the slightly crispy edges. You can prepare this a little ahead of time and pop it in the fridge before baking; the trapped air in the souffle mix will hold up for an hour or so without any real detriment to the final result.

1 Cook the spaghetti for about 6 minutes (half the usual cooking time for al dente pasta), or until it is just bendy. Drain, then toss in 50 g of parmesan and 2 tablespoons of olive oil. Set aside.

2 Melt the butter in a medium saucepan over medium heat. Add the flour and cook, stirring constantly, for 2–3 minutes, without colouring. Gradually add the milk, whisking continuously to prevent any lumps. Cook over low heat until thick, then season heavily with salt and pepper. Add the nutmeg and remove from the heat. Leave to cool for 5 minutes, so that you don't scramble the egg yolks in the next stage.

3 Meanwhile, preheat the oven to 140°C fan-forced (160°C conventional). Grease a 3 litre ovenproof bowl with the remaining tablespoon of olive oil.

4 Add the egg yolks to the seasoned milk and flour mixture one at a time, beating them with a wooden spoon and adding the second egg yolk only when the first has been incorporated. Add the emmental, remaining parmesan and parsley.

5 Whisk the egg whites to a soft peak in a really clean bowl. Fold half of the egg whites into the cheese mixture and combine well, being mindful not to knock too much air out of your egg whites. Add the remaining egg whites and gently fold through, either chopping with a pastry card or folding with your hand – you want to retain the trapped air in the mixture.

6 Line the greased bowl with a fifth of the par-cooked spaghetti. Squish the bocconcini slices up the sides and on the bottom of the bowl, as best you can. Fold the remaining spaghetti into the souffle mixture, then turn it out into the bowl. It may look a bit wet, but the par-cooked pasta will absorb any excess moisture during cooking.

7 Cook in the oven for about 50 minutes or until the souffle is set. Allow to cool for 5 minutes, then slide a spatula down the sides of the bowl to release the baked pasta. Turn it out onto a platter and sprinkle with extra chopped parsley. Drizzle with a little extra olive oil and season with salt, pepper and freshly grated nutmeg for oomph.

ESPRESSO AND FIG BREAD

MAKES 1 LOAF

20 DRIED WILD FIGS, CHOPPED INTO
ROUGHLY 5 MM DICE (OR USE
10 REGULAR FIGS, IF UNAVAILABLE)

½ CUP (125 ML) ESPRESSO COFFEE

2½ CUPS (400 G) STRONG PLAIN FLOUR
(SEE INGREDIENTS)

1 TABLESPOON DRIED YEAST

1 TEASPOON SALT FLAKES

2 TEASPOONS SUGAR

1 TABLESPOON ANISE SEEDS,
PLUS 2 TEASPOONS EXTRA
FOR SPRINKLING

½ CUP (125 ML) WARM WATER

3½ TABLESPOONS EXTRA VIRGIN
OLIVE OIL

1 FREE-RANGE EGG YOLK

1 TABLESPOON MILK

Baking is my Achilles' heel. I make sourdough bread at home and have achieved a certain level of competence through practice and a dogged determination to succeed in at least one area of what I jokingly refer to among my baking-competent peers as 'the dark side of cooking'. But, more often than not, when a recipe has yeast involved, I hit speed-dial on my phone and seek counsel from one of two great bakers/pastry chefs I know. Ernst Schutt was my pastry sous chef for a number of years and is used to me asking the most ridiculously simple (to him) questions, as is Stephanie Vasileff, who gave me this recipe when she was my research assistant during the filming of *The Cook and the Chef*.

This bread is wonderful served fresh out of the oven as a morning-tea snack or toasted and eaten with some blue cheese. If you don't have a pizza stone, transfer the bread to the base of the oven for the final 10 minutes to get a decent bottom crust (assuming your oven has a bottom element).

1 Macerate the figs in the coffee for about 30 minutes. Squeeze out excess coffee from the figs, then set the figs and coffee aside separately.

2 Combine the flour, yeast, salt, sugar and anise seeds in a bowl. Mix the warm water, coffee and 3 tablespoons of olive oil in a jug. Slowly pour into the bowl and incorporate using your hands, until the dough comes together. Turn it out onto a lightly floured benchtop and knead the dough until it's shiny and elastic, about 8 minutes. Add a little more water if required. Place the dough in a bowl dusted with flour, cover with plastic film and leave it to rest in a warm spot until it has doubled in size, about 1 hour.

3 Lightly flour your benchtop and roll out the dough to a rectangle about 20 cm × 10 cm (it should be about 2–2.5 cm thick). Sprinkle the figs down the middle of the dough. Gather the sides and ends and pinch together to make a pasty-shape with the figs inside. Turn the dough upside down so that the seam is on the bottom, then carefully stretch the sides and ends of the dough down and tuck them underneath to form a smooth round ball about 12–15 cm in diameter. Cover with a tea towel. Place it in a warm, draught-free spot and leave to rest for 15 minutes until soft and spongy.

4 Heat a pizza stone in the oven at 200°C fan-forced (220°C conventional). Cut three or four diagonal slashes in the dough in one direction. Cut three or four more slashes at right angles to these to form a crosshatch pattern on the top of the loaf. The slashes need only be 3 mm deep, but use a wetted razor blade or really sharp knife so you do not pull the dough. Mix together the egg yolk, milk and remaining ½ tablespoon of olive oil. Brush this over the dough, slightly pulling apart the slashes. Sprinkle with the extra 2 teaspoons of anise seeds.

5 Lightly dust the pizza stone with flour and immediately place the bread in the oven. Bake it for 30 minutes until it sounds hollow when tapped on the bottom. If the bread is browning too much after 20 minutes, drop the oven temperature by 20°C for the final 10 minutes of baking.

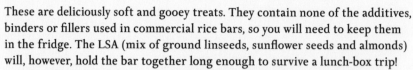

SESAME AND TAHINI PUFFED RICE BARS WITH DARK CHOCOLATE

MAKES 18 BARS

1 CUP (35 G) PUFFED RICE
(OR SUBSTITUTE ROLLED OATS)

½ CUP (75 G) SESAME SEEDS

½ CUP (25 G) TOASTED
DESICCATED COCONUT

½ CUP (75 G) TOASTED
HAZELNUTS, CHOPPED

½ CUP (75 G) DRIED APRICOTS, DICED

½ CUP (75 G) DRIED BABY FIGS
AND/OR DICED DATES

½ CUP (80 G) ALMONDS, LIGHTLY
ROASTED, THEN CHOPPED

½ CUP (75 G) PUMPKIN SEEDS
(PEPITAS), TOASTED

½ CUP (140 G) TAHINI

½ CUP (180 G) HONEY

½ CUP (175 G) GOLDEN SYRUP

½ CUP (60 G) LSA (MIX OF GROUND
LINSEEDS, SUNFLOWER SEEDS
AND ALMONDS)

500 G DARK COUVERTURE CHOCOLATE
(80 PER CENT COCOA)

These are deliciously soft and gooey treats. They contain none of the additives, binders or fillers used in commercial rice bars, so you will need to keep them in the fridge. The LSA (mix of ground linseeds, sunflower seeds and almonds) will, however, hold the bar together long enough to survive a lunch-box trip!

The chocolate coating creates a hard shell that sandwiches the ingredients and makes the bar a little easier to handle, but if I am feeling lazy, I often just coat the top half. If you're feeling all cheffy, you can temper the chocolate to achieve a mirror gloss and snap to the surface, but I rarely bother.

Don't forget that you have the opportunity to make a difference to a worker and their family, and raise a community's standard of living, if you choose fairtrade chocolate. Get yours from Oxfam (oxfam.org.au) and leave a better taste in everyone's mouth.

1 Preheat the oven to 100°C fan-forced (120°C conventional).

2 Place all of the dry ingredients on a baking tray, and the tahini (if using), honey and golden syrup in separate heatproof ramekins. Warm everything in the oven for 30 minutes. This will soften the tahini and honey, and help with mixing the ingredients together.

3 Transfer the warm dry ingredients to a big bowl and add the warm tahini, honey and golden syrup. Mix well, then add the LSA to bind the mixture together.

4 Grease a 26 cm (or thereabouts) square baking tray and line it with baking paper. Spread the mixture evenly into the tray. (The mixture should be about 1.5 cm deep.) Place in the fridge for about 20 minutes to set.

5 Grate 200 g of the chocolate and set it aside. Melt the remaining chocolate in a bowl over a saucepan of gently simmering water (making sure the bottom of the bowl does not touch the water). Stir in the grated chocolate, then immediately remove the pan from the heat. Set aside and allow the grated chocolate to melt, stirring occasionally.

6 While the mixture is still in the tray, cut it into 9 cm × 4 cm bars. Gently (because they're gooey and a little soft), lift the bars out of the tray and spread them out on a large sheet of baking paper. Coat the tops of the bars with half of the chocolate using a spatula. Allow the chocolate to set (you can speed this up by popping the bars in the fridge for 10 minutes or so), then flip the bars over and coat the other side. (Alternatively, just dip the bars into the melted chocolate with a fork, shake off any excess and lay them on a cooling rack to set.) The bars will keep in the fridge for a couple of weeks.

BASIC RECIPES

CHAPATTIS

These chapattis make the perfect accompaniment to plenty of dishes in this book, including the Mushroom dal (see page 141), Tomato rasam (see page 34) and Chickpea and kipfler potato curry (see page 203). You can cook them several hours ahead. Just wrap them in a tea towel, then foil. Warm them through for 5–10 minutes in a preheated 110°C fan-forced (130°C conventional) oven before serving.

MAKES 12

2 CUPS (300 G) ATTA FLOUR (SEE INGREDIENTS)

1 TEASPOON SALT FLAKES

2 TABLESPOONS GHEE (SEE INGREDIENTS), AT ROOM TEMPERATURE, PLUS 1 TABLESPOON EXTRA, FOR FRYING

1 Combine the atta flour and salt in a bowl, then blend in the ghee by rubbing the mix through your palms as if washing your hands with the flour. When combined, add 1 cup (250 ml) of room-temperature water to the bowl and gather the dough into a lump by bringing it all together with your hands. Turn the dough out onto your benchtop and knead for 10 minutes until it is soft and elastic. Rest the dough in a floured bowl, covered with a tea towel, at room temperature for 1 hour.

2 Dust your hands and the benchtop with flour and divide the dough into 12 balls. Roll them into rounds about 2–3 mm thick. Preheat a heavy-based frying pan over really high heat. Very lightly oil the pan with 2 teaspoons of ghee for the first chapatti and immediately add a round of dough to the pan. Let it just set for 30 seconds or so, then flip it over and, using a thick tea towel, press down quite firmly so that the chapatti makes full contact with the pan. When the bread is ready (about a minute or so), it will puff slightly around the tea towel and squeal a little as steam escapes. It should also have little black patches. Flip it over and repeat on the other side. The dough will become less opaque when fully cooked. Repeat with the remaining dough, re-oiling the pan with another 2 teaspoons of ghee halfway through cooking. Cover the finished chapattis with a tea towel to keep them warm.

SHIITAKE STOCK

I'm not a huge fan of regular vegie stock. I believe if you use top-quality ingredients and a sound method, you'll achieve enough flavour as you cook. However, this shiitake stock adds depth and earthiness to dishes, and it only takes a jiffy to whip up.

MAKES ABOUT 1 LITRE

1 CUP (30 G) DRIED SHIITAKE MUSHROOMS

1.6 LITRES COLD WATER

2 CM PIECE GINGER, BRUISED

2 SPRING ONIONS

1 Place the shiitakes in a large saucepan and add the water. Leave them to soak for a couple of hours.

2 Add the ginger and spring onions (folded up to fit) to the saucepan, then bring to a gentle simmer over medium heat. Simmer for 1 hour, then strain through a muslin-lined sieve, pressing lightly with the back of a ladle to extract as much liquid as possible without mangling the mushrooms.

3 The stock can be kept for 1 week in an airtight container in the fridge or frozen for up to 6 months. The drained shiitakes will keep for 1 week in an airtight container in the fridge. You can use them for the Corn short soup with silken tofu and egg threads on page 99, if you like.

BURNT CHILLI SAMBAL

A big nod to Thai chef Dang who taught me how to make this brilliant burnt chilli sambal. You don't have to use soybean oil, but you do want an oil with a high smoke point to achieve the slight blackening of the dried chillies. Rice bran or grapeseed oils are good alternatives, and, like soybean oil, they won't add unwanted flavour (see Ingredients).

MAKES ABOUT 2 CUPS (500 ML)

450 ML SOYBEAN OIL, PLUS EXTRA TO COVER

2 LARGE OR 4 SMALL HEADS OF GARLIC, PEELED BUT LEFT WHOLE

4 ONIONS, PEELED AND HALVED

40 DRIED LONG RED CHILLIES

4 TABLESPOONS VEGETARIAN OYSTER SAUCE (SEE INGREDIENTS)

4 TABLESPOONS TAMARIND CONCENTRATE

60 G GRATED COCONUT PALM SUGAR (SEE PAGE 52)

1 Warm the oil in a wok over medium heat. Add the garlic and onion and fry for about 10 minutes, stirring occasionally until well caramelised. (After about 5 minutes the onion will start to separate – this will allow it to cook evenly with the garlic.) Remove the garlic and onion from the oil with a slotted spoon, then drain on paper towel and set aside.

2 Turn up the heat until the oil is almost smoking (you should probably turn up your exhaust fan too at this point). Add the chillies in small batches and cook until they slightly change colour to deep aubergine. Do not blacken them completely, but don't be alarmed if they have a slightly burnt smell and you are coughing a little! This is a sign that they're just right. Remove the chillies from the wok with a slotted spoon and allow both the chillies and oil to cool slightly.

3 Blend the chillies, garlic and onion to a fine paste in a food processor, then add 100 ml of the wok oil. Add the oyster sauce and tamarind and blend until a thick sauce is achieved, then add the palm sugar and blend until it's folded through evenly. You want to attain a balance between sweetness, acidity and heat, with pleasant burnt-caramel overtones. Store in sterilised jars (see page 223) covered with a thin layer of oil. It will keep forever (well, about a year).

HARISSA

This harissa is especially good with the Artichoke and lemon tagine (see page 175) and Dukkah soft-boiled eggs with rocket (see page 19). I like to grill a few capsicums at the end of summer and plonk them in oil, but you can always skip this step and use jarred or tinned capsicums for the harissa if you prefer.

MAKES ABOUT 200 ML

2 RED CAPSICUMS (PEPPERS)

EXTRA VIRGIN OLIVE OIL, FOR BRUSHING AND DRIZZLING

4–6 SMALL RED CHILLIES, SEEDS AND ALL

1 CLOVE GARLIC, PEELED

1 TEASPOON CUMIN SEEDS

2 TEASPOONS CORIANDER SEEDS, ROASTED

3 TEASPOONS SALT FLAKES

1 For the capsicums, preheat a grill-plate to medium. Brush the capsicums with a teeny amount of olive oil and place them on the grill-plate. Cook until blackened on all sides, turning as you go. Transfer the capsicums to a bowl, cover tightly with plastic film and leave for 10 minutes to sweat off the skins.

2 With very clean hands (any bacteria will spoil the capsicums and reduce storage time), cut the capsicums in half, scrape out the seeds and rub off the blackened skins. Don't be tempted to rinse them under water, as half the flavour will be lost down the drain! You can store the capsicums in a sterilised jar (see page 223) in the fridge for up to 6 months.

3 To make the harissa, place the grilled capsicums, chillies, garlic, cumin seeds, coriander seeds and salt in a food processor and add a drizzle of olive oil. Blend to a smooth paste.

4 Store the harissa in a sterilised jar in the fridge for up to 6 months.

COCONUT CHUTNEY

I serve this delicious coconut chutney with the Pea rice pancakes on page 50, but it's equally at home used as a lovely cooling condiment for most Indian meals, including the Mushroom dal on page 141.

MAKES ABOUT 200 ML

3 TABLESPOONS DESICCATED COCONUT, SOAKED IN 3 TABLESPOONS WATER

1 GREEN CHILLI, FINELY CHOPPED

1 SMALL BUNCH CORIANDER, LEAVES PICKED AND FINELY CHOPPED

½ TEASPOON SALT FLAKES

3 TABLESPOONS LEMON JUICE

1½ TABLESPOONS GHEE (SEE INGREDIENTS)

½ TEASPOON BROWN MUSTARD SEEDS

1 SPRIG CURRY LEAVES

1 Combine the coconut, chilli, coriander, salt and lemon juice in a small bowl.

2 Heat the ghee in a small saucepan over medium heat, then add the mustard seeds and curry leaves and wait for the seeds to pop, about 10 seconds. Pour the mustard seeds and curry leaves over the coconut mixture.

3 Store the chutney in a sterilised jar (see page 223) in the fridge for up to 2 weeks.

TAMARILLO AND TOMATO CHUTNEY

This recipe came about one autumn when I had a tree bursting with tamarillos. I love their slightly acidic clean finish, subtle sweetness and deep red flesh, but there is a limit to how many of them you can eat. So I was thinking about creative ways to use them up and decided to adapt a favourite mango chutney recipe. I was so pleased with the result that I now make the chutney every year. It's perfect with the Pea and potato samosas (see page 157) and is pretty good with the Preserved lime pilaf (see page 196) too.

MAKES ABOUT 200 ML

400 G TAMARILLOS

50 ML FLAVOUR-NEUTRAL OIL (SEE INGREDIENTS)

2 CLOVES GARLIC, CRUSHED

2 TABLESPOONS CHOPPED GINGER

1 ONION, CHOPPED

2–4 SMALL RED CHILLIES, CHOPPED (SEEDS AND ALL, IF YOU LIKE)

½ TEASPOON GROUND TURMERIC

½ TEASPOON GROUND CUMIN

½ TEASPOON CURRY POWDER

½ TEASPOON WHITE-WINE VINEGAR OR TAMARIND CONCENTRATE

1 TEASPOON SUGAR

½ TEASPOON SALT FLAKES

½ BUNCH CORIANDER, LEAVES PICKED AND ROUGHLY CHOPPED

1 Halve the tamarillos and scoop out the flesh and seeds with a spoon. Set the flesh and seeds aside, discarding the skins.

2 Preheat a heavy-based sauteuse or frying pan over low–medium heat and add the oil. Fry the garlic, ginger and onion for 5 minutes, stirring occasionally, then add the chilli and spices and cook for another minute or so.

3 Add the tamarillo flesh and seeds, vinegar or tamarind, sugar and salt. Cover the pan, reduce the temperature to low and simmer gently for 10 minutes. Leave the chutney to cool.

4 Store the chutney in a sterilised jar (see page 223) in the fridge for up to 6 months. Add the coriander just before serving.

CHILLI PEANUT SAUCE

This chilli peanut sauce is really handy to have in the fridge. I nearly always have a batch in there. I serve the sauce with the Carrot and fried tofu salad (see page 43) and the Potato potstickers (see page 127) or, if I am feeling really lazy, I just chuck some on top of some steamed jasmine rice for a quick dinner.

MAKES ABOUT 400 ML

2 LARGE DRIED RED CHILLIES, FINELY CHOPPED, SEEDS AND ALL

1 TABLESPOON RICE VINEGAR (SEE INGREDIENTS)

1 TABLESPOON FLAVOUR-NEUTRAL OIL (SEE INGREDIENTS)

1 CLOVE GARLIC, CRUSHED

½ CUP (75 G) COARSELY CRUSHED ROASTED PEANUTS (I USUALLY LEAVE SKINS ON, BUT FEEL FREE TO REMOVE THEM IF YOU PREFER A FINER TEXTURE)

1 TABLESPOON LIGHT SOY SAUCE (SEE INGREDIENTS)

1 TABLESPOON KECAP MANIS (SEE INGREDIENTS)

1 TEASPOON GRATED COCONUT PALM SUGAR (SEE PAGE 52)

1 CUP (250 ML) COCONUT CREAM

1 Place the chilli in a tiny bowl, splash over the vinegar and leave to soak for 15 minutes.

2 Preheat a small heavy-based sauteuse or frying pan over medium heat. Add the oil and when hot, add the garlic and saute until softened, then add the chilli and vinegar mix and fry for a few seconds, stirring.

3 Add all the other ingredients, then reduce the heat to low and gently simmer, stirring occasionally, for about 10–15 minutes or until the peanuts suck up the coconut cream and the sauce becomes thick.

4 Store the chilli peanut sauce in a sterilised jar (see page 223) in the fridge for up to 1 month.

APPLE, HONEY AND MINT RAITA

This is my favourite raita recipe. It is sweet, aromatic and cooling and the besan (chickpea) flour gives it a thick richness. I pretty much use it with any Indian dish, from the Onion bhajis on page 178 to the Spinach pakoras on page 119. I sometimes just simply serve it alongside a few pappadams as a simple snack.

MAKES ABOUT 500 ML

400 G GREEK-STYLE YOGHURT

2 TEASPOONS BESAN (CHICKPEA) FLOUR (SEE INGREDIENTS)

2 TABLESPOONS HONEY

½ GREEN APPLE, FINELY GRATED

1 TABLESPOON GROUND CORIANDER

2 TEASPOONS SALT FLAKES

JUICE OF ½ LEMON

1 TABLESPOON GHEE (SEE INGREDIENTS)

1 TABLESPOON BROWN MUSTARD SEEDS

1 LONG GREEN CHILLI, SEEDED AND FINELY DICED

1 HANDFUL EACH MINT AND CORIANDER LEAVES, FINELY CHOPPED

1 Place a small heavy-based frying pan over low heat to warm up.

2 Meanwhile, place the yoghurt in a mixing bowl and slowly rain in the flour, whisking it through the yoghurt as you do so. Add the honey, apple, ground coriander, salt and lemon juice and combine.

3 Add the ghee to the warm pan and wait a few seconds for it to heat up, then add the mustard seeds and let them crackle for a few seconds. Pour the ghee and mustard seeds into the yoghurt. Finally, fold in the chilli, mint and coriander. (You can whiz this up in a food processor if you prefer a vibrant green sauce as opposed to a white one with flecks of green.)

4 Store the raita in the fridge for up to 1 week.

CRISPY SHALLOT CHIPS

I sprinkle these crispy shallot chips over quite a few recipes in this book, including the Eggplant curry with green chilli and coconut (see page 105), Ginger and mushroom congee (see page 130) and Coconut and macadamia laksa (see page 191). They're simple to make and will last for ages if cooked and stored correctly, but you can always cheat and buy them from Asian grocers if you're short of time.

MAKES 200 ML JAR

4–6 GOLDEN SHALLOTS, THINLY SLICED FROM BULB TO TIP

600 ML FLAVOUR-NEUTRAL OIL (SEE INGREDIENTS)

SALT FLAKES

1 Place the shallots and oil in a small–medium saucepan and place over low heat. Allow the oil to gradually heat up; bringing the shallots up from cold in oil means the sugars convert slowly and the shallots can get really sweet and crispy without burning.

2 Simmer the shallots in the oil, without disturbing them. When they turn golden, about 6–10 minutes, remove them with a spider or slotted spoon and drain on paper towel. Season well with salt immediately, as this will help draw out excess oil. Leave to cool.

3 Store the crispy shallot chips in an airtight jar for up to 1 year.

PICKLED CHERRIES

When cherries hit rock-bottom price, it's time to pickle! Visit the markets after New Year and grab a couple of kilos. Pickled cherries go well with cheese (including the Twice-cooked cheese souffles on page 151) and they are delicious in salads with a little of the pickling vinegar incorporated into the dressing. I like my desserts with savoury overtones, so I even chuck them over ice-cream. When it comes to pickling, I have no idea what I am doing half the time, but I will pickle anything just to see what happens. I favour recipes that keep the main ingredient at the fore of the pickle and not buried under a whole heap of flavours, so the recipe here is pretty basic. Jazz things up with spices, if you like, but remember to use good-quality vinegar to do your pickle justice.

MAKES 1.75 LITRE JAR

750 G CHERRIES, WASHED AND DRAINED, PIPS AND STEMS INTACT

½ CUP (125 ML) REALLY GOOD WHITE-WINE VINEGAR

100 G DARK BROWN SUGAR

1 TABLESPOON FINE SALT

1 To sterilise the jar, preheat the oven to 100°C fan-forced (120°C conventional). Wash the jar and lid well, then place them in a large pan of boiling water for 10 minutes. Shake off excess water, then when cool enough to handle, transfer the jar to the oven for 20 minutes to dry out. It sounds like a lot of fuss, but you really do need an immaculately clean, dry jar and lid to ensure that the contents will not spoil during storage.

2 Wash your hands. Prick each cherry with a clean skewer down to the stone and place in the jar. Combine 1 cup (250 ml) of water and the vinegar in a small saucepan over medium heat and add the sugar and salt. Boil until the sugar and salt have dissolved. Pour the boiling liquid into the sterilised jar over the cherries, filling to 4 mm below the lid, then immediately seal the jar. Store in the fridge. The cherries will take a couple of weeks to pickle, and they will last for up to 1 year.

ACKNOWLEDGEMENTS

While there's no single recipe for becoming a good chef, there are some vital ingredients. You definitely need a big pinch of inspiration, a sprinkling of curiosity and a dollop of hard work, but, for me, the key ingredient is generosity of spirit. The best chefs start out as keen learners and become great teachers themselves. Everything I've ever learnt is due to the generosity of others: all those people who guided, supported and inspired me. My biggest thank you is to all of you who took the time to teach me over the years. (And to those who didn't: I still looked over your shoulder/ate at your restaurant/drew inspiration from you regardless, so I owe you a big thanks as well!)

To the people who cook stuff
Firstly and mostly, my favourite cheffy Stephy, for the above-and-beyond support and help during *The Cook and the Chef*, and for making me look way better than I really am. So many of these recipes came about through doing the show, and because you were so generous with your knowledge. I am in your debt . . . I owe you a puppy! Dang, Chef Baba and Mui, for those early days of woks and curry pots. 'BOP' Singham, for opening that first door to the kitchen for me. Beth: Respec'! And because you were silly enough to hire me even though I never wore my hat. Cheong, for your 'no secrets' approach to running a kitchen and for sharing that amazing database of knowledge in your head. Maggie, I know how busy you were that day when you sat down and typed and *made me* start this book: absolute gratitude that words cannot express for this and all the other stuff you bring to the table. You have changed the way I cook (and this is a good thing!). Blanksey: Get a measuring spoon, you b@#*h! No, seriously, I love you, and I'd never have finished this book without your help. You are my special, lovely, number one lady (not just in the kitchen). Ah, anyone and everyone who was over or under me in a kitchen and actually put up with me, particularly my entire Hilton Adelaide kitchen brigade.

To the people who grow stuff
Pete the Yardstick Garden man, for designing my garden and teaching me the virtues of permaculture organics. Food Forest and Tony Scarfo, for growing the good stuff. House of Organics, for going that extra mile. Margy and Chris of AMJ Produce, for always delivering the goods. Pat, because your hands are magic and your vegies are gold (and Daniel, you are 'Patman's Robin').

To the people who helped grow the book
Fi R and Jacqui W, for getting me over the line in the first place with lovely snaps and a helping shove. Fran Moore, for wheeling and dealing. Julie Gibbs and all the other kids at Penguin, especially Ingrid Ohlsson, Clio Kempster, Evi Oetomo and, extra-super especially, Ariane Durkin. Alan Benson and his magic camera lens: I can't thank you enough for making my food look so good – and you're a nice guy to boot! Thanks also to stylist Michelle Noerianto. Margot, for letting me be on the telly and for the chats in the car. (P.S. You never bought me that pillow, though.) Caro, the little one – actually you do look like my PA. Scott and Jade at InFront Management for managing the unmanageable (me).

To the people who grew me
Iggy, for teaching me how to dig again. Sid, for being lovely (but please stop digging up the vegies!). All the farmers/producers/growers who only take what the land can give. Your food is grown with real care, and for that I salute you. And Mum, for knocking table manners into my teeny head. There isn't a day when I don't miss you terribly, but I understand you had to leave the dinner table a little early. You were never really one to sit still and hang around long enough for dessert and coffee anyway. Oh, and thanks for buying me my first spade (sorry about the rhubarb – I really did think it was a weed).

Luff,
Simon xxx

INDEX

LANTERN

Published by the Penguin Group
Penguin Group (Australia)
707 Collins Street, Melbourne, Victoria 3008, Australia
(a division of Penguin Australia Group Pty Ltd)
Penguin Group (USA) Inc.
375 Hudson Street, New York, New York 10014, USA
Penguin Group (Canada)
90 Eglinton Avenue East, Suite 700, Toronto, Canada ON M4P 2Y3
(a division of Penguin Canada Books Inc.)
Penguin Books Ltd
80 Strand, London WC2R 0RL England
Penguin Ireland
25 St Stephen's Green, Dublin 2, Ireland
(a division of Penguin Books Ltd)
Penguin Books India Pvt Ltd
11 Community Centre, Panchsheel Park, New Delhi – 110 017, India
Penguin Group (NZ)
67 Apollo Drive, Rosedale, Auckland 0632, New Zealand
(a division of Penguin New Zealand Pty Ltd)
Penguin Books (South Africa) (Pty) Ltd, Rosebank Offi
Rosebank Office Park, Block D, 181 Jan Smuts Avenue, Parktown North,
Johannesburg 2196, South Africa
Penguin Beijing, Ltd
7F, Tower B, Jiaming Centre, 27 East Third Ring Road North, Chayong District,
Beijing 100020, China

Penguin Books Ltd, Registered Offices: 80 Strand, London, WC2R 0RL, England

First published by Penguin Group (Australia), 2012

5 7 9 10 8 6 4

Design by Evi O. © Penguin Group (Australia)
Photography by Alan Benson
Props by Michelle Noerianto

Typeset in Delicato by Post Pre-Press Group, Brisbane, Queensland
Colour reproduction by Splitting Image Colour Studio Pty Ltd, Clayton, Victoria
Printed and bound in China by 1010 Printing International Ltd

National Library of Australia
Cataloguing-in-Publication data:

Bryant, Simon.
Simon Bryant's vegies / Simon Bryant; Alan Benson, photographer.
9781921382703 (pbk.)
Includes index.
Cooking (Vegetables)
641.65

penguin.com.au/lantern